Matt Hills is Professor in Film and TV Studies at Aberystwyth University. He is the author of five previous books, including *Fan Cultures* (2002) and *Triumph of a Time Lord* (2010). He is a regular reviewer for doctorwhonews.net, and has published widely on *Doctor Who* and media fandom.

'A pop-cultural matrix of a show, *Doctor Who* needs exploratory missions from as many different worlds and disciplines as possible. Chewy, provocative ideas and sly insights combine in unexpected ways here, making sure this book will spark many more useful conversations than "who's your favourite Doctor?"'

– **Tat Wood, author of *About Time 7***

READING CONTEMPORARY TELEVISION
Series Editors: Kim Akass and Janet McCabe
janetandkim@hotmail.com

The *Reading Contemporary Television* series offers a varied, intellectually groundbreaking and often polemical response to what is happening in television today. This series is distinct in that it sets out to immediately comment upon the TV *zeitgeist* while providing an intellectual and creative platform for thinking differently and ingeniously writing about contemporary television culture. The books in the series seek to establish a critical space where new voices are heard and fresh perspectives offered. Innovation is encouraged and intellectual curiosity demanded.

PUBLISHED AND FORTHCOMING

Mad Men: *Dream Come True TV* edited by Gary R. Edgerton
Makeover Television: Realities Remodelled edited by Dana Heller
New Dimensions of **Doctor Who** edited by Matt Hills
Quality TV: American Television and Beyond edited by Janet McCabe and Kim Akass
Reading **CSI**: *Television under the Microscope* edited by Michael Allen
Reading **Deadwood**: *A Western to Swear By* edited by David Lavery
Reading **Desperate Housewives**: *Beyond the White Picket Fence* edited by Janet McCabe and Kim Akass
Reading **Little Britain**: *Comedy Matters on Contemporary Television* edited by Sharon Lockyer
Reading **Lost**: *Perspectives on a Hit Television Show* edited by Roberta Pearson
Reading **Sex and the City** edited by Kim Akass and Janet McCabe
Reading **Six Feet Under**: *TV to Die For* edited by Kim Akass and Janet McCabe
Reading **The L Word**: *Outing Contemporary Television* edited by Kim Akass and Janet McCabe, with an introduction by Sarah Warne
Reading **The Sopranos**: *Hit TV from HBO* edited by David Lavery
Reading **24**: *Television Against the Clock* edited by Steven Peacock
The Queer Politics of Television by Samuel A. Chambers
Third Wave Feminism and Television: Jane Puts It in a Box edited by Merri Lisa Johnson
TV's Betty Goes Global: From Telenovela to International Brand edited by Janet McCabe and Kim Akass
Loving **The L Word**: *The Complete Series in Focus* edited by Dana Heller

NEW DIMENSIONS OF
DOCTOR WHO

Adventures in Space, Time and Television

Edited by Matt Hills

Published in 2013 by I.B.Tauris & Co Ltd
6 Salem Road, London W2 4BU
175 Fifth Avenue, New York NY 10010
www.ibtauris.com

Distributed in the United States and Canada
Exclusively by Palgrave Macmillan
175 Fifth Avenue, New York NY 10010

Copyright Editorial Selection and Introduction © 2013 Matt Hills
Copyright Individual Chapters © 2013 Melissa Beattie, Piers D. Britton, Will Brooker, David Butler, Elizabeth Evans, Ross P. Garner, Bonnie Green, Matt Hills, Catherine Johnson, Andrew O'Day, Rebecca Williams, Chris Willmott

The right of Matt Hills to be identified as the editor of this work has been asserted by him in accordance with the Copyright, Designs and Patents Act 1988.

All rights reserved. Except for brief quotations in a review, this book, or any part thereof, may not be reproduced, stored in or introduced into a retrieval system, or transmitted, in any form or by any means, electronic, mechanical, photocopying, recording or otherwise, without the prior written permission of the publisher.

ISBN: 978 1 84511 866 2

A full CIP record for this book is available from the British Library
A full CIP record is available from the Library of Congress

Library of Congress Catalog Card Number: available

Printed and bound in Great Britain by Page Bros, Norwich

CONTENTS

Contributors   vii

Acknowledgements   x

Introduction: *Doctor Who* Studies?   1
Matt Hills

PART I   NEW *DOCTOR WHO*

1   A Good Score Goes to War: Multiculturalism, Monsters and Music in New *Doctor Who*   19
David Butler

2   Making 'a Superior Brand of Alien Mastermind': *Doctor Who* Monsters and the Rhetoric of (Re)design   39
Piers D. Britton

3   The Cybermen as Human.2   54
Bonnie Green and Chris Willmott

4   Talking to the TARDIS: *Doctor Who*, Neil Gaiman and Cultural Mythology   71
Will Brooker

PART II   NEW TELEVISION, NEW MEDIA

5   *Doctor Who* as Programme Brand   95
Catherine Johnson

6   On Speed: The Ordering of Time and Pace
    of Action in *Doctor Who*   113
    Andrew O'Day

7   Learning with the Doctor: Pedagogic Strategies
    in Transmedia *Doctor Who*   134
    Elizabeth Evans

8   Tweeting the TARDIS: Interaction, Liveness and Social
    Media in *Doctor Who* Fandom   154
    Rebecca Williams

PART III   NEW SPACES AND TIMES

9   The '*Doctor Who* Experience' (2012—) and
    the Commodification of Cardiff Bay   177
    Melissa Beattie

10 Remembering Sarah Jane: Intradiegetic Allusions,
    Embodied Presence/Absence and Nostalgia   192
    Ross P. Garner

11 Anniversary Adventures in Space and Time:
    The Changing Faces of *Doctor Who's* Commemoration   216
    Matt Hills

Further Reading   235

CONTRIBUTORS

Melissa Beattie is a PhD student studying the construction of national identity in the telefantasy series *Torchwood* at Aberystwyth University, Wales. Melissa co-edited *Impossible Worlds, Impossible Things: Cultural Perspectives on Doctor Who, Torchwood and the Sarah Jane Adventures* (Cambridge Scholars, 2010) and has contributed to *Time Unincorporated Vol. 3* (Mad Norwegian Press, 2011) and *Who Needs Experts? Counter-Mapping Cultural Heritage* (Ashgate, 2013).

Piers D. Britton is Associate Professor and Director of Visual & Media Studies at the University of Redlands, southern California. He is co-author, with Simon Barker, of *Reading Between Designs: Visual Imagery and the Generation of Meaning in The Avengers, The Prisoner and Doctor Who* (University of Texas Press, 2003) and the author of *TARDISbound: Navigating the Universes of Doctor Who* (I.B.Tauris, 2011).

Will Brooker is Professor of Film and Cultural Studies at Kingston University, London. He is the author of *Batman Unmasked*, along with its sequel, *Hunting the Dark Knight: Twenty-First Century Batman* (I.B.Tauris, 2012). Other books include *Using the Force* and *Alice's Adventures*, and he has edited *The Audience Studies Reader* and *The Blade Runner Experience* as well as writing a BFI Film Classics volume on *Star Wars*. Will is the first British editor of *Cinema Journal*.

David Butler is Senior Lecturer in Screen Studies at the University of Manchester. He is the editor of *Time and Relative Dissertations in Space: Critical Perspectives on Doctor Who* (Manchester University Press, 2007), and the author of *Fantasy Cinema: Impossible Worlds on Screen*

NEW DIMENSIONS OF *DOCTOR WHO*

(Wallflower, 2009). David's recent work includes a chapter in *Music in Science Fiction Television* (Routledge, 2013) and research on one of the pioneering figures in British electronic music, Delia Derbyshire.

Elizabeth Evans is Lecturer in Film and TV Studies at Nottingham University. Her research focuses on the relationship between technology and the experience of narrative, tackling issues such as interactivity, agency and immersion. Elizabeth's first book *Transmedia Television: Audiences, New Media and Daily Life* (Routledge, 2011) explores the development of the internet and mobile phone as extensions and alternatives to the television set.

Ross P. Garner is Lecturer in Media and Cultural Studies at Cardiff University, Wales. He has recently completed his PhD on discourses of nostalgia in post-2005 British time travel television dramas and has contributed to forthcoming edited collections on *Doctor Who* and *Torchwood*, as well as co-editing *Impossible Worlds, Impossible Things: Cultural Perspectives on Doctor Who, Torchwood and the Sarah Jane Adventures* (Cambridge Scholars, 2010).

Bonnie Green has an MSc in social research methods and social psychology from the London School of Economics and Political Science. She studied for a PhD in sociology at the University of Exeter. Bonnie was previously a research assistant on the BioethicsBytes project at the University of Leicester, and has contributed work to *Doctor Who and Philosophy: Bigger on the Inside* (Open Court, 2011).

Matt Hills is Professor in Film and TV Studies at Aberystwyth University, Wales. He is the author of five books, including *Fan Cultures* (Routledge, 2002), *The Pleasures of Horror* (Continuum, 2005), and *Triumph of a Time Lord: Regenerating Doctor Who in the Twenty-First Century* (I.B.Tauris, 2010). Matt has published widely on cult film/TV, media fandom, and *Doctor Who*, and is a regular reviewer for doctorwho-news.net. He is currently working on an academic study of *Torchwood*.

Catherine Johnson is Associate Professor at the University of Nottingham. Her research examines the Western television industries and the impact of industrial shifts on the cultural artefacts that they produce. She is the author of *Telefantasy* (BFI, 2005) and *Branding*

Television (Routledge, 2012) as well as the co-editor of *ITV Cultures* (Open University, 2005) and *Transnational Television History* (Routledge, 2012).

Andrew O'Day is the co-author of *Terry Nation* (Manchester University Press, 2004) and editor of *Doctor Who, The Eleventh Hour* (I.B.Tauris, 2013). Andrew's other recent work includes a chapter on satire in *Ruminations, Peregrinations and Regenerations: A Critical Approach to Doctor Who* (Cambridge Scholars, 2010), and chapters on the social history of *Who* fandom in *Doctor Who in Time and Space* (McFarland, 2013).

Rebecca Williams is Lecturer in Communication, Cultural and Media Studies at the University of South Wales. She is the editor of *Torchwood Declassified: Investigating Mainstream Cult Television* (I.B.Tauris, 2013) and has contributed work on *Doctor Who*, David Tennant and female fandom to *British Science Fiction Film and Television* (McFarland, 2011). She is currently working on a book about 'post-object fandom' for Bloomsbury, and is on the editorial board of the *Journal of Fandom Studies*.

Chris Willmott is Senior Lecturer in the Department of Biochemistry at the University of Leicester, and a National Teaching Fellow. He has established www.bioethicsbytes.wordpress.com, a web-based repository of materials for teaching about the science and ethics of biomedicine. Chris is a trustee of the British Universities Film and Video Council, a member of the education committee for the Nuffield Council on Bioethics and has contributed work to *Doctor Who and Philosophy: Bigger on the Inside* (Open Court, 2011).

ACKNOWLEDGEMENTS

This book has had an unusual and lengthy genesis (indeed, it's pretty much regenerated along the path to publication). First and foremost, I'd like to thank David Mellor, who first developed the idea, Benjamin Earl who helped on the way, and everyone who submitted material for the book's earlier incarnation. I would also like to extend my particular thanks to all those who joined *New Dimensions of Doctor Who* with me, and helped it into this final configuration.

In Cardiff, thanks to my former colleagues Inaki Garcia-Blanco, Emma Gilliam, Justin Lewis and Karin Wahl-Jorgensen.

In Aberystwyth, hello to my new workmates and all-round fine folk: Daniel Chandler, Glen Creeber, Beck Edwards, Kate Egan, Merris Griffiths, Kim Knowles, Jamie Medhurst, Paul Newland, Tom O'Malley and Sarah Thomas.

I'd also like to thank and acknowledge my past and present PhD students (a small number of whom are represented in these pages) for having helped to make academia such a pleasure.

At Doctor Who News, my appreciation goes to Harry Ward and Chuck Foster.

At I.B.Tauris, thanks to Philippa Brewster (editor extraordinaire), Cecile Rault and Dawn Rey. And thanks also to the series editors of 'Reading Contemporary Television', the fantastic Kim Akass and Janet McCabe who helped guide this project.

Outside academia, cheers to Paul, Helen, Tim and Amy for (mostly) tolerating my foibles.

And, as always, much love to Mum, Dad, Pendy, Stu, Teresa, and their beautiful new arrival, Eleanor.

INTRODUCTION
DOCTOR WHO STUDIES?

Matt Hills

I f 'it always begins with the same two words,' then those words have formed a question echoing through time – from 'An Unearthly Child' (1963) to 'The Snowmen' (2012) and beyond – namely, 'Doctor *Who*?'. But this mystery, this puzzle of identity, partly crosses over into scholarship on the programme, meaning that we can also ask what '*Doctor Who* Studies' might, or even should, look like. That is something I will explore briefly here, as well as setting out the reasons behind this specific collection of essays.

Doctor Who has, of course, displayed and traversed many new dimensions across its history: in a sense, new dimensions are business as usual for the Doctor. When the show began back in 1963, there were no Time Lords or Gallifrey; there was just a mysterious figure identified by title alone. Perhaps the most significant change in the programme's history did not come until 1966, when regeneration was introduced, and lead actor William Hartnell was replaced by Patrick Troughton. Other major shifts emerged when the programme moved into colour and an altered, Earth-based format in 1970 with third Doctor Jon Pertwee, and again when John Nathan-Turner took over as producer with season 18, not to mention the 'golden age' popularity of Tom Baker arriving in between. And another new dimension just as important as regeneration loomed in the form of cancellation, both with the 1985 hiatus, after which the Doctor was on trial for his life, and in *Doctor Who*'s eventual 1989 departure from TV screens.

But this volume would not exist without further seismic shifts – a US/UK co-produced movie in 1996,[1] and a triumphant BBC Wales' reinvention in 2005, often still thought of as 'new *Who*' or nu*Who*.[2] This incarnation of *Doctor Who* has since moved on to a second showrunner, and is soon to feature its fourth lead actor.[3] And, more than that, the show has multiple lives beyond TV, in original fiction following long in the wake of 1966's *Doctor Who and the Invasion from Space*,[4] merchandising,[5] computer games, and a fan culture that has moved through fan clubs or appreciation societies and into TV production as well as all sorts of digital fandom,[6] and even academia. Again, novelty is actually rather ordinary in the many worlds of *Doctor Who*. In the wake of its noughties' transformation into a flagship BBC programme, timely books have been written detailing *Timeless Adventures: How Doctor Who Conquered TV*,[7] and the series has been subjected both to a British Film Institute 'TV Classics' volume,[8] and a Wayne State University Press 'TV Milestones' appreciation.[9] Scholars have widened their scope, studying the cultural history of fandom,[10] *Doctor Who*'s novels and audios as well as its TV episodes,[11] and the series' marketing and reception in America.[12] Despite *Who*'s rampantly mainstream status of late, the programme continues to fascinate those studying cult TV, cropping up as a case study in *The Cult TV Book*,[13] *The Essential Cult TV Reader*,[14] and *Cult Telefantasy Series*.[15]

A fellow TV studies' researcher interested in new dimensions – specifically tackling *Television in Transition* – also features a thoughtful analysis of *Doctor Who*, arguing that the Doctor is 'incrementally losing his particular cultural perspectivism'.[16] By this, Shawn Shimpach means that the character – once an outsider, and seemingly beyond sentiment and sexuality – is increasingly a part of normative contemporary culture within TV narratives that depict an accessible, 'relatable' figure who loves his female companions, gets married, and gets grey hairs.[17] US pop culture scholar Lynnette Porter goes a step further than Shimpach and describes *Doctor Who* itself as 'a franchise in transition', noting: 'Just as the Time Lord must deal with temporal and spatial changes, so too must *Doctor Who* confront the challenges of changing times.'[18]

whether these concern how BBC Worldwide sells the programme, how Twitter alters audience interactions, or how the show fares in international markets, especially America.

As in Porter and Shimpach's work, it is the current *Doctor Who* that frequently draws the most engaging analytical commentary – often showrunner-oriented – and this crops up in book-length discussions of Russell T Davies's work from 2008,[19] along with more recent books, journal articles and blogs specifically theorizing Steven Moffat's *Who*.[20] Writers are obsessed with writers, it would seem. Regardless of this fact, bibliophile *Who* fans are well served both by niche, fan-targeted presses (for example Mad Norwegian, Miwk and Telos) and also by academic publishers who have specialised in *Doctor Who*, such as I.B.Tauris and its '*Who* Watching' series, McFarland,[21] and Cambridge Scholars Publishing.[22] Furthermore, *Doctor Who* has found itself the topic of religious,[23] philosophical[24] and mythological[25] critiques. When Paul Cornell wrote in *Licence Denied* that 'Thomas Noonan was the first New Fanboy' to use lit crit readings and terminologies, tracking fans' 'Analysis' of the show made sense,[26] but by 2013 multiple generations of New Fanboys, Fangirls,[27] acafans and fan-scholars had got in on the act, making such analysis far more dispersed, diverse and differentiated.

All of this suggests that Paul Magrs may not have been too hyperbolic when he proclaimed in 2007 that 'we're at the start of *Doctor Who* Studies. And it really is about time.'[28] For me, *Doctor Who* studies implies something cohesive, something cumulative, where shared bibliographies are amassed. All too often, however, I think there's a danger of writers on *Who* actually writing across each other rather than building this shared, communal project: philosophers don't bother with TV studies (and sometimes *vice versa*); fan-scholars don't always bother with academia (and *vice versa*); and academics sometimes write as if they're slotting fandom into a favoured theory (or *Doctor Who* itself, for that matter). Rather than a developing, unfolding body of knowledge there are instead pockets of wisdom. Capacious pockets, mind you, but overly separate philosophical or theoretical or disciplinary pockets nonetheless.

I think Paul Magrs' statement should be dwelt upon. Anyone who can write deftly humorous, moving academic articles and a book as beautiful as *Diary of a Dr Who Addict*[29] deserves a thoughtful hearing. Because surely '*Doctor Who* Studies' shouldn't just be a quick-fire provocation or a punchy closing line. And nor – to be self-reflexive for a moment – should it simply be the outcome of a market-led glut of anniversary-targeted book titles, despite the 'current economy of television studies [...] underpinning this book'.[30] When the buzz dies down, perhaps it'll truly be about time for the many silos of academic productivity and enclaves of fan theorisation to intersect far more, aiming to create something genuinely worthy of the name '*Doctor Who* Studies' rather than 'academic merchandising'.[31] Of course, there's a prehistory to *Doctor Who* studies as well – tales from the olden days about 'semiotic thickness', structuralism, and reading formations[32] – but contemporary scholarship is generally marked by plurality and multiplicity rather than Big Ideas and schools of thought. In such a context, it increasingly seems to be media texts and audience emotions that drive whatever coherence emerges out of the rushing time-tunnel vortex of analysis and publication.

If there is a danger of *Doctor Who* studies being less joined-up than it could be – a kind of *textual exclusionism* where different disciplines/cultures use the programme for their own ends, excluding alternative readings – then perhaps there's also an accompanying risk of *textual exceptionalism*. In this second case, fans and academics who love 'The Show' might focus solely on *its* production details and narrative worlds rather than placing it in industrial, cultural, intertextual, generic, technological, transnational, audience and other contexts. Although we may well believe that *Who* is magical, unique, and deserving of its own pure scholarship, I would argue that any *Doctor Who* studies up to the task of exploring so many years of adventures needs to articulate *Who* with a range of other texts, histories and concepts. As such, *Doctor Who* studies might profitably learn from other programme-centred scholarship, thus avoiding a retreat into intratextual and intradiegetic isolation.[33] And above all, I suspect that *Doctor Who* studies should be a playful pursuit and not a wholly solemn ritual: a sort of '*Who*dology'.[34] Although theorisation and logical debate have very different aims to the creation of fan parody[35] or fan-made 'Next Time' trailers, like the latter they also:

> add nothing new *per se* to the textual world, they arrange the preexisting content in such a way that a new iteration [...] is created. [...] an expression and ordering of what [... scholars] believe to be the most important features of the narrative [...]. Importantly, the rules of the textual world are maintained through this paratextuality [...] but the

reorganization of [...] material seems clearly to be a ludic activity in its own right.[36]

And given the huge range of fan, scholar, scholar-fan and fan-scholar[37] ludic activity surrounding *Doctor Who* (and the fact that new dimensions have indeed been endemic to the programme), then why this book, and why now? Well, almost the academic equivalent of a multi-Doctor story, it brings together the authors of *Triumph of a Time Lord*[38] and *TARDISbound*,[39] along with editors of *Time and Relative Dissertations in Space*[40] and *Doctor Who, The Eleventh Hour*,[41] two co-editors of *Impossible Worlds, Impossible Things*,[42] contributors to *Doctor Who and Philosophy*,[43] and the editor of *Torchwood Declassified*.[44] It also reaches further afield to academic experts on *Branding Television*[45] and *Transmedia Television*[46] as well as asking *the* leading international writer on Batman – another cultural mythology/franchise subject to reinvention and multiple authorship – to turn his attention from Dark Knight[47] to Time Lord.

Aside from the assembled contributors, there are three further rationales underpinning this book that broadly correspond with the essays grouped into Parts 1, 2 and 3. First, *as the division between 'new' and 'classic'* Who *recedes somewhat in production and marketing discourses, now is a good time to compare these iterations more carefully*. Thus, a number of writers in Part 1 focus on matters such as how music and design have developed or shifted in the new *Who*. In Chapter 1, 'A Good Score Goes to War: Multiculturalism, Monsters and Music in New *Doctor Who*', David Butler addresses the emphasis on orchestral scoring – and Western tonalities and melodies – in composer Murray Gold's work. Otherness and alien-ness, often generically coded through electronic sound in science fiction, have been assimilated into a relatively homogenising framework, Butler argues, meaning that although monstrosity has been challenged visually and narratively by BBC Wales' *Doctor Who*, the show's incidental music and leitmotifs have sometimes worked against this. Butler therefore raises questions of musical 'authorship' and authority – Gold is, after all, working to a brief from executive producers – while also innovatively linking musicology to theories and debates around multiculturalism. This produces new readings of *Doctor Who*'s musical dimensions – an area often still under-researched in TV studies.

Monstrosity has clearly been a central part of *Who*'s (classic and new) textual identities,[48] and it provides a linking strand through the three opening essays. In Chapter 2 – 'Making "a Superior Brand of Alien Mastermind": *Doctor Who* Monsters and the Rhetoric of (Re)design' – Piers D. Britton analyses promotional discourses that have surrounded old monsters' returns to BBC Wales' *Who*. Although this practice of reinvention is shared across the Russell T Davies and Steven Moffat eras (indeed, note Butler's preceding interpretation of series five's Silurians), Britton discerns some new dimensions to the latter authorial phase of the programme. Unlike Davies, Moffat has been represented as less intensely focused on details of design,[49] and there is also a greater sense of (fannish) pleasure conveyed in relation to 'cool' redesigns. Overall, though, Britton argues that a significant aspect of post-2005 *Who* has been its 'responsible modernisation' of older monster designs, usually with an emphasis on the 'realism' of fantastical creatures, or at least their functional plausibility. Although 'responsible modernisation' appears to link classic and new *Doctor Who* in branded continuity, Britton argues that it simultaneously distances new *Who* from its predecessor, very much positioning contemporary monster (re)designs as superior – 'new and improved' – to those embedded in the series' longer history. Part of the crucial work of redesign is therefore discursive and rhetorical as well as visual/material, being linked to authorship, and especially to showrunners' public images.

While Britton links themes of monstrosity and authorship, Chapter 3 – 'The Cybermen as Human.2' – by Bonnie Green and Chris Willmott considers how *Doctor Who*'s monstrous cyborgs can be linked to shifting philosophies of science and technology.[50] Green and Willmott adopt a different disciplinary approach to both Butler and Britton, moving beyond TV studies and into debates drawn from bioethics.[51] At the same time, though, they reflect on how new *Who* represents the Cybermen, suggesting that it displays a specific incoherence: sometimes characters' identities are locked in their brains (therefore persisting after cyber-conversion) and sometimes human essence is seen to be embodied, and hence destroyed by threatening, gothic Cyber-villains. Green and Willmott approach the Cybermen through theories of post-humanism and trans-humanism. They argue that one of the new dimensions of *Doctor Who* is not simply that it updates classic monsters, but also – read partly against the grain – that it can open up positive considerations of whether, as smartphone users and connected,

INTRODUCTION

networked selves, 'we are all posthuman now.' Perhaps the upgraded Cybermen are more like us than *Who*'s body-horror narratives want to imply.

If monstrosity has been vital to new *Who* in terms of its bombastic sounds, redesigned visuals and contemporary meanings, then authorship has been no less significant to the programme. We are now firmly in an age of 'auteur' *Who* linked to showrunners and 'big name' creatives such as Richard Curtis and Neil Gaiman.[52] Although classic *Who* had its luminaries[53] (often celebrated by fans rather than achieving widespread publicity value and public recognition), there can be little denying that the series today is more intensely and pervasively linked to notions of authorship via the industry showrunner model. Indeed, this is one of its most visible new dimensions. Previously broached in Britton's essay, the topic of authorship is also tackled by Will Brooker in Chapter 4, 'Talking to the TARDIS: *Doctor Who*, Neil Gaiman and Cultural Mythology'. As I have already noted, studies of showrunners and their eras have proliferated of late, but Brooker does something else – he thinks about the encounter between *Who* as a mythology and Neil Gaiman as a 'hired hand' rather than a supposedly authoritative showrunner. Gaiman, nevertheless, has an established authorial persona and 'author-function' outside new *Who*, leading Brooker to contrast fans' *Who*-centric and his own Gaiman-oriented interpretations of 'The Doctor's Wife' (2011). Ultimately, Brooker argues, readings that prioritise either *Who* or Gaiman as *the* 'source' of episodic meaning fail to consider their many cultural, generic intersections and interactions. Audiences may increasingly be industrially disciplined to read via authorial codes, but whether this is about executive producers/showrunners or 'big name' contributors, perhaps thinking in terms of 'the auteur' closes down popular television's dialogic, mythic status.

All of which takes me onto the second reason for this book, and Part 2 of its structure: *new dimensions of* Doctor Who *are also significant because of pronounced changes in the TV industry*, and thus developments in production contexts and practices.[54] Perhaps most crucially, *Doctor Who* is now a *brand* rather than merely a text; this profound change in how TV drama is professionally imagined and exploited provides a theme that runs through a number of essays. It is most obviously and directly tackled in Catherine Johnson's analysis in Chapter 5, '*Doctor Who* as Programme Brand', but in fact it also weaves through the book as a whole, appearing in Piers Britton's work on design in Part 1, and in my own chapter on *Who*'s changing anniversary moments at the end of Part 3, as well as in Melissa Beattie's approach to Cardiff as a 'city brand' symbiotically linked to post-2005 *Doctor Who*. In Part 2, however, Johnson focuses squarely on how new *Who* has been conceptualised within production and marketing, drawing on original interview material with those responsible for its brand management. Johnson also points out that while the modern BBC might be assumed to operate in some monolithic corporate fashion, its policies and practices can be rather more open to variations in emphasis and activation. A key concern remains, though, regarding the BBC's use of branding: might this be detrimental to public service television, or can commercial and public service logics be brought together by the programme brand?

In the TV industry of the twenty-first century, exactly how *Who* works aesthetically as television drama has also evolved, and this is something that Andrew O'Day addresses in Chapter 6, 'On Speed: The Ordering of Time and Pace of Action in *Doctor Who*'. O'Day combines a close reading of particular episodes with a desire to place new *Who*'s aesthetics in their industry context rather than simply legitimating the programme (as 'quality TV', for instance, or even TV art). This leads O'Day to think of 'narrative speed' as something that is thematised in a number of stories, along with obstructions and delays to the Doctor's movement through diegetic worlds. Akin to Britton's analysis in Part 1, O'Day also considers how Russell T Davies and Steven Moffat deploy specific approaches to fast-paced narrative. Where Davies favoured *in medias res* storytelling, and technology used as a narrative shortcut (for example the psychic paper) Moffat favours rapid character montages, and a more deliberately disorientating use of juxtaposition, jolting audiences along via self-conscious and showy narrative leaps, for example '1, 894 years later...' in a series finale, or '50 years later' in a story setting up *Who*'s 50th anniversary year.

As well as developments in branding and aesthetics, paratexts – such as DVD extras, online prequels, e-books, downloads, games, and so on – are becoming increasingly significant to sectors of the TV industry as the consequences of multiplatform, digital media sink in, meaning that *Doctor Who* is now a coordinated transmedia franchise[55] rather than simply a merchandised TV show, as it has been in the past. As such, analysing material like the British Academy of Film and Television Arts Cymru award-winning computer game 'The Gunpowder

Plot' (2011) is important, especially given that this production seemingly returns *Doctor Who* to its very earliest Reithian roots – to inform, educate and entertain audiences. Hence in Chapter 7, 'Learning with the Doctor: Pedagogic Strategies in Transmedia *Doctor Who*', Elizabeth Evans considers how educational and entertainment-oriented responses are brought together in 'The Gunpowder Plot'. Theorising different learning strategies that are drawn on by the game's designers, and highlighted in teachers' resource packs, Evans shows how notions of player interactivity and choice are linked to the possibility of choosing *not* to learn (or consume historical information), instead simply pursuing goal-oriented play.

Approaching transmedia *Who* also means addressing online, digital fan practices, something that Rebecca Williams ponders via a case study of Steven Moffat's Twitter participation in 'Tweeting the TARDIS: Interaction, Liveness and Social Media in *Doctor Who*'. Alongside developments in TV texts and industry contexts, transmedia and social media like Tumblr and Twitter represent emergent dimensions of *Who* that are difficult for fans and academics to ignore. In Chapter 8, Williams considers the idea that fans can now interact with showrunners and other production personnel more easily and rapidly than ever before, arguing that behind the Twitter hype ongoing structural inequalities remain between producers and fans. Despite this, Twitter's 'presentism' and informational pace put a premium on 'liveness', transforming *Doctor Who*'s texts into ongoing events: of promotion, of mediated closeness between fans and producers, of fan commentary and emotional expression. *Doctor Who* studies may be prefigured in the concept of TV *Who* as an 'unfolding text', but by analysing how Cardiff's Official *Doctor Who* Convention was tweeted, Williams moves towards analysing Twitterverse *Who* as an unfolding *event*.

Mention of Cardiff brings me to the third major reason for this book, and to the essays in Part 3. If *Who* has been thought of as essentially (although variably) British,[56] only recently getting 'the props it deserves in the States',[57] it still has not been geographically positioned in the past in quite the way it is today. Based historically at BBC TV Centre for much of its run, the show generally used to film within a certain radius of London,[58] but it was not specifically mediated, publicized or thought of as 'metropolitan'. *Another pronounced new dimension of* Who *thus lies in its newfound connection with the city of Cardiff, its symbolic 'home'.* This novel sense of space is partly reflected on by Rebecca Williams at the end of Part 2, but it is picked up as a central topic in Part 3. Melissa Beattie's Chapter 9, 'The *"Doctor Who* Experience" (2012—) and the Commodification of Cardiff Bay', focuses on the exhibition and walk-through 'Experience' that was relocated from London to Cardiff in June of 2012. The 'Experience', situated very close to *Doctor Who*'s latest production studios Roath Lock, provides a commodified focal point for *Who*'s articulation with Cardiff which fans can gain access to (unlike Roath Lock Studios, which usually permit no public access). Beattie analyses how the 'Experience' walk-through constructs a sense of 'entering' diegetic space for its visitors, and wonders why it is that the free, non-commodified availability of filming locations and 'cult geography' around Cardiff Bay doesn't harm the commercial viability of the 'Experience'. Her answer takes us beyond the issue of how BBC Worldwide makes money out of *Who* and fan tourism, suggesting that fans and governmental/corporate authorities all cooperate in blurring diegetic and extra-diegetic realities. And by collaboratively coproducing Cardiff as the modern, 'cool' and glossy 'home of *Doctor Who*', both fans and marketing folk problematically rewrite Cardiff Bay's history, silencing its past.

Further to issues of space and place, *Who*'s *newly auratic spaces are paralleled by new times*, not just the show's latest 'golden age', but also times of nostalgia and remembrance – even mourning – occasioned by the programme's lengthy, multigenerational history. Chapter 10, 'Remembering Sarah Jane: Intradiegetic Allusions, Embodied Presence/Absence and Nostalgia' by Ross P. Garner tackles some of these difficult issues. He argues against postmodernist attacks on nostalgia, instead seeking to positively revalue the term. Garner also distinguishes between audience nostalgia occasioned by redesigned monsters – harking back to Britton's detailed design analysis in Part 1 – and nostalgia premised on the return of actors/characters. After all, actors cannot (yet) be redesigned and modernised in the way that the Daleks, Cybermen, Sontarans and others have been. Rather, the embodied presence of actors such as Elisabeth Sladen has reminded fans of the passage of time. Garner covers a range of topics, including 'intradiegetic allusion', before turning to the matter of Elisabeth Sladen's unexpected and untimely death in 2011. Along with embodied presence, traumatic absence also spurs on nostalgic memories, but in a very different register. This time, fans sought to manage the emotional shock and

INTRODUCTION

upset of Sladen's loss by projecting their cultural identities back into a comforting past, thus restoring a sense of basic or 'ontological security'.

If bleaker times of mortality and sadness have recently circled around *Who* – Sladen's passing was preceded by the loss of Nick Courtney, and followed shortly after by the deaths of Caroline John and Mary Tamm – then these dark dimensions also run up against brighter times of commemoration and celebration, especially in *Doctor Who*'s golden year of 2013. Although *Who* has celebrated multiple anniversaries before, in Chapter 11 – 'Anniversary Adventures in Space and Time: The Changing Faces of *Doctor Who*'s Commemoration' – I argue that the 50th is actually unique. It combines mass audience popularity with branding logics and practices, leading to a cross-media, coordinated and extended 11-month or year-long event quite unlike 10th, 20th or even 40th anniversaries. By analytically categorising *Who*'s different celebrations into four types – naive, hybrid, niche and hyped – I suggest that changing industry and fan discourses have informed concepts of 'the *Doctor Who* anniversary' from 1973 through to today. To contemporary fandom, for instance, it may seem extremely odd that 'The Three Doctors' was actually broadcast almost a year ahead of *Who*'s tenth birthday. Our notion of a TV anniversary is now far more date-and-time specific (it is 'event' TV, after all, to use that term again) rather than being linked to cyclical notions of ephemeral, ritualised and seasonal TV drama. Given these changes, it is surprising that TV studies has not had much to say on the subject of television anniversaries.

Of course, a closing piece on *Who*'s anniversaries is suitably fitting for this volume's 2013 publication. But more than that, it is immensely fitting that a TV programme representing adventures in space and time has itself undergone – and is still undergoing – vital transformations in space, time and media. Ultimately, if there isn't just one answer to 'The Question' of what *Doctor Who* studies should or could be (given *Who*'s ever-shifting identity), I hope that readers will nevertheless appreciate the essays, and the ludic activity, that follow.

NOTES

1   See Segal, Philip with Russell, Gary, *Doctor Who Regeneration: The Story Behind the Revival of a Television Legend* (HarperCollinsEntertainment, London, 2000). Academic accounts of the TV film include Cull, Nicholas J., 'Tardis at the OK Corral: *Doctor Who* and the USA' in John R. Cook and Peter

Wright (eds) *British Science Fiction Television: A Hitchhiker's Guide* (I.B.Tauris, London, New York, NY, 2006), pp. 52–70, and Wright, Peter, 'Expatriate! Expatriate! *Doctor Who: The Movie* and commercial negotiation of a multiple text' in Tobias Hochscherf and James Leggott (eds) *British Science Fiction Film and Television: Critical Essays* (McFarland, Jefferson, MO, 2011), pp. 128–42.

2   Hills, Matt, *Triumph of a Time Lord: Regenerating Doctor Who in the Twenty-First Century* (I.B.Tauris, London, New York, NY, 2010); Bould, Mark (2008) 'Science fiction television in the United Kingdom' in J.P. Telotte (ed.) *The Essential Science Fiction Television Reader* (University Press of Kentucky, Lexington, KY, 2008), pp. 209–30.

3   O'Day, Andrew, *Doctor Who, The Eleventh Hour* (I.B.Tauris, London, New York, NY, 2013).

4   Marlow, Christopher, 'The folding text: *Doctor Who*, adaptation and fan fiction' in Rachel Carroll (ed.) *Adaptation in Contemporary Culture: Textual Infidelities* (Continuum, London, 2009), pp. 46–57.

5   Gray, Jonathan, *Show Sold Separately: Promos, Spoilers and Other Media Paratexts* (New York University Press, New York, NY, London, 2010); Howe, David J. and Blumberg, Arnold T., *Howe's Transcendental Toybox Update No. 2: The Complete Guide to 2004–2005 Doctor Who Merchandise* (Telos, Tolworth, 2006).

6   Booth, Paul *Digital Fandom: New Media Studies* (Peter Lang, New York, NY, 2010); *Fan Phenomena: Doctor Who* (Intellect, Bristol, 2013); Cherry, Brigid, 'Squee, Retcon, Fanwank and the Not-We: Computer-mediated discourse and the online audience for nu*Who*' in Chris Hansen (ed.) *Ruminations, Peregrinations, and Regenerations: A Critical Approach to Doctor Who* (Cambridge Scholars Publishing, Newcastle upon Tyne, 2010), pp. 209–32; Hadas, Leora, 'The Web planet: How the changing Internet divided *Doctor Who* fan fiction writers' *The Journal of Transformative Works and Cultures* III (2009) available online at http://journal.transformativeworks.org/index.php/twc/article/view/129, accessed 30 April 2013; Sarachan, Jeremy, 'Doctor Who fan videos, YouTube, and the public sphere' in Chris Hansen (ed) *Ruminations, Peregrinations, and Regenerations: A Critical Approach to Doctor Who* (Cambridge Scholars Publishing, Newcastle upon Tyne, 2010), pp. 249–61.

7   Robb, Brian J., *Timeless Adventures: How Doctor Who Conquered TV* (Kamera Books, Harpenden, 2009).

8   Newman, Kim, *BFI TV Classics: Doctor Who* (BFI Publishing, London, 2005).

9   Leach, Jim, *Doctor Who: TV Milestones* (Wayne State University Press, Detroit, MI, 2009).

10 Booy, Miles. *Love and Monsters: The Doctor Who Experience, 1979 to the Present* (I.B.Tauris, London, New York, NY, 2012).

11 Hills, Matt, 'Televisuality without television? The Big Finish audios and discourses of "tele-centric" *Doctor Who*' in David Butler (ed.) *Time and Relative Dissertations in Space: Critical Perspectives on Doctor Who* (Manchester University Press, Manchester, New York, NY, 2007), pp. 280–95; Smith, Dale, 'Broader and deeper: the lineage and impact of the Timewyrm series' in David Butler (ed.) *Time and Relative Dissertations in*

INTRODUCTION

Space: Critical Perspectives on Doctor Who (Manchester University Press, Manchester, New York, NY, 2007), pp. 263–79; Parkin, Lance, 'Truths universally acknowledged: how the "rules" of Doctor Who affect the writing' in Pat Harrigan and Noah Wardrip-Fruin (eds) Third Person: Authoring and Exploring Vast Narratives (MIT Press, Massachusetts, MA, 2009), pp. 13–24; Cornell, Paul and Orman, Kate, 'Two interviews about Doctor Who' in Pat Harrigan and Noah Wardrip-Fruin (eds) Third Person: Authoring and Exploring Vast Narratives (MIT Press, Massachusetts, MA, 2009), pp. 33–40; Britton, Piers D., TARDISbound: Navigating the Universes of Doctor Who (I.B.Tauris, London, 2011).

12   See Porter, Lynnette, The Doctor Who Franchise: American Influence, Fan Culture and the Spinoffs (McFarland, Jefferson, MO, 2012).

13   Booy, Miles (2010) 'Doctor Who' in Stacey Abbott (ed.) The Cult TV Book (I.B.Tauris, London, New York, NY, 2010), pp. 189–90.

14   Hills, Matt, 'Doctor Who' in David Lavery (ed.) The Essential Cult TV Reader (University Press of Kentucky, Lexington, KY, 2010), pp. 97–103.

15   Short, Sue, Cult Telefantasy Series (McFarland, Jefferson, MO, 2011).

16   Shimpach, Shawn, Television in Transition (Wiley-Blackwell, Malden, 2010), p. 178.

17   Amy tells the 11th Doctor he has 'seven grey hairs' in a scene cut from 'The Angels Take Manhattan'; see Moffat, Steven (2012) 'Production Notes' in Doctor Who Magazine 453 (2012), p. 6.

18   Porter: The Doctor Who Franchise, p. 167.

19   Aldridge, Mark and Murray, Andy, T is for Television: The Small Screen Adventures of Russell T. Davies (Reynolds and Hearn Ltd., Kew Gardens, 2008); and for a useful volume published after Davies's departure from the show, see also Bradshaw, Simon, Keen, Antony, and Sleight, Graham (eds) The Unsilent Library: Essays on the Russell T. Davies Era of the New Doctor Who (Science Fiction Foundation, London, 2011).

20   Collins, Frank, The Pandorica Opens: Exploring the worlds of the Eleventh Doctor (Classic TV Press, Cambridge, 2010); Charles, Alec, 'The crack of doom: the uncanny echoes of Steven Moffat's Doctor Who' in Science Fiction Film and Television IV/1 (2011), pp. 1–23; Hills, Matt (2011) 'A showrunner goes to war: Doctor Who and the almost fans' Antenna, 6 June 2011, available online at http://blog.commarts.wisc.edu/2011/06/06/a-show-runner-goes-to-war-doctor-who-and-the-almost-fans/, accessed 30 April 2013; Peacock, Steven (2011) 'Against Dr. Who', CST Online, 8 June 2011, available online at http://cstonline.tv/against-dr-who, accessed 30 April 2013.

21   Layton, David, The Humanism of Doctor Who: A Critical Study in Science Fiction and Philosophy (McFarland, Jefferson, MO, 2012); Leitch, Gillian I. (ed.) Doctor Who in Time and Space: Essays on Themes, Characters, History and Fandom, 1963–2012 (McFarland, Jefferson, MO, 2013); Porter, Lynnette, Tarnished Heroes, Charming Villains and Modern Monsters: Science Fiction in Shades of Gray on 21st Century Television (McFarland, Jefferson, MO, 2010).

22   Garner, Ross P., Beattie, Melissa, and McCormack, Una (eds) Impossible Worlds, Impossible Things: Cultural Perspectives on Doctor Who, Torchwood

and *The Sarah Jane Adventures* (Cambridge Scholars Publishing, Newcastle upon Tyne, 2010); Hansen, Chris (ed.) *Ruminations, Peregrinations, and Regenerations: A Critical Approach to Doctor Who* (Cambridge Scholars Publishing, Newcastle upon Tyne, 2010).

23 Couch, Steve, Watkins, Tony, Williams, Peter S., *Back in Time: A Thinking Fan's Guide to Doctor Who* (Damaris Books, Bletchley, 2005).

24 Lewis, Courtland and Smithka, Paula (eds), *Doctor Who and Philosophy* (Open Court Publishing, Chicago, IL, 2011).

25 Burdge, Anthony S., Burke, Jessica and Larsen, Kristine (eds) *The Mythological Dimensions of Doctor Who* (Kitsune Books, Crawfordville, FL, 2010).

26 Cornell, Paul (ed.), *Licence Denied: Rumblings from the Doctor Who Underground* (Virgin Books, London, 1997).

27 For example, Thomas, Lynne M. and O'Shea, Tara (eds) *Chicks Dig Time Lords: A Celebration of Doctor Who by the Women Who Love It* (Mad Norwegian Press, Illinois, IL, 2010); Stanish, Deborah and Myles, L. M. (eds) *Chicks Unravel Time: Women Journey Through Every Season of Doctor Who* (Mad Norwegian Press, Illinois, IL, 2012); Williams, Rebecca, 'Desiring the Doctor: Identity, gender and genre in online fandom' in Tobias Hochscherf and James Leggott (eds) *British Science Fiction Film and Television: Critical Essays* (McFarland, Jefferson, MO, 2011), pp. 167–77.

28 Magrs, Paul, 'Afterword: My adventures' in David Butler (ed.) *Time and Relative Dissertations in Space: Critical Perspectives on Doctor Who* (Manchester University Press, Manchester, New York, NY, 2007): p. 308.

29 Magrs, Paul, *Diary of a Dr. Who Addict* (Simon and Schuster UK, London, 2010).

30 As noted by Booy: *Love and Monsters*, p. 107; see also Hastie, Amelie, 'The epistemological stakes of *Buffy the Vampire Slayer*: Television criticism and marketing demands' in Elana Levine and Lisa Parks (eds) *Undead TV: Essays on Buffy the Vampire Slayer* (Duke University Press, Durham, NC, 2007), pp. 74–95.

31 Hastie: 'The epistemological stakes of *Buffy the Vampire Slayer*', p. 88.

32 Tulloch, John and Alvarado, Manuel, *Doctor Who: The Unfolding Text* (Macmillan, Basingstoke, 1983); Tulloch, John and Jenkins, Henry, *Science Fiction Audiences: Watching Doctor Who and Star Trek* (Routledge, London, 1995).

33 See Parkhurst, Roy, 'The critic as vampire: Parasitic relations in media studies and popular culture' in Gareth Schott and Kirstine Moffat (eds) *Fanpires: Audience Consumption of the Modern Vampire* (New Academia Publishing, Washington DC, WA, 2011), pp. 291–312; Lavery, David (2004) '"I wrote my thesis on you!" *Buffy* studies as an academic cult', *Slayage* 4.1-2/ Nos. 13–14, available online at http://slayageonline.com/essays/slayage13_14/Lavery.htm, accessed 30 April 2013.

34 Hoge, Charles William, 'Whodology: Encountering *Doctor Who* fan fiction through the portals of play studies and ludology', *Journal of Transformative Works and Cultures* VIII (2011) available online at http://journal.transformativeworks.org/index.php/twc/article/view/262/223, accessed 30 April 2013.

INTRODUCTION

35 See, for example, on the 'Inspector Spacetime' phenomenon: Booth, Paul (2012), 'Fan I am: hyperreal fandom and parody', available online at http://www.youtube.com/watch?v=DWQUNJQ1fec, accessed 30 April 2013.
36 Hoge: 'Whodology'.
37 For good recent examples of such work – produced primarily for a fan readership but drawing on media/cultural theory – see Collins: *The Pandorica Opens*, and Sandifer, Philip, *TARDIS Eruditorum – A Unauthorized Critical History of Doctor Who Volume 1: William Hartnell* (CreateSpace Independent Publishing Platform, 2011), and *TARDIS Eruditorum – An Unauthorized Critical History of Doctor Who Volume 2: Patrick Troughton* (CreateSpace Independent Publishing Platform, 2012).
38 Matt Hills (Chapter 11 in this book) was previously responsible for Hills: *Triumph of a Time Lord*.
39 Piers D. Britton (Chapter 2 in this book) is author of the outstanding Britton: *TARDISbound*.
40 David Butler (Chapter 1 in this book) put together the impressive Butler, *Time and Relative Dissertations in Space: Critical Perspectives on Doctor Who*.
41 Andrew O'Day (Chapter 6 in this book) has edited a strong collection of essays on 'the Matt Smith and Steven Moffat era'; see O'Day: *Doctor Who, The Eleventh Hour*.
42 Namely Melissa Beattie (Chapter 9 in this book) and Ross Garner (Chapter 10), two of the editorial triumvirate behind Garner, Beattie, and McCormack: *Impossible Worlds, Impossible Things*.
43 Bonnie Green and Chris Willmott (Chapter 3 in this book) are the previous authors of 'Ain't we all the same? Underneath, ain't we all kin?' in Courtland Lewis and Paula Smithka (eds) *Doctor Who and Philosophy: Bigger on the Inside* (Open Court, Chicago, IL, 2011), pp. 99–109.
44 Rebecca Williams (Chapter 8 in this book) has overseen *Torchwood Declassified: Investigating Mainstream Cult Television* (I.B.Tauris, London, New York, NY, 2013).
45 Catherine Johnson (Chapter 5 in this book) is author of the ground-breaking *Branding Television* (Routledge, London and New York, NY, 2012).
46 Elizabeth Evans (Chapter 7 in this book) has written the extremely timely *Transmedia Television: Audiences, New Media and Daily Life* (Routledge, London, 2011).
47 Will Brooker (Chapter 4 in this book) is, among many other studies, most recently the author of *Hunting the Dark Knight: Twenty-First Century Batman* (I.B.Tauris, London, New York, NY, 2012).
48 Britton: *TARDISbound*, p. 56.
49 For useful work on *Doctor Who Confidential*'s representations of Davies as showrunner see Cornea, Christine, 'Showrunning the *Doctor Who* franchise: A reply to Denise Mann' in Vicki Mayer, Miranda J. Banks and John Thornton Caldwell (eds) *Production Studies: Cultural Studies of Media Industries* (Routledge, New York, NY, London, 2009) pp. 115–22.
50 Sleight, Graham, *The Doctor's Monsters: Meanings of the Monstrous in Doctor Who* (I.B.Tauris, London, New York, NY, 2012).

51 And for another relatively unusual disciplinary take on *Doctor Who*'s monsters, see Dixit, Priya, 'Relating to difference: Aliens and alienness in *Doctor Who* and international relations' in *International Studies Perspectives* XIII/3 (2012), pp. 289–306.
52 See Hills, Matt, 'What ever happened to the Time Lord? Mythology and fandom in Neil Gaiman's contributions to unfolding texts' in Anthony S. Burdge, Jessica Burke and Kristine Larsen (eds) *The Mythological Dimensions of Neil Gaiman* (Kitsune Books, Crawfordville, FL, 2012), pp. 64–80.
53 See, for example, Bignell, Jonathan, and Andrew O'Day, *Terry Nation* (Manchester University Press, Manchester, 2004); Murray, Andy 'The talons of Robert Holmes' in David Butler (ed.) *Time and Relative Dissertations in Space: Critical Perspectives on Doctor Who* (Manchester University Press, Manchester, New York, NY, 2007), p. 217–32.
54 For one example of these shifting production practices, where BBC Wales' *Doctor Who* is made with its own promotion in mind, see Hills, Matt, 'The dispersible television text: theorising moments of the new *Doctor Who*', *Science Fiction Film and Television* I/1 (2008), pp. 25–44. Such practices have continued, inflected in new ways, in the Moffat era, for example in the high concept 'movie posters' approach of series seven.
55 For more on this shift, specifically in relation to the *Doctor Who* spin-off *Torchwood*, see Hills, Matt, '*Torchwood*'s trans-transmedia: Media tie-ins and brand "fanagement"', *Participations: Journal of Audience and Reception Studies* IX/2 (2012), available online at http://www.participations.org/Volume%209/Issue%202/23%20Hills.pdf, accessed 30 April 2013.
56 See, for example, Selznick, Barbara, 'Rebooting and re-branding: The changing brands of *Doctor Who*'s Britishness' in Chris Hansen (ed.) *Ruminations, Peregrinations, and Regenerations: A Critical Approach to Doctor Who* (Cambridge Scholars Publishing, Newcastle upon Tyne, 2010), pp. 68–84.
57 D'Arminio, Aubry, '*Doctor Who* is No. 1', *TV Guide* 10–23 December 2012, p. 15.
58 Bignell, Richard, *Doctor Who On Location* (Reynolds and Hearn Ltd., Kew Gardens, 2001).

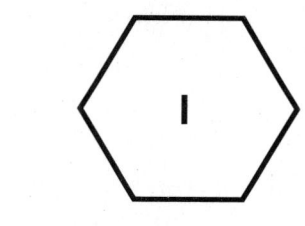

NEW *DOCTOR WHO*

# 1

A GOOD SCORE GOES TO WAR
Multiculturalism, Monsters and Music in New *Doctor Who*

David Butler

When *Doctor Who* returned to BBC television in 2005, one of the underlying themes in the first series was the acceptance of difference and coming to terms with the alien. Rose struggles to adjust to the aliens she encounters in 'The End of the World' (2005) but finds it easier when she learns that she has things in common with Raffalo, the alien plumber she befriends. However, in the very next episode, 'The Unquiet Dead' (2005), the Doctor berates Rose for being unable to recognise the validity of another (alien) cultural practice ('It is different yeah – it's a different morality – get used to it or go home') yet by the mid-season point it is Rose who calls attention to the Doctor's inability to see beyond his own prejudices in the climax to 'Dalek' (2005). As new *Doctor Who* has continued, the programme has repeatedly portrayed the monstrous figure, one of the staple sources of fear in classic *Doctor Who*, as sympathetic. From the Dalek–human hybrid in 'Evolution of the Daleks' (2007) to the Krafayis in 'Vincent and the Doctor' (2010), one of the values of the new series, as Matt Hills asserts, is that 'monstrous appearances can be deceptive and that "monsters" [...] can be understood rather than narratively repressed or destroyed'.[1] All of the examples from the new series mentioned above revolve around the tension generated by the 'problem' of difference and its (mis)recognition, with the alien or monster operating as a metaphor for the human Other.

Following the work of Charles Taylor (1994), the concept of recognition is at the core of debates over multiculturalism, debates that have increased dramatically in the US and Britain in the years following the terrorist attacks of 9/11 in 2001 and 7/7 in 2005, respectively.[2] Whether one is a champion of multiculturalism such as Tariq Modood, a stern critic like Rumy Hasan or a more balanced advocate such as Anne Phillips, those engaged in the debate over multiculturalism tend to agree on the nature of the solution. Despite their opposing views, in Hasan's[3] call for intercultural fusion and Modood's[4] support for the benefits of a multilogical process, both scholars are united in their recommendation of the need for interaction between different cultures rather than separation and the dangers of ghettoization. But to what extent does the music for new *Doctor Who* 'recognise' the monster or alien cultures and species? If, as Matt Hills says, monstrous appearances can be deceptive then can that be extended to 'monstrous' sounds and music?

The original run of *Doctor Who* (1963–89) was often reliant on music and sound design to enhance the realisation of the multitude of alien worlds visited by the Doctor and the various species that inhabited (or invaded) them. As Kevin Donnelly has noted, 'sound and music had to carry out a lot of the "imagining" for a programme beset with cheap sets, basic lighting and unconvincing special effects'.[5] Alien worlds and monstrous invaders were often accompanied by the prominent use of electronic timbres and music rejecting the more conventional techniques of mainstream approaches to scoring narrative fictions. In this respect, much of the music for the alien and monstrous in 'classic' *Doctor Who* corresponds with the third and fourth of five phases of science fiction film music identified by Philip Hayward, emphasising discordant, atonal and experimental aspects of orchestration and instrumentation.[6] Murray Gold's scores for new *Doctor Who*, however, have moved the programme's overriding sound into Hayward's fifth phase: the prominence of classic Hollywood-derived orchestral scores fused with popular idioms. Gold's musical style is part of what Matt Hills characterises as an overall 'anti-science-fictional' shift in the programme.[7] This chapter argues that one of the effects of this shift has been a homogenisation of the musical cultures and soundworlds encountered by the Doctor and a condensation of the range of music featured in the programme, privileging the human at the loss of the alien. The programme's sound champions a fusion of classical and popular genres of music with the BBC National Orchestra of Wales grounding the predominant sound in the traditions of Western tonality and the European classical concert hall. If the extensive electronics of classic-era scores such as 'The Sea Devils' (1972), 'Earthshock' (1982) and 'Revelation of the Daleks' (1985) suggest that their respective hostile species have taken over our sound waves as well as the diegesis, the music of the aliens and monsters in new *Doctor Who* tends to assimilate these species into the symphony orchestra and renders them, in the words of the Cybermen, 'like us'. Analysing this new dimension of music that's associated with the alien/monstrous in BBC Wales' *Doctor Who*, I focus in particular on 'The End of the World' (2005) and two linked Silurian episodes: 'The Hungry Earth' and 'Cold Blood' (both 2010). By selecting these episodes, I hope to avoid the pitfalls identified by Piers Britton when cultural historians studying *Doctor Who* 'treat contemporary ideological referents as the natural, even inescapable, basis for finding irreducible meaning in the *Who* texts'.[8] Rather than projecting subtext onto a *Doctor Who* story, each of my case studies focuses explicitly on the tensions created by encounters with cultural difference. The Silurian episodes, in particular, address the problem of recognition and coexistence. In a story about the need for two races, humans and Silurians, to share their planet and learn to live together, whether one endorses Hasan's intercultural fusion or Modood's multilogue, is there evidence for mixing and cultural exchange within Gold's scores for 'The Hungry Earth' and 'Cold Blood'?

The Problem of Recognition

Why has the 'politics of recognition' proven so contentious within debates about multiculturalism? When multiculturalism first began to emerge in public discourse in the West during the late 1960s and early 1970s, one of its principal concerns was the need to secure justice for minority rights. As Anne Phillips summarises, by the end of the 1990s it was widely accepted that: 'states can harm their citizens by trivialising or ignoring their cultural identities, and that this harm (commonly described, following Charles Taylor's work, as a failure of recognition) can be as damaging to people as denying them their civil or political rights.'[9] That recognition of difference, however, was not without potential and equally damaging consequences. Critics of multiculturalism in the West have argued that by recognising and tolerating cultural practices that are at odds with the dominant culture (the examples most often mentioned tend to include forced marriages, honour killings and female circumcision via genital mutilation), the result has been that certain minority cultures have become ghettoised rather than integrating more fully within mainstream society. In this understanding, the implications of multiculturalism go far beyond the localised problems of a minority culture being distanced from wider society. Multiculturalism's opponents perceive it as being illiberal and inegalitarian, 'undermining social cohesion, dissipating national identity, and emptying citizenship of much of its content'[10] but as Tariq Modood, one of the leading defenders of multiculturalism in Britain alongside figures such as Bhikhu Parekh, counters:

> Multiculturalism is much more than toleration or the co-presence of mutually indifferent communities. Dialogue necessarily implies openness and the possibility of mutual learning but not uncritical acceptance [...]. Parekh emphasizes that the ultimate value of multiculturalism lies in cross-cultural and cross-civilizational understanding through which we simultaneously appreciate the varied ways to be human whilst more profoundly understanding our own distinctive location.[11]

Modood rejects the sanitised notion of multiculturalism as being a fuzzy 'mutual admiration' society and calls instead for a more plural and 'multilogical process'. Yet the challenge facing the dominant culture, if it aims to remain unified, is, as Rumy Hasan notes, how to ensure that '*oppressive* beliefs and practices' are abandoned 'from wherever they emanate' while, in critiquing certain practices, the dominant culture risks the charge of being intolerant and disrespectful.[12]

Hasan complicates the assumption in the work of C. W. Watson that there are two choices for multiculturalism:

> destroy multiculturalism and transform society into being mono-cultural, or celebrate and encourage multiculturalism so that all cultures are

endorsed by the state and thus risk an *unequal* state in which certain oppressive practices are allowed to continue when they would be strongly discouraged (and perhaps even result in criminal proceedings) if practiced within the dominant culture.[13]

The related potential consequence here is of ghettoization, whereby the tolerance shown to all cultures means that integration and interaction might be less likely. For Hasan, however, there is a third, more preferable option whereby 'ethnic minorities adopt significant elements of the dominant culture while the indigenous majority society adopts aspects of minority cultures to bring about cultural fusion and transformation'.[14] For Hasan, then, this process is not a one-way hierarchical route in which the minority culture is inevitably assimilated into the dominant culture at the expense of its cultural distinctiveness. Hasan thus echoes aspects of Roy Jenkins's 1966 speech as British Home Secretary in which Jenkins defined integration 'not as a flattening process of assimilation but as equal opportunity, coupled with cultural diversity,' a diversity which would avoid the melting pot that would 'turn everybody out in a common mould, as one of a series of carbon copies of someone's misplaced vision of the stereotyped Englishman'.[15] Hasan is quick to challenge the assumption that cultures are fixed and that 'fixity is an unalloyed good' as opposed to being open to the possibility of change.[16] Instead, a genuine process of mixing and exchange would result in something new thanks to:

> ... meaningful contacts between different people of cultural and racial groups, which stimulates the creation of new cultural patterns and altered identities by the absorption of parts of more than one culture [...] bringing in its wake the existence of 'new people', that is, those of 'mixed heritage'.[17]

Applying Hasan's ideas to BBC Wales' *Doctor Who*, it is apparent that visually the series provides 'positive' examples of cultural and 'racial' mixing, from Mickey and Rose to Brannigan and Valerie (cat-person and human) in 'Gridlock' (2007) or Madame Vastra and Jenny (reptile and human) who join the Doctor's band alongside a Sontaran nurse in 'A Good Man Goes to War' (2011), returning to assist him in later episodes. But are there equivalent prominent examples of cultural and racial mixing in the *music* for new *Doctor Who*? In order to better understand the principal approach to scoring, and so by extension recognising cultural difference in the new *Doctor Who*, it is necessary to establish first how Murray Gold's music for the series relates to other traditions in film and television music and the scoring of science fiction in particular.

Scoring the Alien

One of the core functions of music in mainstream screen fictions is, as Claudia Gorbman states in her influential list of the principles of classical film music, to provide 'narrative cueing' in order to help establish setting and character.[18] Simon Frith notes how film music often has to quickly establish a specific mood or situation by employing 'musical shorthand' through the use of generic conventions.[19] This shorthand often relies on and ensures the perpetuation of stereotypes, especially in terms of ethnicity – a quick burst of bagpipes and (assuming we are familiar with the cultural code at work) we know we are in Scotland, an accordion means we're probably in Paris, brass bands Yorkshire – which, at worst, can result in a cultural or 'racial' essentialism (all Scots like bagpipes, all African Americans love the blues and have innate natural rhythm and so on). When science fiction began to flourish as a Hollywood genre in the 1950s, it soon acquired a musical shorthand of its own. As James Wierzbicki argues in his analysis of the ground-breaking score for *Forbidden Planet* (1956):

> ... recent developments in science and the suddenly widespread belief in UFOs had given [aliens] at least a soupçon of credibility [...]. Like the various ethnic Others who preceded it to the screen, the suddenly ubiquitous and conceptually graspable alien/mutant Other of the postwar years demanded a sonic calling card. With no anthropological materials to guide them in their search for a musical stereotype, Hollywood composers turned to technology.[20]

The technology that provided that initial distinctive science fiction sound was the theremin, but in time it would also include other uses of electronics, such as the cybernetic circuits constructed by Bebe and Louis Barron in *Forbidden Planet* or the synthesisers employed by Vangelis for *Blade Runner* (1982). The legacy of the connection between science fiction and electronic music is, of course, evident in abundance throughout the scores of 'classic' *Doctor Who*, particularly in the contributions of Tristram Cary, Brian Hodgson and Malcolm Clarke during the 1960s and 1970s, which often abandoned recognisable melody in favour of atypical tone–colour and ambience. Science fiction cinema and television has often encouraged the use of unusual sounds, but these have not necessarily always been electronic. Nor does it follow that music outside of the conventional sounds of mainstream film music, which are rooted in Western tonality and the traditions of late nineteenth century orchestral romanticism, has always been negatively associated with hostile alien menaces. Claudia Gorbman is quite right in her observation that:

> There is little that's progressive or subversive about [...] the electronic sounds that waft over the strange *Forbidden Planet*, or the electronically generated music complicit with the alcoholic dementia of Ray Milland in *The Lost Weekend*. David Bordwell in fact cites *Hangover Square's* score to argue for Hollywood's capacity for 'non-disruptive differentiation,' as the film's discordant music is narratively motivated by its connection to a deranged character.[21]

But in rare instances, alien sounds can also be associated with positive qualities that *do* disrupt prevailing ideological assumptions. In *2001: A Space Odyssey* (1968), for example, the atonal and non-melodic 'difficulty' of György Ligeti's *Requiem for Mezzo Soprano, Two Mixed Choirs and Orchestra* (1963–5) is associated with an alien presence that, in its absence of familiar rules of melody, harmony and rhythm, appears to be threatening but can also be interpreted, in Timothy Scheurer's argument, as conveying the chaos of creative energy out of which can come development, progress and evolution through the rejection of established order.[22] Each time the *Requiem* is heard, those individuals encountering the alien are stimulated to make a profound advance for their species.

By the late 1970s and early 1980s, however, the success of the *Star Wars* films, with their lavish orchestral scores harking back to the romantic flourishes of classical Hollywood, and the heroic orchestral themes associated with the *Star Trek* films had encouraged a new emphasis on the large-scale orchestra in the scoring of epic science fiction adventure films and series. This approach to science fiction scoring would become the prevailing model, so much so that by 2004 Lawrence Miles and Tat Wood could assert that

... in the twenty-first century, music in television (and fantasy television especially) is even more standardised, even more banal than it was in the [...] '60s. Modern SF isn't supposed to sound peculiar, or alien, or alarming. It's supposed to sound like Jerry Goldsmith and that's about all.[23]

As one of the most versatile of Hollywood composers, sounding like Jerry Goldsmith could, of course, mean anything from the atonal, primal modernism of *Planet of the Apes* (1968) to the bittersweet swing-infused nostalgia of *Chinatown* (1974) or the surging orchestral optimism of his main theme for *Star Trek: The Motion Picture* (1979), which became the title theme for *Star Trek: The Next Generation* (1987–94). It is this latter style, however, that would dominate (Hollywood) science fiction scoring in the 1990s and 2000s and it is revealing that when Bear McCreary was approached to provide the music for the re-imagined *Battlestar Galactica* (2004–9) the one thing the production team did not want was a brass-heavy orchestral sound as they felt it had become a cliché. As McCreary (2006) has explained, 'they felt that strong, orchestral fanfare had been done to death in science fiction'.[24] Instead of the sounds of the European symphony orchestra, McCreary turned to instruments from around the world based on a concept of wanting to use musical instruments that were as ancient as possible. Prominent instruments in McCreary's soundworld for *Battlestar Galactica* include the Armenian duduk, Japanese taiko drums, Indian tabla and sitar, Balinese gamelan, Irish uilleann pipes, Chinese erhu, Portuguese guitar and glass (h)armonica. In a narrative about the remnants of humanity struggling for survival, McCreary's extremely unusual combination of instruments conveys the diversity and rich heritage of the human race rather than the narrower range of human cultures that would have been audible through the dominant and more Eurocentric sounds of a conventional orchestra. The Federation of *Star Trek* may well applaud the presence of diverse ethnicities and even species on the bridge of its starships, but the prevailing music in the franchise suggests that this optimistic future is still driven by European traditions and concerns.

At the same time that Bear McCreary was reinventing not just the approach to music in the original *Battlestar Galactica* (1978–80) but science fiction film/television music more generally, the new series of *Doctor Who* also appeared with a commitment to reimagining its own musical heritage, in this case the prominent use of electronic music.

Murray Gold has scored the entirety of new *Doctor Who* thus far, working in close collaboration with Ben Foster as orchestrator. As with McCreary, Gold received clear directions from his producers as to the kind of music they wanted, but with markedly different choices to those for *Battlestar Galactica*:

> There was only one type of music they specifically didn't want, and that was Radiophonic Workshop-style electronic stuff. They said they wanted an orchestra. Or rather [. . .] the *sound* of an orchestra – there wasn't the budget for a real one![25]

Following its initial series, with the first *Doctor Who* Christmas special in 2005, Murray Gold secured the services of the BBC National Orchestra of Wales to give the show a flamboyant orchestral feel, one that has remained its musical trademark ever since. The motivations behind this choice include the perceived cinematic grandiosity of the symphony orchestra, helping to distance the programme from its association with low-budget production values during its original run and providing it with the strong, familiar and emotional cinematic feel deemed necessary to secure and maintain a large, popular mainstream audience. Electronic sounds and smaller ensembles have not been entirely excluded from the music for new *Doctor Who*, and Gold demonstrates a joyous willingness to blend popular, classical and 'serious' idioms, but orchestral sound and memorable melodic themes remain the twin heartbeats of the programme's music. Gold's introduction in the liner notes to the series four soundtrack CD underlines the priority given to the orchestra:

> The first [version of this] disc [. . .] sounded like an old radiophonic record [. . .]. The point is, you could make lots of *Doctor Who* albums – even just from this series. The orchestral material sits alongside, and sometimes on top of, the electronic material. I loved [the first version of the disc]. I didn't recognize it, but I really liked it. All the same, I asked [album editor and engineer Jake Jackson] to go back and put all the tunes back in, so here we are, back to normal. Thank goodness. Because the point of this show is to tell stories and to tell them in the most vivid, bold and exuberant way imaginable. And although the music performs a separate function of creating ominous moods, it is working best when it is narrating and jumping and punching the air and bounding along with the story.[26]

This emphasis placed on the familiar sounds of the symphony orchestra and the programme's 'anti-science-fictional shift' have had a notable effect on the way new *Who* has portrayed the aliens and monsters encountered by the Doctor. The first real test of the new series' approach to science fiction came in its second episode, 'The End of the World' (2005), with the Doctor taking Rose on a proper trip in the TARDIS: the year 5 billion and the point at which the Earth is about to be engulfed by the Sun. One by one, a series of alien dignitaries arrive on the space station Platform One to observe the Earth's final moments. Gold's scoring of the arrival of the aliens is revealing of the programme's tonal shift under Russell T Davies. As the station steward begins to announce the alien guests, small blue menial workers and attendants scurry into action and the aliens enter in turn. The reaction shots of Rose suggest that she is taken aback by the aliens' appearance, whereas the Doctor seems to be gleefully enjoying her culture shock.

If 'Rose' was told primarily from Rose's point of view, Gold's music at the outset of this scene seems to express the perspective of a different character or group of characters. The jaunty march that accompanies this sequence does not distinguish between, or tell us anything much about, the different alien cultures – or indeed Rose's subjective response to them unless it conveys her attempt to make sense of these little blue people and various alien races by relating them as best she can to her own experience (the chirpy upbeat music associated with the *Teletubbies* [1997–2001] perhaps, or the Oompa-Loompas of *Willy Wonka and the Chocolate Factory* [1971]). Instead, the music conveys an overall mood of cheery busyness as the aliens' perceived strangeness is sonically downplayed. If the music is articulating any character's feelings and auditory point here, it is arguably that of the blue attendants or the Doctor himself, none of whom perceive the situation as odd or alien. In other words, the music is not emphasising 'alien' and 'science fiction' but 'recognisable situation and mood', in a similar vein to the jazz music played by the alien band in the Mos Eisley cantina in *Star Wars* (1977). The visuals might be surprising and exotic (or estranging, following Darko Suvin's (1979) classic definition of science fiction as the dialectic between cognition and estrangement), but the music implies familiarity and the suggestion that, beneath their extraordinary exteriors, these creatures have similar feelings, desires and concerns to our own, which is partly the Doctor's message to Rose in this episode.[27]

There is a revealing contrast between the arrival of alien guests in 'The End of the World' and the arrival of alien delegates in 'Day of Armageddon' (1965), episode two of 'The Daleks' Master Plan'(1965–6). The two occupy very different contexts, of course, both in terms of their production and their respective narratives. The former is a gathering for a social event and in effect the guests are attending a cosmic firework display. The bright music underlines that for them, unlike Rose, it is not a sombre occasion. In contrast, the scene in the 1960s story takes place at a serious conference with military intent. Tristram Cary's electro-acoustic music for this sequence has an uneasy tonality and a combination of instrumentation (electronically-treated woodwind, brass and vibraphone) that, although not denoting the aliens as being necessarily malevolent, certainly identifies them as inhabiting an unfamiliar world. Neither cue in these respective episodes makes significant distinctions between the various species on-screen: the classic cue assimilates the aliens into an overall sense of unease whereas Gold's cue similarly unifies the different aliens but with humour and benevolence (although brief, underlying lower-register minor chords hint at the threat posed by the Adherents of the Repeated Meme). The contrasting approach to instrumentation, tonality and musical idiom is largely representative of the prevailing attitudes towards aliens and the monstrous in the new and original series of *Doctor Who*. Notably, the one character on Platform One to receive the most obvious 'science fiction' and stereotypical 'alien' scoring is the last 'pure' human, Cassandra, who is criticised by Rose for being anything but ('You're not human – anything human got chucked in the bin – you're just skin Cassandra, lipstick and skin'). Cassandra's theme is a delicate waltz with the melody entrusted to a high-pitched theremin sound, placing her in the tradition of science fiction film scoring and the conventions of scoring ethnicity, in this case the non-human alien, as discussed by Wierzbicki.[28] Cassandra may claim she is human but her musical theme suggests otherwise and codes her as alien instead.

'The End of the World' establishes the new series' musical approach towards the alien and monstrous. Attempts at creating alien sounds and musical worlds in the series are rare (the alien musical instrument in 'Dalek' is a momentary exception in series one) with the most sustained example to date being the haunting wordless vocals, pulsing electronics and minimalist percussion for 'Planet of the Ood' (2008). Even here, by the end of the episode the liberated Oods' 'Song of Freedom' unfurls with more recognisable melodic development and instrumental accompaniment. When the new series has made the most extensive use of unconventional and 'difficult' sounds, phrasing and playing techniques, it has been in association with creatures such as the Weeping Angels or the nameless alien entity in 'Midnight' (2008), reinforcing Matt Hills's suggestion that the Weeping Angels 'resemble conventional horror monsters, monsters who have no role other than being monsters [suggesting] that a strand of reactionary horror runs through new *Who*, despite its professed, progressive value systems'.[29] The score for the Steven Moffat-scripted 'Asylum of the Daleks' (2012) also underlines this possibility. Prior to the episode's broadcast, Moffat spoke of his desire to make the Daleks scary for children again ('they'd become cuddly') and to reinvest them with a monstrous malevolence ('they are the nastiest beasts in *Doctor Who*').[30] The episode features a maximum security installation, the Asylum, where the Daleks leave those of their own kind who have gone insane and over which they have no control. For much of the sequences set within the Asylum establishing the Dalek menace, Gold provides brooding cues shorn of the implied 'rationality' of melody.[31] The portentous choral music for his earlier Dalek scores is rejected in favour of a sinister two-note ostinato, non-melodic electronic sound, stark percussive beats and rumbling bass clarinet. Perhaps the clearest evidence of a progressive versus reactionary tension within the production process, however, is audible in the dissonance between the music and script for the reptilian Silurians in 'The Hungry Earth' and 'Cold Blood'.

More Similarities than Differences? 'The Hungry Earth' and 'Cold Blood'

In classic *Doctor Who*, the 'monsters' that repeatedly stimulated the most overt stories about coexistence between species were the civilised reptilian Silurians (otherwise known more accurately as the Eocenes or *Homo reptilia*) in 'Doctor Who and the Silurians' (1970), 'Warriors of the Deep' (1984) and, to a lesser extent, 'The Sea Devils' (1972), which featured the Silurians' aquatic cousins. The Silurians would eventually resurface in new *Doctor Who* in the series five linked episodes 'The Hungry Earth' and 'Cold Blood', written by Chris Chibnall. If 'Warriors of the Deep' was intended by its writer Johnny Byrne to be an analogy for

Cold War tensions between the Soviet Union and the West, Chibnall's story realigns the Silurians with twenty-first century concerns informed by heightened anxieties over immigration and the impact of multiculturalism.

A once proud and thriving civilisation long before the human race, the Silurians have been in hibernation deep beneath the earth for millennia until a number are awoken by a scientific drilling project operating from the Welsh mining village of Cwmtaff in the year 2020 AD. Several humans are abducted by the Silurians, including the husband and son of Ambrose whose father, Tony Mack, is one of the principal workers on the drill. When the Doctor, Rory and Amy arrive, they manage to capture a Silurian warrior, Alaya, but not before she has infected Tony with venom. Alaya's sister, Restac, is intent on all-out war with the humans but the Doctor attempts to defuse the situation by instigating peace talks between the Silurian leader, Eldane, and the leader of the drilling project, Nasreen Chaudhry. These talks collapse after Alaya is killed by Ambrose, and Restac seeks revenge, but not before Eldane commits the Silurians to another thousand years of hibernation in the hope that both sides will be better prepared to negotiate and share the planet in future.

'The Hungry Earth' begins with an interesting audio-visual juxtaposition, but one that is not developed in the music. As the episode opens on an establishing shot of the village of Cwmtaff, we hear the voice of Mo reading from *The Gruffalo*[32] to his son, Elliot: 'But who is this creature with terrible claws and terrible teeth in his terrible jaws?'. The immediate visual answer to this question is provided by a figure approaching in the distance from a row of terraced houses nestling in the valley: Elliot's mother, Ambrose. It's a foreboding audio-visual clue, as Ambrose's actions in 'Cold Blood' threaten to trigger a war and jeopardise any immediate hopes of peaceful coexistence between humans and Silurians. In many ways Ambrose is the story's 'terrible creature' who, as the Doctor tells her frankly, fails to be 'the best of humanity'. Although dialogue in the two episodes frequently draws parallels between the two opposing species, noting the virtues and flaws of both and suggesting that neither should be dismissed or essentialised as terrible creatures (as the Silurian scientist Malokheh says to the prejudiced military commander Restac, 'We're not monsters and neither are they'), the music for the story and the choice of instrumentation for key cues privileges the humans and suggests that aggression and refusal to accept the Other are Silurian traits as opposed to being shared by both species.

Both 'The Hungry Earth' and 'Cold Blood' make use of several of Gold's established *leitmotifs* for the series, but they also extensively feature a new four-note motif that is associated directly with the Silurians. This motif returns incessantly throughout the story, often in quick succession at moments when the Silurian menace is ascendant and is informed, as Gold explains in the liner notes for the series five soundtrack CD, by the 'inflexible and contrary character of the Silurians. The musical phrase that represents them twists and turns quite stridently through both episodes.'[33] Gold's brief account of the Silurian motif is telling, as it conflates the entire Silurian race into those negative characteristics displayed by only two of its representatives: the twin warrior sisters Alaya and Restac. Elsewhere in the story, the only other speaking Silurians, Eldane and Malohkeh, are far from inflexible – both are rational, good-humoured and open to discussion with the Doctor and human characters.

The Silurian motif's instrumentation undergoes a number of transformations but is heard most frequently in brass and woodwind, particularly in bass and even contrabass clarinets. The lower instrumental registers associated with the Silurians are an effective analogue to their habitat in the lower depths of the Earth. There are parallels here with Bernard Herrmann's thinking behind the emphasis on woodwinds, brass and percussion in his score for *Journey to the Center of the Earth* (1959). As Herrmann explained, 'I decided to evoke the mood and feeling of inner earth by using only instruments played in the lower registers'.[34] Carey Blyton's acoustic score for the original Silurian story from 1970 also employs similar conceptual thinking, with woodwind and percussion to the fore. Blyton's striking score takes his conceptual thinking even further, however, by associating the Silurians with the sound of the crumhorn: a pre-modern wind instrument that, as Mark Ayres observes in the DVD feature *Musical Scales* (2008), functions as a logical musical solution to the notion of the Silurians as an ancient civilisation that flourished on Earth before apes had evolved into humans.[35]

The Silurian motif is heard repeatedly in relation to their menacing presence – their impending arrival, their hostile actions or their threats of future violence towards the 'apes' or humans. Yet the most notable use of the Silurian motif is when it is passed on to the human Ambrose.

Alaya goads Ambrose into killing her, knowing that this action has the potential to trigger a war between Silurians and humans. As Ambrose tasers Alaya to death, the Silurian motif is heard in a strident, martial variation in brass instrumentation, and it is heard again in relation to Ambrose later in the episode when she tries to persuade her father to drive the drill into the Silurian city. There are two ways of reading this association of the Silurian motif with the actions of a human female. The first is that Ambrose's actions will fulfil the desires of aggressive, racist Silurians for a 'just' war with the humans – in other words, Ambrose is an unwitting agent of the hawkish Silurians' wish for war. An alternative reading, however, is that in conferring the Silurian motif onto Ambrose she is also being associated with Silurian traits of hostility, inflexibility and violence. Although the Doctor is at pains to point out to the humans that Silurians are no more evil than they are, and that from the Silurian perspective the humans are clearly the invaders, the score for the story gives no sense of there being an equivalent 'inflexibility' or 'hostility' motif for the humans. Despite revenge, aggression, inflexibility and murderous desire being displayed by humans in the story (principally by Ambrose), the score can only convey human hostility by passing the Silurian cue for these traits onto humans displaying them. In other words, Gold's score and the placement of the Silurian motif implies that Ambrose has *become* a Silurian rather than displaying traits that are just as inherent in humans.

Perhaps, as the Doctor says at the end of the 1984 Silurian story, 'there should have been another way'. An alternative approach to the score might have echoed that demonstrated by Ennio Morricone (one of Gold's favourite film composers) for Gillo Pontecorvo's powerful film about the 1954–8 Algerian struggle for independence from French colonialists, *The Battle of Algiers* (1966). The film makes use of recordings Pontecorvo made of Algerian music and a score by Morricone that combines classical European and Arabic idioms with more modern styles and techniques. A member of the Italian communist party, Pontecorvo made the film with state funding from the Algerian government. With such a background, it might seem inevitable that the film would vilify the French and depict them as imperialist monsters, but we get something more shaded. One of the most remarkable things about *The Battle of Algiers* is the way that it offers the different perspectives of the participants in the struggle. If the film ultimately sides with the Algerians (via editing and point-of-view shots) it does not demonise the French colonists in order to get us to share its sympathies, and this approach is extended to the film's music. The same basic theme, an insistent rising and falling ostinato bassline, is associated with the violent activities of both the French military and the Algerian rebels, yet each side gets their own distinctive instrumentation. Unlike Gold's approach to hostility and the Silurians, Morricone's score makes a clear statement about violence being a trait shared by *both* populations and not one that is more characteristic of a particular culture. By the end of the film, the theme associated with Ali, one of the principal Algerian rebels, with non-European inflections in the solo recorder and hints of Arabic tonality in the strings, is heard played on the harpsichord, a distinctively European instrument. Both cultures, French/Western European and Algerian/Arabic are fused, suggesting that their fates are bound together and will require on-going dialogue. In 'Cold Blood', however, distinctive Silurian sounds are lost at the negotiating table and in resolution scenes, replaced with measured, legato strings. In terms of coexistence, the hope for the future, musically, is not a blending of human and Silurian sounds but the reassertion of the calm and harmonious European orchestra. Ultimately, Silurian civilisation and identity is inaudible in the music for the final stages of the story when Eldane's voiceover describes the moment that his race finally emerged from hibernation. The fact that the scene is less about the Silurian people and more about the Doctor's on-going fate and story is emphasised through the music playing a variation on the Doctor's motif.

Conclusion

Through music, the alien in new *Doctor Who* is frequently coded less as an estranging (and so threatening) 'Other', but this comes at the cost of lessened cultural distinctiveness. Unlike Bear McCreary's music for the new *Battlestar Galactica*, which rejects the prominence of the large-scale orchestral score and features instead a fusion of non-Western styles and instruments, the emphasis on the European symphony orchestra in new *Who* creates markedly different ideological connotations, particularly in narratives about coexistence and encounters between different cultures and species. Rumy Hasan stresses the need for representations of cultural interaction and fusion to become a 'prominent feature of the mass media so that it is viewed as the norm'.[36] Visually and in script and performance, there are clear examples of intercultural fusion and hybridity within new *Doctor Who*. By the end of 'Cold Blood', Eldane is agreeable to dialogue with the humans in the future when both sides are better prepared to negotiate; Tony Mack is mutating into something new as a result of the Silurian venom in his bloodstream; and, more positively, in Tony's relationship with Nasreen the story includes a romance between a white Welshman and British Asian woman.

But where the music is concerned, there is far less evidence of genuine hybridity and musical interaction at work. Gold's scores gleefully collapse boundaries between genres by combining popular idioms with the symphony orchestra. There is indeed cultural fusion here but, in Homi Bhabha's understanding of the term, it's not quite the same thing as hybridity. For Bhabha, as Janet Staiger summarises, the hybrid is an authentic cross-cultural encounter – two or more languages speaking to each other:

> To recognise a hybrid forces the dominant culture to look back at itself and see its presumption of universality. Hybridity always opens up the discriminatory presumptions of purity, authenticity, and originality from which this textual hybrid is declared to be a deviation, a bastard, a corruption.[37]

Following Bhabha's thinking, then, the music for new *Doctor Who* has tended not to be hybrid. As Staiger points out,[38] most American multi-genre films are not about two different languages interacting – because all the genres tend to come from the same language family of Western culture. For example, the genres being mingled in a film like *Blue Velvet* (1986) are all from the Hollywood system: film noir, horror and teen-college movies. In this sense, *Blue Velvet* is not a hybrid but is rather inbred and, in the priority given to the orchestra and various influences from Hollywood film music, the potential for hybridity in *Doctor Who*'s music is similarly downplayed with instances of cross-cultural fusion, such as the Indian-inflected cue 'Hanging on the Tablaphone' from the climax of series four being less prevalent.[39]

An emphasis on the sounds of the European classical orchestra is perhaps surprising for a character like the Doctor, who is after all the programme's most prominent alien and a compassionate individual who celebrates encounters with difference. Over the course of both classic and new *Doctor Who*, the Doctor has demonstrated an eclectic fondness for a diverse range of music (nursery rhymes, English music hall, Courtney Pine and modern jazz, Italian opera and Puccini, Soft Cell and Ian Dury) but genres that are nonetheless all grounded in the principles of Western tonality. If the programme provides what Anne Cranny-Francis calls an 'almost fetishistic celebration of "the human", most notably by the Tennant Doctor' then in musical terms the human tends to equate solely with the Western European.[40] Yet there have been glimpses of an openness to sounds beyond Western tonality that might be more fitting for an alien character who has lived for centuries and who has a thirst for travelling to cultures and galaxies far and wide. In the short episode 'Music of the Spheres' (2008), designed to be shown as part of the *Doctor Who* prom at the Royal Albert Hall, the Doctor delights in the abstract, ambient noise generated by the gravity patterns of the planets, suns and galaxies revolving around each other (and which sounds like a blend of breathing, whale song and harmonic whirlies). Later he revels in his cacophonous composition 'Ode to the Universe' (ten seconds of all the instruments in the orchestra playing simultaneously in a similar if less structured fashion to Ligeti's *Atmosphères* [1961] used by Kubrick in *2001*) and closes the episode with a speech about the music inside everybody's head, encouraging the audience to shut their eyes when they're on their own and listen to their own internal music. This speech, evocative of John Cage's openness to the music of sounds in everyday life, points to a more inclusive approach to music than the dominant, albeit glorious, tones and melodies of the new *Doctor Who*'s prevailing orchestral soundworld on TV. Encouraging each individual to nurture his or her own internal song, the Doctor complicates the musical essentialism present in scores such as those for 'The Hungry Earth' and 'Cold Blood', and calls for an acknowledgement of the difference in us all.

NOTES

1 Hills, Matt (2010) *Triumph of a Time Lord: Regenerating Doctor Who in the Twenty-First Century* (I.B.Tauris, London), p. 135.

2 Taylor, Charles (1994) 'The Politics of Recognition', in C. Taylor, A. Gutmann (eds) *Multiculturalism: Examining the Politics of Recognition* (Princeton University Press, Princeton, New Jersey), pp. 25–73.

3 Hasan, Rumy (2009) *Multiculturalism: Some Inconvenient Truths* (Politico's, London).

4. Modood, Tariq (2007) *Multiculturalism* (Polity Press, Cambridge).
5. Donnelly, Kevin J. (2007) 'Between prosaic functionalism and sublime experimentation: *Doctor Who* and musical sound design', in D. Butler (ed.) *Time And Relative Dissertations In Space: Critical perspectives on Doctor Who* (Manchester University Press, Manchester), p. 190.
6. Hayward, Philip (2004) 'Sci-fidelity: Music, sound and genre history', in P. Hayward (ed.) *Off the Planet: Music, Sound and Science Fiction Cinema* (John Libbey Publishing, Eastleigh), p. 2.
7. Hills: *Triumph of a Time Lord*, pp. 197–8.
8. Britton, Piers D. (2011) *TARDISbound: Navigating the Universes of Doctor Who* (I.B.Tauris, London), p. 56.
9. Phillips, Anne (2007) *Multiculturalism without Culture* (Princeton University Press, Princeton, New Jersey), p. 11.
10. Ibid., p. 13.
11. Modood: *Multiculturalism*, p. 65.
12. Hasan: *Multiculturalism: Some Inconvenient Truths*, p. 23.
13. Ibid., p. 22.
14. Ibid., p. 22.
15. Quoted in Phillips: *Multiculturalism without Culture*, p. 4.
16. Hasan: *Multiculturalism*, p. 52.
17. Ibid., pp. 244–5.
18. Gorbman, Claudia (1987) *Unheard Melodies: Narrative Film Music* (British Film Institute, London), p. 73.
19. Frith, Simon (1996) *Performing Rites: Evaluating Popular Music* (Oxford University Press, Oxford), p. 120.
20. Wierzbicki, James (2005) *Louis and Bebe Barron's Forbidden Planet: A Film Score Guide* (Scarecrow Press, Inc, Lanham, Maryland), p. 25.
21. Gorbman: *Unheard Melodies*, p. 153.
22. Scheurer, Timothy (1998) 'The score for 2001: A Space Odyssey,' *The Journal of Popular Film and Television*, xxv/4, pp. 172–82.
23. Miles, Lawrence and Wood, Tat (2004) *About Time: The Unauthorised Guide to Doctor Who 1970–1974 Seasons 7 to 11* (Mad Norwegian Press, New Orleans), p. 81.
24. McCreary, Bear (2006) 'Themes of Battlestar Galactica, Pt I' available online at http://www.bearmccreary.com/#blog/battlestar-galactica-3/themes-of-battlestar-galactica-pt-i/, accessed 27 May 2013.
25. Quoted in Matt Bell (2007) 'Murray Gold: Composing for Doctor Who', available online at http://www.soundonsound.com/sos/jun07/articles/dr-who.htm, accessed 27 May 2013.
26. Gold, Murray (2008) Liner notes for *Doctor Who: Original Television Soundtrack – Series 4*, BBC, Silva Screen Records SILCD1275.
27. Suvin, Darko (1979) *Metamorphoses of Science Fiction* (Yale University Press, New Haven and London).
28. Wierzbicki: *Louis and Bebe Barron's Forbidden Planet: A Film Score Guide*.
29. Hills: *Triumph of a Time Lord*, p. 136.
30. Moffat, Steven (2012) 'The Return of the Daleks' available online at http://www.bbc.co.uk/programmes/p. 0xz5hp, accessed 27 May 2013.

31. Royal Brown addresses the relationship between melody and rationality (order and structure) in his discussion of the 'irrationality' emphasised by the rejection of (extensive) melodic writing in much of Bernard Herrmann's music for the films of Alfred Hitchcock. See Brown, Royal S. (1994) *Overtones and Undertones: Reading Film Music* (University of California Press, Berkeley and Los Angeles), p. 154.
32. Donaldson Julia (1999), *The Gruffalo* (Macmillan Children's Books, London).
33. Gold, Murray (2010) Liner notes for *Doctor Who: Original Television Soundtrack – Series 5*, BBC, Silva Screen Records SILCD1345.
34. Quoted in Steven C. Smith (2002 [1991]) *A Heart at Fire's Center: The Life and Music of Bernard Herrmann* (University of California Press, Los Angeles), p. 228.
35. *Musical Scales* (2008) DVD special feature on the BBC Video/2 Entertain Video *Doctor Who and the Silurians*.
36. Hasan: *Multiculturalism*, p. 53.
37. Staiger, Janet (1997) 'Hybrid or inbred: The purity hypothesis and Hollywood genre history', *Film Criticism*, xxii/1, p. 16.
38. Staiger, *Film Criticism*.
39. Of course, in making use of different genres of popular music, especially those with their roots in African American culture, Gold's scores for *Doctor Who* do contain traces and instances of hybridity but the central point remains: the emphasis on the large-scale European symphony orchestra and popular idioms grounded in Western tonality limits the potential for hybridity within the music and cues like 'Hanging on the Tablaphone' are rare.
40. Cranny-Francis, Anne (2009) 'Why the Cybermen stomp: Sound in the new Doctor Who', *Mosaic*, xlii/2, p. 124.

2

MAKING 'A SUPERIOR BRAND OF ALIEN MASTERMIND'
Doctor Who Monsters and the Rhetoric of (Re)design

Piers D. Britton

In July 2008, the *Daily Telegraph* ran an article entitled 'Doctor Who: Reinventing Davros' to mark the return of the Daleks' fictional creator in 'The Stolen Earth'. The piece incorporates remarks by both Neill Gorton, who moulded a new prosthetic mask and hand for Davros, and Peter McKinstry, the conceptual artist whose designs formed the basis for Davros's 'half-Dalek' wheelchair. After stressing that Gorton and McKinstry turned for inspiration to the 1975 Davros *ur*-image, as opposed to the prosthetics and props created for the character's appearances in the 1980s, the columnist Andrew Pettie explains that 'alterations were made, of course, partly because modern audiences expect a superior brand of alien mastermind'.[1] To underscore the point, he suggests that readers search YouTube for a clip of the 1980s Davros, warning that they will 'gasp at the Hallowe'en clunkiness' of the rubber prosthetics. This discursive pattern is repeated in relation to McKinstry's concept drawings for Davros's wheelchair. Pettie stresses that the new chair remained faithful to the original 'iconic' design, but quotes McKinstry as saying that he had 'beefed Davros up,' making the chair 'more sturdy' than its 'slightly flimsy' predecessors.[2]

Gorton's and McKinstry's comments in the *Telegraph* article epitomise rhetoric surrounding new *Who*'s redesign of signature images from the classic series. Whenever an iconic monster is reintroduced in the new series, its overhaul is generally characterised in documentaries and press reports in terms of the same conceit: responsible modernisation. The revised design is always bold enough to meet current standards for plausibility, but essential, familiar motifs are carefully maintained. What is particularly interesting about this rhetorical device is its double gesture. Creative personnel and other commentators pay homage to the classic series while simultaneously distancing themselves from it, since the renovated design is always shown to improve upon the original in one way or another. As I shall ultimately argue in this chapter, this seeming dichotomy is resolved by branding logic[3] (which is hinted at, whether by accident or design, in Pettie's comment that 'modern audiences expect a superior *brand* of alien mastermind'). Yet as well as probing what has been said about somatic design – by which I mean not only costume but also the continuum of other practices used in character and creature construction, encompassing make-up and prosthetics, digital imagery, and practical prop fabrication – I also want to reflect on elements of design that go unmentioned in the publicity narrative. Rhetoric surrounding signature images overrides or at least mitigates internal disparities in design for the new series, including, as I shall suggest, changes that have occurred since Steven Moffat took over from Russell T Davies as showrunner. Structuring silences and elisions can again be accounted for in relation to branding imperatives.

Developments from 'Classic' to 'New' *Who*: Above-the-Line and Below-the-Line Somatic Design

Before turning to particular design images and the rhetorical project within which some of their possible meanings are negotiated, it is worth establishing how far design, as process and practice, has changed between the demise of the classic series and *Doctor Who*'s revival. In practical terms, the primary locus of design within the production process has undergone a massive shift. The relative affordability of new technologies and practices in the past 15 years has heavily determined the visual character of the new *Doctor Who*, and separated it radically from the classic series. For example, the new series regularly incorporates monsters produced solely with computer animation. In every season this technique has been used for flying creatures, which would either have been sparingly realised with overlay effects or eschewed completely in the old series. Every season has also introduced entities that could not have been rendered as slickly with 'monster suits' or puppets, such as a werewolf and a rock creature with a glowing magma core (in 'Tooth and Claw' and 'The Fires of Pompeii', respectively). This is the most conspicuous manifestation of the general shift in emphasis from pre- to post-production manufacture. Drawing upon a new dimension of computer imagery has also enabled the creation of believable epic-scale settings and solved longstanding problems; for example, the Daleks *en masse* have been spectacularly liberated from the frustration of a cosmos full of staircases.[4]

Other changes in design processes and techniques are less immediately obvious. Shared responsibility for design and realisation is now more usual than in the era of the classic series. Before the restructuring of the BBC in the 1990s, the departments comprising the BBC's Design Group worked for the most part independently of one another, each exerting complete artistic control over the elements within its purview. Today, design is phased and collaborative to a much greater extent, with consultants and credited concept artists more frequently initiating or participating in the design process. A prime example is the design for the new TARDIS interior in 2005, which originated from conceptual art by the comic-book artist Bryan Hitch and was subsequently developed by members of the *Doctor Who* art department under the aegis of production designer Edward Thomas.

The *Telegraph* article on Davros typifies the attention given to these new technologies and processes in *Doctor Who*'s surrounding paratexts. Dominant rhetoric has tended to elide design as an imaginative act with design as the prelude to manufacture. In stressing improved construction techniques for characters such as Davros, the publicity narrative often tacitly implies that *stylistic* improvements are an inevitable corollary – and that both are unavoidable in the face of audience expectation.

In fact, some of the most significant changes between somatic design in classic and new *Doctor Who* are not related at all to the use of new technologies (except, perhaps, in terms of budget allocation). Ironically, for all the trumpeting of revision and improvement, the visual character of monsters in the revival has overall been much more consonant with elements of the old series than costume for humans. Yet the marked change in costume design sensibility for 'ordinary' supporting characters has attracted little comment. After the first few episodes of the initial 2005 season, costume received short shrift in publicity and press coverage (except when a new lead actor's arrival led to the predictable feeding frenzy over the incoming Doctor's 'look'). It is certainly hard to imagine one of today's Dalek episodes being heralded in the *Radio Times* only by an article about the costume designer's creations for *non*-Dalek characters, as was the case for 'Destiny of the Daleks' in 1979.

Given its relative lack of visibility in new *Who*'s paratextual relay, it can hardly be coincidental that costume design in the Davies era was also unobtrusive within the narrative itself. In particular, costumes for episodes set in future and alien worlds were studiedly self-effacing in comparison with the gorgeously flamboyant and inventive imagery created by designers such as June Hudson and Amy Roberts in the classic series – and, for that matter, the bold and striking imagery introduced by Barbara Kidd and Howard Burden in the new, after Steven Moffat became showrunner. Except in the case of the three related stories all set around the year 5 billion – 'The End of the World' (2005), 'New Earth' (2006) and 'Gridlock' (2007) – human characters in futuristic episodes during the Davies era invariably wore contemporary dress, ranging as appropriate from combat fatigues and overalls to jeans and funnel-neck fleeces, and even two-piece business suits. Although 'New Earth' and 'Gridlock' departed somewhat from this tendency, they featured mostly straightforward vintage or period dress, with 'Gridlock' invoking cultural clichés (such as the old-fashioned city gent in his bowler hat) and well-known art images (such as the unprepossessing subjects of Grant Wood's *American Gothic*).

To summarise, somatic design in *Doctor Who* was sharply stratified under Davies's tutelage. Monsters occupied a privileged level of visibility and distinctiveness. They represented what might be called 'above-the-line' imagery, while costume for 'ordinary' characters was correspondingly 'below-the-line' and generally occupied a neutral position within the screen narrative itself. This stratification was tacitly underscored when Davies spoke out in 2006 against BAFTA's failure to nominate *Doctor Who* for a costume design award. In arguing that costume design for his series was as deserving of recognition as the 'antique lace collars' that routinely won plaudits for period productions, Davies chose 'a birdwoman from the 57th century' as exemplary of *Doctor Who*'s imagery, *not* the series' host of human characters.[5]

It is surely no accident that so much of the costume design in Davies's *Doctor Who* was thoroughly reticent and unremarkable. Assuming that aesthetic as well as fiscal considerations were in play, the consistent use of contemporary dress implied a preference for understatement and for a flavour of naturalism. One could speculate that this approach was either meant, as in the 're-imagined' *Battlestar Galactica*, to underscore parallels between the fictional and real world and to stress immediacy, or that it was an intentional retreat from the supposed camp of the old series from the 1970s onwards, or indeed that both concerns were in play within production discourse.[6] Whatever the stimuli, it seems clear that the discreet, not to say bland, costuming under Davies reflected a general policy to avoid any visual motifs that might test viewers' credulity.

In marked contrast to the classic series, there seemed to be no real place in the new for the kind of costumes that Tom Baker used to describe enthusiastically as 'operatic.'[7] More generally, there was little truly stylised design imagery in the Davies era, which is to say little that was simplified or exaggerated far beyond the quotidian norm. In spite of the fact that some of the narratives entailed patent absurdities – such as monsters whose human disguises have zip openings in the forehead – the *visual* presentation of these absurdities never partook of the joke. Computer-generated shots, editing, lighting and of course fabrication were contrived to shore up believability even in face of the most adverse odds. So while 'real life' was in no absolute sense the benchmark for this fantasy narrative, the wish to ground fantasy in the visually familiar and real(istic) seemed to be a key aesthetic concern for programme makers. The idea that dress in every future period would resemble that of the early twenty-first century may logically be *un*realistic, but this is hardly the point. Consistent visual reference to the contemporary was surely meant to enhance the narrative's believability at an affective, not a rational, level.

One fruitful way to think about the Davies-led *Doctor Who* design idiom is in terms of the series' generic verisimilitude. In other words, it is useful to consider the way in which the new series was calibrated to prevailing conventions, and therefore to a standard of believability, within the science-fiction/fantasy genre.[8] Whether or not *Battlestar Galactica* or other naturalistic science fiction directly influenced stylistic choices in Davies's *Doctor Who*, early 2000s telefantasy provided the context within which the new series was intelligible to new viewers, and hence the terms within which it was likely to be judged credible or otherwise. The legacy of *The X-Files* and *Buffy the Vampire Slayer*, both of which were strongly rooted in the everyday, loomed large in the telefantasy of the noughties. Although its inherently capricious time-travel narrative in principle allows for stylistic diversity, *Doctor Who* might have run the risk of being unacceptably out of step with generic norms if it incorporated too little that was grittily contemporary and too much that was operatically stylised.

With all this in mind, it would be a mistake to think of somatic design for monsters as aesthetically replete and the (more prevalent) contemporary-based costumes in Davies's new *Doctor Who* as aesthetically void. In fact, the 'invisible' costuming of most human characters in the series' first four seasons had an important persuasive role to play, conditioning the whole programme aesthetic. The contemporary bias in *Doctor Who* costuming furnished an ethos to which everything, including the spectacular elements, had to conform. Stylised costumes in the old series arguably accommodated the presence of 'hokey' monsters, because in a world where nothing corresponds with viewers' day-to-day experience, the benchmark for realism is slippery.[9] In the new series under Davies, where a critical mass of imagery was drawn unmediated from the contemporary environment, monsters and other fantastic elements could not be allowed to jar with this everyday norm, even if they were by their very nature extraordinary.

Yet it is not sufficient simply to draw a line between monsters and other characters in *Doctor Who*, for iconic images carried over from the classic series occupy a special position in terms of the programme's identity, history, and reputation. In other words, returning menaces such as the Daleks are not directly comparable to *ex novo* creations like the Slitheen, the Weeping Angels or the Silents: the former present a particular rhetorical problem that the publicity narrative of responsible modernisation is clearly meant to overcome. Whether or not the original Cybermen, Daleks and Sontarans number among those classic monsters that supposedly now seem clunky or hokey (as the 80s Davros apparently does), they potentially call to mind three decades of the British press's affectionate but nonetheless pejorative teasing about 'Blue Peter monsters' and 'wobbly sets' in the classic series. Consequently, iconic monsters' visual transformation (however slight the changes might seem to anyone but a hard-core fan) allows for *conceptual* transformation. Through documentary making-of and media coverage of the process of reinvention, these old-school aliens are changed from a liability into an asset; ironically, for all that they embody nostalgia,[10] these creatures simultaneously become the most potent of distancing devices.

Catherine Johnson has remarked on the fact that primetime British telefantasy of the past dozen years has been devised and publicised in such a way as to disavow a prior tradition associated with weak production values and implausible special effects. She stresses that this is not simply a matter of imitating US telefantasy, but rather 'working *against* a notion of British telefantasy as aesthetically inferior and less appealing to British (and international) audiences'.[11] Johnson's comments were focused primarily on the 2000 series *Randall and Hopkirk (Deceased)*, which was a remake rather than a revival, but her observations are just as applicable to *Doctor Who*. What I should like to examine now are the particular strategies by which this differentiation is accomplished.

Rhetorics of Modernisation and Functionalism

Apart from plaudits in the press, *Doctor Who*'s design makeovers for classic monsters have also been treated minutely in the documentary production that 'shadowed' the new series on BBC Three until 2011, *Doctor Who Confidential*, and also in a range of short behind-the-scenes videos on the BBC's official *Doctor Who* website. Here, reinvention was generally expounded in part by designers and fabricators such as Edward Thomas and Neill Gorton, and in part by the incumbent showrunner. These paratexts almost invariably ascribe authorial control of *Doctor Who*'s visual style to Russell T Davies. Thus one of the series' cinematographers, Ernie Vincze, noted in interview that Davies was 'very, very detail oriented,'[12] while in *Confidential* Gorton and others consistently alluded to what 'Russell want[ed]' for revised monster designs. It is interesting that this hands-on, detail- and design-oriented form of showrunner authority has been much less paratextually present in relation to Steven Moffat. Unlike his successor, Davies was in effect identified as a Kubrick-like, late modernist *auteur*.[13] At the time of *Doctor Who*'s revival there was strong generic precedent for constructing this kind of *auteurism* in telefantasy: as well as Joss Whedon, much vaunted 'creator' of *Buffy the Vampire Slayer*, Ronald D. Moore may be cited for *Battlestar*, Chris Carter for *The X-Files*, and of course Gene Roddenberry for *Star Trek*.[14]

Two conceits dominated programme makers' comments on reinvented monsters in Davies's *Doctor Who*. The first was modernisation itself (and this has persisted since Moffat took over as showrunner). The second was functionalism, by which I mean the machine aesthetic that privileges the appearance, at least, of form following function.[15] Of the new Daleks that appeared first in the 2005 season, Edward Thomas noted that the art department had added elements to 'make them a lot more chunky,' directly comparing them with another recently updated icon of 1960s modernism, the Mini Cooper. The overriding aim was that the new Dalek should seem 'more powerful [...] as if it's got a lot more attitude'.[16] In further implied contradistinction to the classic series versions, Thomas observed that the new model 'needed to look like a metal piece of kit that could really do some harm'.[17] In short, the Dalek shell had to be appropriately functional-looking, given that it is in effect a one-man tank with formidable killing power. Actions demonstrating strength were not in themselves enough; the Dalek literally needed to *embody* machine-age force, even in a still photograph. Gone, therefore, were the clean geometries of Ray Cusick's original design. While the overall silhouette was unchanged, the surface of the new Dalek was riddled with breaks of contour, etched lines, rivets and reinforcing flanges. And the greys and whites of earlier Dalek colour schemes were supplanted by more optically assertive bronze and gold – arguably the most immediately arresting design change, which was consistently attributed to Davies.[18]

When the revamped Cybermen debuted in 2006, this narrative of functionalist modernisation was even more emphatically voiced in *Doctor Who Confidential*. For Davies, it was important that the Cybermen look 'like something made in a science fiction programme in the year 2006'; for Gorton, similarly, the new design 'had to be a Cyberman for the twenty-first century'. As with the Daleks, the necessity of the Cybermen's appearing heftier and thus more plausible was duly rehearsed. Gorton emphasised that they had to look 'really like metal,' adding that, 'Russell really wants them to look machined.' Davies correspondingly insisted that 'one of the most important things [...] was to stop calling them silver,' presumably because that metal is relatively soft: 'steel – that's what they're made of.'[19] The functionalist sentiment was echoed yet again in 2008, not only apropos the 'beefed-up,' 'sturdier' Davros but also in relation to the Sontarans. The 'padded' uniforms worn by the Sontarans in the classic series were replaced by what Davies called 'something more armour-like' and which he considered 'just sort of stronger'. These curious blue, articulated outfits were apparently supposed to be 'metal shells', in Davies's view appropriate to the Sontarans 'because they're soldiers'.[20]

As the above should attest, press and documentary coverage of returning icons from classic *Doctor Who* heavily stresses a *necessity* for modernisation. But what are the programme makers' self-imposed – or at least self-described – limits in this updating process? What are the tensions between the nisus to 're-imagination' and the perceived demands of upholding tradition? For all returning monsters under Davies except the Daleks, which is to say those with some relationship to the bipedal human form, the most marked alterations in design are from the neck down. Conversely, when Davies and others spoke of the iconic elements they sought to retain, the focus was always on the cranium and facial features. Gorton recalled that the brief for the Sontarans was to replicate the original form of the head, 'that lovely dome shape'.[21] For the Cybermen, Davies commented that 'you want to keep the earhandles, the black, blank eyes' and the 'brilliant detail' of the 'little teardrop in the corner of their eye, that says somehow that they're sad underneath for what's happened to them'.[22] And Gorton's claim that the fabricators could not replicate 'a hokey rubber mask' for Davros is very deliberately juxtaposed with acknowledgement of the need 'to make [him] recognisable'.[23] Thus it is the part of the body usually considered the most expressive, and therefore central to the vast majority of shots both on-screen and in still photography, which was apparently treated with the greatest caution by Davies and those who reported to him. This interestingly mirrors the new focus on character under Davies: monsters' accoutrements might change, but prime indicators of 'personality' were to remain unaltered.

Redesigns are Cool

Since Steven Moffat took over as showrunner, the narrative of responsible modernisation has in itself been subject to adjustment. While the necessity for revision remains a leitmotif, change is not always justified in the same way, and the coherent, functionalist narrative, so often articulated under Davies, has been abandoned. Thus, when the Silurians were reintroduced, the writer Chris Chibnall noted, predictably, in *Confidential* that 'from the very first moment [...] it was about making sure we reinvent [the] Silurians for 2010'. Yet, sounding a far less familiar note, Chibnall claimed that Moffat left him 'absolutely [...] free to reinvent the Silurians'.[24] This apparent mandate for creative latitude is interesting both because it contrasts with numerous accounts of Davies's 'detail oriented' input into design, and because it frames the fact that the reinvention of the Silurians was the most extreme monster makeover to date on the new *Doctor Who*. Indeed, as the director Ashley Way noted, there was evidently agreement that the creatures should seem 'human' and 'not particularly monster-like'.[25] Thus the original, largely static, pull-on mask for the Silurians, with its markedly *non-human* three-eyed physiognomy and 'beak' was replaced by a thin, silicone appliance of green scaling that retained rather than disguised the main, expressive elements of human physiognomy. Only the bony 'crests' flaring out backwards from the cheekbones and brow were kept from the original 1970 design. Chibnall also went beyond the Davies-era emphasis on dramatic expressiveness, noting that he 'really wanted the Silurians to be *beautiful*' [my italics] in addition to having 'credibility as characters'.[26] In this version of the reinvention narrative, stylistic shifts are to be understood less as imperatives than as choices.

During Moffat's first series as showrunner, the Daleks also (and more controversially) underwent radical renovation in Mark Gatiss's 'Victory of the Daleks.' This redesign again produced a significant variation on the official rhetoric of the Davies era, with expressions of personal preference and affect looming large in the accompanying *Doctor Who Confidential* episode, 'War Games', and in the parallel *Monster Files*. As usual, claims for the necessity of updating the design were offered, but they were tempered with something new: rather than stressing audience expectations of credibility (i.e. the functionalist conceit), issues of tone and emotional impact were paramount. According to Moffat, speaking in *Doctor Who Confidential*, it was 'time just to have [...]

a really noticeably different and more frightening Dalek'.[27] Most of the rest of the commentary by cast and crew in *Doctor Who Confidential* echoes Moffat's comments on the increased scale and number of the new props, with Edward Thomas specifically linking greater size to the intention of making the Daleks 'more scary'.[28]

Other comments on the Daleks in the 'War Games' *Confidential* represented a shift away from the narrative of responsible modernisation and towards a much more ludic approach. Rather than intoning earnestly about the necessity of honouring the legacy of the classic series, both Moffat and Gatiss linked the new Daleks with the tall, brightly coloured, 'non-canonical' Daleks that appeared in two 1960s theatrical releases starring Peter Cushing, Gatiss commenting that there was 'something gorgeously impressive about those big, big bloody Daleks with their colourful liveries'.[29] His pleasure in the production team's decision to 'just go for it' in echoing this chromatic richness is strongly projected in *Confidential*. Elsewhere in the programme, the epithet most freely used to characterize the new Daleks is 'cool', again eroding any sense of portentousness. Karen Gillan twice describes the new props as cool in separate interview clips. Similarly, Steven Moffat, commenting that he and Gatiss 'had great fun making up names for the Daleks,' notes that one of these names, the 'Eternal', stuck simply because it 'sounds cool'.[30]

In short, all these comments are conspicuously infused with delight – with the sense, one might say, that reinvention is a joyous adventure, not a sober responsibility. Strikingly, Edward Thomas claimed in 'War Games' that his 'heart skips a beat when he opens a script and [sees] "the Daleks",' because 'you just know it's going to be fun'.[31] Nor was the expression of such sentiment unique to 'War Games'. For example, during the episode of *Monster Files* dealing with the return of the Cybermats in the 2011 episode 'Closing Time', the hitherto dour Neill Gorton is quoted as saying that the challenge of a returning 'classic' creature – which is to say updating the design while keeping it recognisable – is 'always fun'.[32]

If there has been alteration in, or at least complication of, the rhetoric surrounding 'above-the-line' somatic design under Steven Moffat, then 'below-the-line' costume design has also subtly changed. Just as with Davies, little of this incidental design imagery has been discussed in official publicity narratives and paratexts. Moreover, the stylistic shift in design, just like the shift in rhetoric, has been limited: for example, in each season since Moffat became showrunner, contemporary dress has remained an anchor for costuming in most of the futuristic episodes. Even so, there has been a greater visual richness and diversity, especially in Barbara Kidd's work as costume designer. Episodes such as 2010's unabashedly Dickensian yuletide special 'A Christmas Carol' represented a return to 'operatic' design imagery. To characterise the overall shift in tone, one could do worse than speak of a postmodern sensibility under Moffat replacing a 'modernist' one under Davies, recapitulating in miniature a shift that occurred in the classic series over the course of the 1970s.

Yet it would be easy to go too far in periodising the Davies and Moffat 'eras', at least in the context of a chapter primarily concerned less with design itself than with the publicity narrative built around design. As I have emphasised, there are clear, continuous threads in that narrative. Rhetorical effort has only ever been expended on signature design elements in the series (which of course go beyond the recurring adversaries discussed here to encompass the Doctor's costume, the TARDIS, and also monsters clearly envisaged as recurring, such as the Silents). While the conceit of responsible modernisation of iconic design has been slightly adjusted under Moffat, what remains constant is the underlying rhetorical assertion that reinventions are always *timely*.

Conclusion

If the rhetoric of new *Who*'s (re)design remains fundamentally consistent in import and focus, despite the shift from functionalist to ludic sensibility, the question remains: why should this be? What is at stake in the ongoing effort to circulate and reaffirm those key values that supposedly underpin the renewal of iconic designs? One useful way to approach these questions, as noted at the outset, is to reflect on the role of branding as a determinant factor in the way that television series, franchises and networks are organised and presented in the era of TVIII.[33] I have suggested that there is in one sense a dichotomy between overt homage and implicit one-upmanship in all the on-message accounts of new *Who*'s reinvented design imagery. However, from the point of view of brand discourse, the very act of highlighting and examining these reinventions serves to weld the new series to the old – and this is obviously not accidental.

'Monsters' were from the first among the brand values – somewhat curiously set alongside such abstract terms as 'friendship' and 'optimism' – delineated by the new series' original brand manager, Ian Grutchfield.[34] It is therefore hardly surprising that new monsters should occupy so central a position in the web of paratexts constituting and supporting the *Doctor Who* brand, most notably the BBC's own *Doctor Who Confidential* (2005–11). Still less surprising is that the timely reinvention of traditional enemies has been such a theme in publicity narratives. In the *Confidential* accompanying 'Victory of the Daleks', Matt Smith notes that 'everyone in Britain' knows the shape of a Dalek. In terms of brand discourse, the potential of an episode such as this, specifically designed to highlight the revision of a universally-known image, does not merely reside in the merchandising opportunities it creates.[35] Beyond the 'toyetic' potential of new Daleks or Cybermen, the reinvention of signature designs transmutes the past into the present, affirming the wholeness of *Doctor Who* as a self-continuous, distinctive and instantly recognisable brand, and hence perpetuating the currency of key elements. In other words, each new redesign reinforces both the brand's historical coherence and its on-going vitality.

NOTES

1. Pettie, Andrew (2008) 'Doctor Who: Reinventing Davros', *The Telegraph*, 3 July. Available online at http://www.telegraph.co.uk/culture/tvandradio/3555652/Doctor-Who-Reinventing-Davros.html, accessed 27 May 2013.
2. Pettie: 'Doctor Who: Reinventing Davros'.
3. For more on this in relation to BBC Wales' *Doctor Who*, see Catherine Johnson's Chapter 5.
4. In the classic series only two Daleks were ever (separately) seen to levitate, both in the 1988 adventure 'Remembrance of the Daleks'. Here the effect was achieved by physically manhandling the full-size, practical prop on a lift.
5. Thomas, Liz (2006) 'Davies "fury" as Doctor Who costumes snubbed by BAFTA', *The Stage*, 11 April, http://www.thestage.co.uk/news/2006/04/-davies-fury-as-doctor-who-costumes-snubbed-by-bafta/, accessed 27 May 2013.

6   On camp in *Doctor Who*, see Cull, Nicholas (2001), '"Bigger on the Inside ..." *Doctor Who* as British cultural history,' in *The Historian, Television and Television History* (University of Luton Press, London), pp. 105–6.
7   Britton, Piers and Barker, Simon (2003) *Reading Between Designs: Visual Imagery and the Generation of Meaning in The Avengers, The Prisoner and Doctor Who* (University of Texas Press, Austin), p. 165.
8   Johnson, Catherine (2005) *Telefantasy* (London), p. 4; Neale, Steven (2000) *Genre and Hollywood* (Routledge, London and New York), p. 32.
9   Neale: *Genre and Hollywood*, p. 38.
10 Chapter 10 further addresses the extent to which nostalgia has been significant for new *Doctor Who*, although it considers the embodied presence of actors rather than the 'responsible modernisation' of monster designs. However, Ross Garner argues that the very recognisability of actors such as Elisabeth Sladen and Peter Davison has formed a significant part of BBC Wales' construction of *Who* nostalgia – suggesting that iconic *Doctor Who* actors, rather like iconic monsters, are also called upon to demonstrate a strong degree of visual continuity with their former selves/appearances.
11 Johnson: *Telefantasy*, p. 141.
12 Johanson, MaryAnn (2006) 'Showing an old Doctor (Who) new tricks', *Film and Video*, 20 December, http://www.studiodaily.com/2006/12/showing-an-old-doctor-who-new-tricks/, accessed 27 May 2013.
13 On Davies as auteur, see Hills, Matt (2010) *Triumph of a Time Lord: Regenerating Doctor Who in the Twenty-First Century* (I.B.Tauris, London), pp. 25–48.
14 Hills, Matt (2002) *Fan Cultures* (Routledge, London and New York), p. 132.
15 Jencks, Charles (1973) *Modern Movements in Architecture* (Harmondsworth), p. 73; Banham, Reyner (1960) *Theory and Design in the First Machine Age* (Architectural Press, London), pp. 320–30.
16 Miles, Rupert and Page, Adam (producers) (2005) 'Dalek', *Doctor Who Confidential*, 30 April [Television broadcast], British Broadcasting Corporation, Cardiff.
17 Miles and Page, 'Dalek.'
18 Arnopp, Jason (2005) 'Tucker's luck', *The Doctor Who Companion: Series One (Doctor Who Magazine Special Edition #11)* (Panini Publishing, Tunbridge Wells), pp. 67–8.
19 Rushton, Zoë (producer) (2006) *Doctor Who Confidential*, 'Cybermen', 13 May [Television broadcast], British Broadcasting Corporation, Cardiff.
20 Rushton, Zoë (producer) (2008) *Doctor Who Confidential*, 'Sontar-Ha!', 3 May [Television broadcast], British Broadcasting Corporation, Cardiff.
21 Rushton: 'Sontar-Ha!'
22 Rushton: 'Cybermen.'
23 Pettie: 'Doctor Who: Reinventing Davros.'
24 Rushton, Zoë (producer) (2010) *Doctor Who Confidential*, 'After Effects', 22 May [Television broadcast], British Broadcasting Corporation, Cardiff.
25 Rushton: 'After Effects.'
26 Rushton: 'After Effects.'
27 Rushton, Zoë (producer) (2010) *Doctor Who Confidential*, 'War Games', 17 April [Television broadcast], British Broadcasting Corporation, Cardiff.

28 Rushton, 'War Games.'
29 Rushton, 'War Games.'
30 Rushton, 'War Games.'
31 *The Monster Files: Cybermats* (2011) *Doctor Who: The Complete Sixth Series* [DVD] BBC Worldwide.
32 Johnson, Catherine (2007) 'Tele-branding in TVIII: the network as brand and the programme as brand', *New Review of Film and Television Studies* v/1, pp. 15–19.
33 Hills, *Triumph of a Time Lord*, p. 68.
34 Hills, *Triumph of a Time Lord*, pp. 66–8.
35 Rushton, 'War Games.'

3
THE CYBERMEN AS HUMAN.2

Bonnie Green and Chris Willmott

> POSTHUMAN: Posthumans will be persons of unprecedented physical, intellectual and psychological ability, self-programming and self-defining, potentially immortal, unlimited individuals. Posthumans have overcome the biological, neurological and psychological constraints evolved into humans [...]. Posthumans may be partly or mostly biological in form, but will likely be partly or wholly postbiological – our personalities having been transferred 'into' more durable, modifiable, [...] faster, and more powerful bodies and thinking hardware.[1]
>
> PRESIDENT: [...] these people – who were they? [...]
> CYBERMAN: We have been upgraded.
> THE DOCTOR: Into what?
> CYBERMAN: The next level of mankind. We are Human Point Two.
> ('Rise of the Cybermen', 2006)

In this chapter we'll consider how new *Who*'s 'return of the Cybermen [...] is [...] emblematic of the way in which the new series revises and updates old concepts'.[2] But by remaking the Cybermen as a timely cultural and technological threat, BBC Wales' *Doctor Who* also opens up a popular-televisual – and sometimes incoherent – space for the consideration of humanist, posthumanist and transhumanist philosophies. Defining and exploring these terms, we will suggest the series can potentially be read 'against the grain', as a way of imaginatively engaging with what it means to be (post-)human, rather than simply as a gothic tale of evil and anti-humanist Cybervillains.

It barely needs stating that we live in times of phenomenal technological advancement. A new raft of high-tech gadgets and devices seem to appear on a daily basis, and many of the technologies that we now take for granted would have been unimaginable just a few years ago. The home computer has given way to the laptop which, in turn, has been replaced by iPads and similar tablets. The revolutionary invention of a mobile phone small enough to fit into your pocket has been eclipsed by the development of smartphones that allow you to take photographs, videos, and access the internet.

What is even more astounding, however, is the speed at which we are able to integrate these machines into our lives. For many of us today these technologies are part of the fabric of our everyday behaviour. We can no longer imagine a world without them; a world in which we are not 'connected'. These technologies and machines connect us to each other, but insofar as we are also connected to them, they are one of the ways in which we may be becoming 'posthuman' or 'human.2'.

In the same way that computer programs can be upgraded from version 1.0 to version 2.0, Extropians such as Max More suggest that human.1 – the current release – will shortly be followed by human.2, as the next step in the evolution of our species. Although the vision of human.2 in the opening quote above may seem somewhat extreme, many posthumanist thinkers believe that this could be the ultimate endpoint of the interconnectedness with machines that we experience when we use our mobile phones or connect to the internet. Given this, human.2 is often thought of as a cyborg: a fusion of *cyb*ernetic and *org*anic parts. Many artists, authors and scientists have imagined what this posthuman form may look like.[3] However, it is through popular science fiction that some of the most potent cyborg forms have entered our culture. *Star Trek*'s Borg and Darth Vader from *Star Wars* are clear examples of organic beings augmented with mechanical parts. Conversely the *Terminator* or Replicants in *Blade Runner* are entirely artificial cybernetic life forms that behave like, and have many of the characteristics of, organic beings. Though all of these cyborgs give us an idea of what being post*biological* might involve, one of the best examples of the post*human* is found in the Cybermen in *Doctor Who*.

Unlike these other cyborgs, Doctor Who has always presented the Cybermen as quintessentially posthuman; as human beings, transformed through the integration and fusion of organic, mechanical and cybernetic parts.[4]

Across 45 years or so there have been frequent confrontations between Cybermen and the Doctor. From their first appearance in 'The Tenth Planet' (1966) through to, at the time of writing, their most recent incarnation in 'Closing Time' (2011),[5] these part-organic, part-mechanical creatures have regularly run up against the Time Lord. As Graham Sleight has pointed out, there have been many occasions during that time when, in truth, the Cybermen have served as little more than 'generic invaders rather than playing on what is distinctive about them': the plot required an adversary, and it was easier to draw upon an established (and popular) nemesis than to devise a new enemy.[6]

Given the frequency and longevity of the Cybermen's appearances in televised episodes of Doctor Who, it is perhaps inevitable that their external features have been depicted in a variety of forms. Aside from the Doctor's own regenerations, no other regular characters have had quite as many makeovers as the Cybermen, and on-location photographs show that there were further refinements of their external features for episodes broadcast in 2013.[7] It is not only in the details of their helmets, gloves and boots that Cybermen have differed. Over the lifetime of the series, there have been at least two mutually-exclusive accounts of the origins of the Cybermen.

The original 'Mondasian Cybermen'[8] in 'The Tenth Planet' (1966) were, in a very literal sense, technologically-augmented humans (albeit ones that originated on Earth's long-lost sister planet Mondas). As one of the Cybermen explains to the Doctor, growing concerns for their ability to survive had led Mondasian scientists to develop the capacity to make spare parts for their bodies. This process had been continued until their original humanoid parts had become the minority. The Cybermen still had some original biological features, including their hands, though most of their other physical features, including their voices, had been replaced by mechanical systems. Significantly, they retained their brains, but with their emotions removed since these were perceived to be a weakness.

As James Rose has discussed,[9] the BBC Wales series revived the Cybermen in the two-part story 'Rise of the Cybermen' and 'The Age of Steel' (2006). Inhabitants of a parallel Earth, these Cybermen were created by Cybus Industries at the behest of owner John Lumic. These 'Lumic Cybermen', or *Cybus*men, were generated by the direct transplant of human brains into cybernetic bodies in a procedure similar to that imagined by Max More in this chapter's opening quote. New *Who* has therefore placed far greater 'emphasis on the brain' than the classic series' cyberconversions.[10] This cyber-process from series two will be discussed in more detail below. First, we must briefly consider a potential third version of cyberconversion represented more recently in the series six episode 'Closing Time' (2011).

Some time prior to the story's events, a Cyberman ship has crash-landed on Earth. In the meantime a city has been established above the vessel. Recent renovation work conducted by the local council has woken the surviving Cybermen from their dormancy, and they have set about repopulating their crew via the upgrading of humans unfortunate enough to have crossed their path. Among their potential victims is the Doctor's friend Craig Owens. An attempt to convert him is depicted, in which Craig's whole body is encased in a preformed cybersuit. Partway through the process, however, Craig's love for his son Alfie wins out and he manages to override the conversion. Cyberconversion in 'Closing Time' has some similarities to that depicted in, for example, 'The Tomb of the Cybermen' (1967) but it is strongly distinct from the process depicted in the Russell T Davies-era episodes 'Rise of the Cybermen' and 'Age of Steel'. In Sleight's terms, 'Closing Time' is one of those episodes where the presence of Cybermen is somewhat incidental to the story rather than a central focus. It is also relevant that the Cybermen in this episode do not carry the Cybus Industries logo as seen in 'Rise of the Cybermen' and 'Age of Steel'. This may be just as well for Craig; the cyberconversion-halted-by-love scenario would, after all, have been rather more complicated to achieve if his brain had already been removed from the rest of his body!

In truth, perhaps the details of *how* humans are transformed into Cybermen are not as significant as the underlying premise that these steel-clad creatures are 'upgraded' humans or Human.2. Despite differences in the specifics of their creation, both Mondasian and Lumic 'Cyberforms' ('Rise of the Cybermen') provide ways of thinking not only about what a posthuman or human.2 might look like, but also what life as a cyborg could involve. In this chapter we address these issues by considering how the Cybermen appear in the diegetic worlds of new

Who. We will discuss some of the characteristics of the posthuman and explore how human.1 and human.2 might interact outside gothic narratives premised on 'the horror of conversion'.[11] First we turn to the Doctor himself, however, and examine how his character has been used to make features of the posthuman Cybermen more obvious and compelling for audiences.

Is the Doctor Human.1?

In 'Revenge of the Cybermen' (1975) the Doctor baulks at being called human. Strictly speaking this is justified since, being a Time Lord from the planet Gallifrey, the Doctor is not human at all. However, throughout all episodes, in both classic and new series of *Doctor Who*, the Doctor seems to embody many of the values and characteristics we associate with humanity. He looks like a human, can be physically injured, and is a very compassionate and emotional being. He consistently manifests love and concern not only for his companions but also for all occupants of Planet Earth. In many ways this makes him the 'ideal type' for human.1.

In terms of (post)humanist social theory and philosophy, the Doctor displays many of the attributes of what has been called the 'liberal humanist subject',[12] where liberal humanism is conceived as the dominant way of understanding what it means to be human. Within this philosophy, men (and historically it has been men rather than women) are seen as individuals with 'a coherent, rational self' and 'the right [...] to autonomy and freedom, and a sense of agency linked with a belief in enlightened self-interest'.[13] Man is 'a "free and sovereign artificer" determining his "own nature without constraint from any barrier",'[14] with a distinct personality that is his 'unique essence'.[15] That the Doctor is a 'coherent' individual, with a fixed, immutable essence unchanging over time is demonstrated by the persistence of his singular character through many regenerations. His autonomy and freedom are also apparent in *Doctor Who*.[16] The Doctor travels through space and time unfettered not only by the natural laws of today's 'cosmic order',[17] but also by any 'obligation to society'.[18] Further, the Doctor celebrates these values in others. He demonstrates a high regard for self-determination when he suggests that 'the most ordinary person could change the world' ('The Age of Steel'), and a belief in free will through his disconnection of hundreds of cybercontrolled humans in 'Rise of the Cybermen'. These attributes also go hand-in-hand with the Doctor's moral convictions. He displays a hesitancy to kill, and also consistently apologizes before doing harm (for example in 'Army of Ghosts', 2006).

Within many versions of posthumanism, it is against this image of human.1 that human.2 is relationally identified and discussed, and this is also the case in the diegetic world of *Doctor Who*. By endowing the Doctor with many characteristics of the liberal humanist subject, the series provides us with a foil for the posthuman Cybermen. Indeed, many of the similarities and differences between human.1 and human.2 come out through the Doctor's interactions with the Cybermen. One obvious way in which humanism and posthumanism are contrasted in new *Who* is through the Doctor's utter rejection of the Cybermen as living beings. He consistently refers to people who have been converted to Cybermen as 'dead' (for example in 'Rise of the Cybermen'), and insists that they cannot be saved (such as in 'The Age of Steel'). He also reacts badly to the suggestion that becoming emotionless – a characteristic feature of the Cybermen – might be a good thing. When John Lumic, creator of the Lumic Cybermen, suggests that the upgrade could remove the Doctor's pain, rage and grief in 'The Age of Steel', the Doctor replies, 'you might as well kill me'. Thus the Doctor represents everything that is human.1. But what about the Cybermen? In what sense do they narratively represent human.2?

Therapy = Good, Enhancement = Bad?

Hans Moravec (a cybernetician and posthumanist thinker) articulates one of the dreams of *transhumanism*. This variant of posthumanism views the move from human.1 towards human.2 in an unfailingly positive light:

> Many people today are alive because of a growing arsenal of artificial organs and other body parts. In time, especially as robotic techniques improve, such replacement parts will be better than any originals. So what about replacing everything, that is, transplanting a human brain into a specially designed robot body?[19]

Transhumanists consistently see the modifications and technological prostheses that may be involved in this transformation as 'enhancements', and refer to the process itself in terms of an 'upgrade'; a step up the evolutionary ladder. This vision of the future resonates particularly strongly with the Lumic Cybermen in new *Who*. These Cybermen are brains 'welded to a metal exoskeleton' in a process referred to as 'the ultimate upgrade' ('Rise of the Cybermen'). They also seem to have many of the characteristics transhumanists see as integral to human.2. These include being faster and stronger than human.1;[20] more durable and possibly longer-lived;[21] as well as having senses and capacities well beyond anything we can imagine today.[22] One example of this is the way the Lumic Cybermen can apparently detect 'increased adrenaline' in their human victims without any external, technological assistance ('Doomsday', 2006). Another interesting feature of the Lumic Cybermen that aligns them with a transhumanist view of human.2 is the way they were developed out of a therapy for John Lumic's mysterious, terminal condition. In fact, the way the creation of the Lumic Cybermen in 'Rise of the Cybermen' is depicted closely parallels real-world debate on-going within another area of philosophy: bioethics. Bioethical discussion concerns the difference between 'therapy' and 'enhancement', considering the extent to which the distinction between the two is a moral as well as a medical or technological one. Within bioethics the distinction between therapy and enhancement is based on a view of therapies as 'responding to genuine medical need', while enhancements are motivated solely by the desire for 'self-improvement'.[23] In most cases the difference between therapy and enhancement is fairly clear, even where the technology being used is similar or identical. For example, most of us would find it easy to see reconstructive breast surgery following mastectomy as therapy, while breast enlargement for cosmetic purposes might be considered enhancement. However, is this also a moral distinction? Are therapies somehow intrinsically more acceptable than enhancements? This is a more difficult question to answer, particularly in situations such as breast surgery, where the same technique is used in two different contexts.

The difficulty of distinguishing therapies from enhancements has actually been integral to the story of the Cybermen right from their original inception. In the mid-1960s, medical researcher Kit Pedler was invited to bring his expertise to the script-writing process to increase the scientific credibility of *Doctor Who*.[24] It was an era in which both transplant surgery and mechanical implants were starting to become a reality: the first implanted pacemaker had been fitted in 1958, and four years prior to that the first kidney transplant had taken place. There was speculation that other organ transplants would soon be feasible. These suggestions were well founded. In 1966, the year that 'The Tenth Planet' was transmitted, doctors carried out the first successful pancreas transplant and the following year the first liver and heart transplants were achieved.

As has been well documented elsewhere,[25] Pedler's day-job as a medical scientist led him to reflect on the logical extensions of this 'spare part' surgery. In particular, he wondered how many natural organs a person could have replaced by mechanical devices before they were no longer technically human. If procedures of the kind became routine, would people be willing to have their entire body replaced if doing so would grant them immortality? The Cybermen were the fruit of Pedler's deliberations.

Perhaps unsurprisingly, given that these new *Who* episodes amount to a rebooted Cybermen origin story, bioethics' therapy/enhancement tension is particularly prominent in 'Rise of the Cybermen' and 'The Age of Steel'. John Lumic is presented as having a 'genuine medical need'; he is wheelchair-bound and in danger of imminent death. With his human body failing, Lumic devises a therapy for his condition: 'a way of [...] keeping the brain alive' ('The Age of Steel') which 'allows cyber-kinetic impulses to be bonded onto a metal exoskeleton' ('Rise of the Cybermen'). It is out of this process that the posthuman Cybermen are born. Even the Doctor recognizes this as a therapy, and hence an admirable and human pursuit, stating 'Lumic [...] everything you've invented, you did to fight your sickness. And that's brilliant. That is so human' ('Rise of the Cybermen'). However, the ambiguity in Lumic's motives makes the status of his cyberconversion as therapy rather than enhancement highly ambiguous. In seeking approval for the Cyberman project, he makes an appeal based on his own medical needs: 'without this project, you have condemned me' ('Rise of the Cybermen'); while simultaneously presenting the process as: 'the ultimate upgrade. Our greatest step into cyberspace.'

Here cyberconversion is presented as occupying something of a 'gray area between treatment and enhancement'.[26] Lumic is denied permission to continue his Cyberman project on the grounds that this 'upgrade' is not only an enhancement too far, but because it is deemed to be morally 'obscene' ('Rise of the Cybermen'). By the end of the episode even Lumic seems to have difficulty in thinking of the upgrade as an acceptable therapy rather than an unacceptable enhancement. He reacts with fear when the Cybermen force the upgrade upon him, shouting, 'I will upgrade only with my last breath!' ('The Age of Steel'). While this suggests that the upgrade potentially remains a therapy (albeit a treatment of last resort) it also enacts a transhumanist nightmare in which enhanced human.2 turns on its creators and forcibly upgrades them, or else 'deletes' them as 'rogue elements', as Lumic's Cybermen ultimately do.[27]

Could you be Posthuman?

Opening this chapter, we introduced the idea of the posthuman and human.2 by highlighting the way many of us – humans.1, presumably – are in some way connected to our (media) technologies. Here we take this parallel one step further. Again, drawing on theoretical accounts of the development of human.2, we look at how the human and the posthuman – in this context, humans and Cybermen – can be thought of as points on a continuum, rather than as wholly distinct and separate types of beings. As Yvonne Hartman says of the Cybermen in 'Doomsday': 'That's what these things are. They're us.' And this uncanny parallel has been a strong theme in new *Who*'s Cybermen episodes. The audience is presented not only with humans and Cybermen, but also with a variety of liminal, in-between forms sharing characteristics with both groups (indeed, this is arguably Yvonne's own fate). Thus one might ask: when does a human stop being human and become a Cyberman? Does this happen at a particular point or is the transition so gradual that it is hard to tell when human.1 ends and human.2 begins?

Within posthumanism itself this is a hotly debated issue. Many transhumanists argue that the transition from human.1 to human.2 will happen at a particular point in time that they call the 'singularity'.[28] Other schools of thought suggest, in a rather more deconstructionist mode, that 'we have always been posthuman.'[29] Here there is no fundamental difference between the human and the posthuman, only a difference in the degree of interconnectedness with machines and technological systems. In the Cybermen episodes we see elements of both of these views. There is both a continuum of more or less human and posthuman forms, and a specific point at which human and

Cyberman can be separated. Unlike the transhumanists, whose singularity is a point in time, *Doctor Who* draws the line between human.1 and human.2 at a physical point. This boundary is 'the skin'.[30] It is only when Cyberman technology penetrates the skin of a human being – specifically to connect with that person's brain – that he or she becomes fully posthuman.

At one end of the narratives' human–posthuman continuum are 'the Preachers'. In 'Rise of the Cybermen' and 'The Age of Steel' the Preachers are 'freedom fighters' who typify human.1. They reject not only the Cybermen's posthumanity, but also many of the technologies that are routine for other humans.1 within these episodes. A step up from this is the Doctor's companion, Rose Tyler, with her mobile phone. Even on the parallel Earth, where much of the action takes place, Rose's phone automatically connects to a network and provides her with the 'daily download' ('Rise of the Cybermen') that indigenous humans receive through their EarPods. The EarPods represent an additional degree of intimacy between humans and technology. However, since they can be 'overridden' by the Cybermen in order to place humans.1 under cybercontrol, their function further emphasizes continuity between human and posthuman. Humans under cybercontrol are frequently depicted as human.2, although they may be physically indistinguishable from humans.1. Cybercontrolled humans are often made agents of the Cybermen (see 'The Moonbase', 1967; 'The Invasion', 1968; and 'Doomsday'), and like the Cybermen are totally emotionless. Following on from cybercontrolled humans are the fully-converted Cybermen and, ultimately, the figure of the Cyber Controller – a human.2 who can be downloaded into any Cyberman body as required ('Doomsday'). When Yvonne says 'They're us' she is recognizing the Cybermen as a reminder of our own dependence on technology. That is, if they are us, then we are also them. As Graham Sleight has pointed out:

> Cyber-stories have always had an edge of satire to them, directed at humanity's increasing (and excessive?) reliance on technology. [...] in the 1960s, this was directed at transplant surgery and similar intrusions into the body. Four decades later, the choice of mobile phone technology seems rather more apposite, even though Davies-era *Doctor Who* also often features mobile phones as a positive plot device (for Rose Tyler to speak to her mother, for instance).[31]

Piers D. Britton likewise recognizes that an emphasis on EarPods and mobile phone technologies means that new *Who* 'insists on the contemporaneity of the threat it explores',[32] even if the series' multiple uses of mobile telephony grants this technology an ambiguity exceeding the specific narratives of 'Rise of the Cybermen' and 'Age of Steel'. And from our description of a human–posthuman continuum, it becomes clear that the point at which true cyberconversion begins is linked to the placing of humans under cybercontrol. In 'Doomsday' the audience is treated to a graphic illustration of the precise point at which this happens when Yvonne removes an EarPod from one of her cybercontrolled staff and exclaims 'Urgh! Oh, God! It goes inside their brain'. Here it appears that the Cybermen have found a way to alter EarPods to penetrate the skin of the wearer and directly connect cybernetic with organic systems (i.e. the brain). It is also at this point that the characters' emotions are removed and their transformation becomes irreversible. *Doctor Who*'s use of the skin as a boundary that separates human from posthuman – albeit linked to a concept of the brain as a controlling source or motor of selfhood – taps into wider trends in popular culture, including the use of the skin as a metaphorical boundary between self and other.[33] However, in doing this *Who* appears to fall foul of what artist and posthumanist scholar, Robert Pepperell, calls 'the "boxed body" fallacy'.[34] Pepperell claims that the idea that humans are made distinct and separate from the environment around them by bodily boundaries like the skin is misleading. Although the skin appears to be a kind of barrier between a person and the world, there is actually a lot of traffic across this boundary. The skin is not watertight, and many of us absorb a whole host of creams, lotions and potions through this permeable layer every day. Of these, many may be technological products (or at least may claim to be). The penetration of cybertechnology beneath the skin could potentially be seen simply as an extension of this, though of course cybertechnology remains narratively framed as a 'threat' to humanity (and humanism) in new *Who* rather than a consumer product or a straightforward therapy. To read episodes such as 'Rise of the Cybermen' and 'Age of Steel' in line with Pepperell's posthumanist argument – however accurate it may be – would therefore require a significantly oppositional interpretation, reading 'against the grain' of new *Who*'s body-horror.

Could a Human Become Posthuman while Remaining the Same Person?

As humans.1, we all have a sense of self; a sense of who we are, and of being a distinct person in the world, separate and different from all other people and things around us. But where might we find this sense of self? Where is it located? Is it 'contained' in one part of the body? Or, is it more ephemeral than that? An aspect of being that has no precise location? These are important questions for those who would like to become human.2 while retaining their human.1 sense of self and identity. The challenge is to preserve the self, unchanged and independent of the physical modifications and enhancements that mark the change from human to posthuman. With this aim in mind, there are many philosophical positions one might take on the location of the self. Each of these views has different implications for the possibility of isolating the self from the body, and hence offers different answers to the question 'could a current human become posthuman while remaining the same person?'[35]

Hans Moravec locates the self, which he equates with the 'mind', in one particular organ of the biological body: the brain. This view of the self, as *embrained*, is a very common way to think about the location of the self within the body, and one that is frequently associated with René Descartes, the philosopher who coined the famous phrase 'I think, therefore, I am'.[36] According to this Cartesian view, simply preserving the brain intact should – as Moravec suggests – allow humans.1 to retain their sense of self and identity even as they become humans.2:.

> ...transplanting a human brain into a specially designed robot body [...] might overcome most of our physical limitations, [though] it would leave untouched our biggest handicap, the limited and fixed intelligence of the human brain. This transplant gets our brain out of our body. Is there a way to get our mind out of our brain?[37]

An extreme version of this viewpoint is to consider the self as a program inscribed or encoded in the organic material of our bodies. This view of the self reduces it to *information*: to software running on biological 'wetware'.[38] Here the body (including the brain) is ultimately disposable, provided that the program can be deciphered and reproduced in another medium – for example, computer hardware.

At the other end of the spectrum, there are views of the self as distributed. Here the self has no single, precise location; there is no organ or program that our sense of self and identity is contained within. Some posthumanists argue that the self is distributed throughout the body, and that each and every part of that body contributes something to our sense of self and who we are.[39] Others take this even further, and – as in the case of 'the skin' – suggest that, since it is very hard to separate the body from its environment, we should consider the self as extending beyond the body and into the wider world.[40] If we take this view of the self, as *embodied* (or perhaps even inseparable from the world around it), then there is no possibility of isolating it nor preserving it through the transformation from human to posthuman. It would be impossible to become posthuman while remaining the same person.

All of these positions on the location of the self – as embrained, as information, or as fully embodied – are part of our stock of contemporary cultural images and narratives. As such, many of them are present in Cybermen stories of new *Who*. Several of these episodes feature the transformation of human characters into posthuman ones, and depict the effects of becoming posthuman on those characters' sense of self and identity. For example, 'Rise of the Cybermen' culminates in the conversion of hundreds of parallel Earth humans into Lumic Cyberforms, as the brains of these unfortunate humans are transplanted directly into posthuman, Cyberman bodies. Among them is Jackie Tyler's alter ego who, unlike her husband Pete, proves unable to escape the upgrading process. In an effort to rescue Jackie, Pete and Rose infiltrate the Cybermen's facility. Unfortunately they are too late and Jackie has already been converted – as they discover when one of the Cybermen addresses them:

> CYBERMAN (to Pete): I recognize you. I went first. My name was Jacqueline Tyler.
> ROSE: (before she can stop herself) No!
> PETE: What?!... You're lying. You're not her! You're not my Jackie!
> (Pete lunges at the Cyberman who was Jackie.)
> CYBERMAN: No. I am Cyber-form. Once I was Jacqueline Tyler.... Her brain is inside this body ('The Age of Steel').

Here the programme draws upon two of the views on self-location outlined above. First, the idea that the self is fully embodied is highlighted when the Cyberman refers to itself as having been Jackie

Tyler. It uses the past tense: this Cyberman *was* Jackie, but in its new Cyberform body this is no longer the case. However, the Cyberman subsequently suggests a view of the self as embrained – that is, as contained in the brain that is now in the Cyberform body. It is that brain that allows the Cyberman to remember the person it once was. This incoherent coupling of embrained and embodied views is typical of the way the self is represented and located in new *Who*.[41] It is suggested that Lumic cyberconversion – a process that involves doing away with most of the human body – irreversibly changes a character's identity. Therefore, the whole body is depicted as vitally important to the sense of self: the self changes as the body changes. However, since at least some Cybermen can remember who they were prior to upgrading, the programme simultaneously suggests that self and identity are associated with the brain. Despite such incoherence, it can be argued that new *Who* actually privileges the embrained, Cartesian self: it is these narratively potent selves that persist in order to fight back against Cyber-power (Yvonne Hartman) and that most starkly and emotively dramatize cyberconversion as otherwise involving the loss of self (e.g. Sally and Jackie in 'The Age of Steel').

Conclusion: Do Posthumans have to be Evil?

We have introduced the main themes in contemporary posthumanist thought, and shown how the Cybermen in new *Who* can be seen as one (powerfully negative) way of thinking about what posthumans might look like and what becoming human.2 might mean. In doing this we have implicitly taken a particular view of the importance of *Doctor Who* and its role in circulating ideas within wider culture. An important part of posthumanist theory is its view on the significance of science fiction in exploring, developing and coming to terms with scientific and technological changes that characterise our modern world. Sherryl Vint, for example, suggests that popular science fiction provides a valuable 'space in which to explore the consequences of various versions of the posthuman within its imagined worlds'.[42] And for Katherine Hayles, programmes like *Doctor Who* 'reveal [...] the complex cultural, social, and representational issues tied up with [...] technological innovations'.[43]

Finally, we would like to speculate on just how *Doctor Who*'s depiction of the Cybermen contributes to our understanding of, and views upon, posthumanism in the real world. By bringing the known and the unknown together, *Doctor Who* offers its audience the opportunity to imaginatively explore what it might mean to live with posthumans. The picture painted by Cybermen episodes is not at all a happy one; but do posthumans necessarily have to be 'baddies'? Some authors, for example Courtland Lewis, have provocatively suggested that the popular notion of the Cybermen as evil may not be justified. Lewis argues that by providing pain-free immortality the Cybermen are actually fulfilling the ambition of many humans.[44] This altruistic interpretation of their actions must, though, surely be the exception rather than the rule, since the decision about who gets upgraded and when lies entirely with the Cybermen; they ride roughshod over the autonomy of their convertees.[45]

However, is it inevitable that humans.1 and humans.2 should be in conflict? Can we avoid a transhumanist nightmare of the kind seen in 'Rise of the Cybermen'? Earlier we discussed the idea that, even today, we may all be at least a little posthuman; what might be called posthuman 'modes of being' could simply be an extension of our contemporary experience with machines and technologies.[46] Extrapolating from this idea, it seems more likely that – rather than being in conflict – humans.1 and humans.2 in various shapes and forms might coexist together relatively positively. This is another transhumanist dream, to be sure, and the flip side of narrative scenarios presented in *Doctor Who*'s fiction.[47] Yet perhaps we can act as posthumanist textual poachers, reading the BBC Wales' series against its own preferred, gothic meanings.[48] Rather than merely representing a culturally-relevant, emotionally-intensified posthuman threat,[49] new *Who* alerts us to the very proximity of the posthuman era, providing a space in which we – human, transhuman, and posthuman alike – can imagine, shape and create our future together.

NOTES

1. Max More www.extropy.org, quoted in Pepperell, Robert, *The Posthuman Condition: Consciousness Beyond the Brain* (Intellect Books, Bristol, 2003), p. 170.
2. Sleight, Graham, *The Doctor's Monsters: Meanings of the Monstrous in Doctor Who* (I.B.Tauris, London and New York, 2012), p. 144.
3. Hayles, N Katherine, *How We Became Posthuman: Virtual Bodies in Cybernetics, Literature, and Informatics* (Chicago University Press, Chicago,

1999), and Pepperell, *The Posthuman Condition*, give numerous examples of these.
4 See Geraghty, Lincoln, 'From balaclavas to jumpsuits: The multiple histories and identities of *Doctor Who*'s Cybermen', *Atlantis: Journal of the Spanish Association of Anglo-American Studies*, 30/1 (2008), pp. 85–100.
5 A further episode 'Nightmare in Silver' aired in the UK on 11th May 2013, after completion of this chapter.
6 Sleight: *The Doctor's Monsters*, p. 56.
7 See Golder, Dave, 'New look for Doctor Who series 7 Cybermen' (2012), available online at http://www.sfx.co.uk/2012/11/09/new-look-for-doctor-who-series-7-cybermen-2/, accessed 1 June 2013.
8 Doctor Who Reference Guide, 'Rise of the Cybermen/Age of Steel' (2007), available online at http://www.drwhoguide.com/who_tv16.htm, accessed 1 June 2013.
9 Rose, James, 'The suffering of the skin: The uncanny nature of the Cybermen in the Russell T. Davies era of *Doctor Who*' in C. Hansen (ed.) *Ruminations, Peregrinations, and Regenerations: A Critical Approach to Doctor Who* (Cambridge Scholars Publishing, Newcastle upon Tyne, 2010), pp. 283–98.
10 Ibid., p. 288.
11 Britton, Piers D., *TARDISbound: Navigating the Universes of Doctor Who* (I.B.Tauris, London and New York, 2011), p. 78; and see also Rose, James 'The suffering of the skin'.
12 Hayles: *How We Became Posthuman*, p. 3.
13 Ibid., pp. 85-6.
14 Soper, Kate, *Humanism and Anti-humanism* (HarperCollins, London, 1985), p. 14.
15 Barry, Peter J, *Beginning Theory: An Introduction to Literary and Cultural Theory* (Manchester University Press, Manchester, 2005), p. 18.
16 For a fuller discussion of *Who* as a secular humanist text see Layton, David, *The Humanism of Doctor Who: A Critical Study in Science Fiction and Philosophy* (2012).
17 Soper: *Humanism and Anti-humanism*, p. 14.
18 Vint, Sherryl, *Bodies of Tomorrow: Technology, Subjectivity, Science Fiction* (University of Toronto Press, Toronto, 2007), p. 12.
19 Moravec, Hans P, *Mind Children: The Future of Robot and Human Intelligence* (Harvard University Press, Cambridge, Cambridge, 1988), p. 109.
20 Miah, Andy, 'Be very afraid: Cyborg athletes, transhuman ideals & posthumanity', *Journal of Evolution and Technology*, xiii (2003), available online at http://jetpress.org/volume13/miah.html, accessed 1 June 2013.
21 De Grey, Aubrey DNJ and Rae, Michael, *Ending Aging: The Rejuvenation Breakthroughs that could Reverse Human Aging in Our Lifetime* (St. Martin's Press, New York, 2007).
22 Bostrom, Nick, 'The transhumanist FAQ' (2003), available online at http://transhumanism.org/resources/FAQv21.pdf, accessed 1 June 2013; and 'Why I want to be a posthuman when I grow up' (2006), available online at http://www.nickbostrom.com/posthuman.pdf, accessed 191 June 2013.
23 DeGrazia, David, 'Technologies and human identity' *Journal of Medicine and Philosophy*, 30/3 (2005), p. 263.

24. Parsons, Paul, *The Science of Doctor Who* (Icon Books, Cambridge, 2006).
25. Barnes, Alan, 'The Fact of Fiction: Tenth Planet' *Doctor Who Magazine* 352 (2005), pp. 22–31; Richards, Justin, *Doctor Who: The Legend Continues* (BBC Books, London, 2005).
26. DeGrazia: 'Enhancement technologies and human identity', p. 263.
27. See Warwick, Kevin, *In the Mind of the Machine: The Breakthrough in Artificial Intelligence* (Arrow Books, London, 1998); Bostrom: 'The transhumanist FAQ'.
28. More, Max and Kurzweil, Raymond, 'Max More and Ray Kurzweil on the singularity', *KurzweilAI.net*, available online at http://www.kurzweilai.net/articles/art0408.html, accessed 20 October 2008.
29. Hayles: *How We Became Posthuman*, p. 261.
30. Haraway, Donna, 'A Cyborg manifesto: Science, technology, and socialist-feminism in the late twentieth century' in *Simians, Cyborgs and Women: The Reinvention of Nature* (Routledge, New York, 1991), p. 178.
31. Sleight: *The Doctor's Monsters*, p. 146.
32. Britton: *TARDISbound*, p. 78.
33. Wegenstein, Bernadette, *Getting Under the Skin: Body and Media Theory* (MIT Press, Cambridge and London, 2006).
34. Pepperell, Robert, 'The posthuman conception of consciousness: A 10-point guide' in R. Ascott (ed.), *Art, Technology and Consciousness: Mind at Large* (Intellect Books, Bristol, 2000), p. 12.
35. Bostrom: 'Why I want to be a posthuman when I grow up', p. 14.
36. Descartes, René, *A Discourse of a Method for the Well-guiding of Reason, and the Discovery of Truth in the Sciences* (John Holden, London, 1649), p. 51.
37. Moravec: *Mind Children*, p. 109.
38. Rucker, Rudy, Sirius, R. U., and Mu, Queen, *Mondo 2000: A user's Guide to the New Edge* (HarperPerennial, New York, 1992), p. 280.
39. For example Hayles: *How We Became Posthuman*, and Vint: *Bodies of Tomorrow*.
40. For example Pepperell: 'The posthuman conception of consciousness' and Pepperell: *The Posthuman Condition*.
41. For more on this, see Cranny-Francis, Anne and Tulloch, John, 'Vaster than empire(s), and more slow: the politics and economics of embodiment in *Doctor Who*' in P. Harrigan and N. Wardrip-Fruin (eds), *Third Person: Authoring and Exploring Vast Narratives* (MIT Press, Massachusetts, 2009), pp. 343–55.
42. Vint: *Bodies of Tomorrow*, p. 20.
43. Hayles: *How We Became Posthuman*, p. 24.
44. Lewis, Courtland, 'Cybermen evil? I don't think so!' in L. Lewis and P. Smithka (eds) *Doctor Who and Philosophy* (Open Court Publishing, Chicago, 2011), pp. 199–209.
45. See Layton: *The Humanism of Doctor Who*, p. 185 for a discussion of Cybermen as 'the very definition of anti-humanist'.
46. Bostrom: 'Why I want to be a posthuman when I grow up', p. 3.
47. Bostrom: 'The transhumanist FAQ'.
48. Rose: 'The suffering of the skin'.

4

TALKING TO THE TARDIS
Doctor Who, Neil Gaiman and Cultural Mythology

Will Brooker

Pre-Credits Sequence

Poststructuralist theory invites us to see stories of all kinds as dialogic, in conversation with each other across an intertextual network.[1] They speak back to earlier stories, cross-referencing, borrowing, echoing, pastiching and homaging; they speak forward, to future stories, as they encourage the next generation of writers to engage with them, to challenge them, to pick up the narrative thread and take it somewhere new. And they speak to us, of course, as readers – though 'we' are no homogenous group, and we are not just readers but co-creators. We come to popular texts, like *Doctor Who*, as if joining a conversation; we are part of the process that makes meaning. We do not enter the conversation cold; rather, we bring a host of preconceptions and expectations that shape our interpretation.

I came to the conversation around 'The Doctor's Wife' (series six, episode four of the BBC Wales *Doctor Who*) with an interpretive framework both broad and specific. Broadly, I have followed the career of Neil Gaiman for the last 25 years – since his first published graphic novel, *Violent Cases*, in 1987 – but for the most part, only in comics. Gaiman's work ran alongside and intersected with my on-going interest in superheroes – primarily of the reworked, revised and rebooted variety – through the four-part *Black Orchid* (1988) and *The Books of Magic* (1993) and the epic, seventy-five issue *Sandman* (1989–96) to his elegiac Batman story *Whatever Happened to the Caped Crusader?* (2009).[2] I have seen his *Neverwhere* (1996), *Stardust* (2007) and *Coraline* (2009) but not read his *American Gods* (2001), *Anansi Boys* (2005), or *The Graveyard Book* (2009).[3] I am, in this context, a comics fan, a superhero fan; a fan of Gaiman's work where it overlaps with my existing generic interests, rather than a fan of Gaiman as individual author, a devoted follower of his stories across modes and media. This particular approach to *Doctor Who* – what we might call *Gaiman-oriented* (expertly but selectively aware of Gaiman's work in other forms) rather than either *Gaiman-centric* (focused exclusively on the writer's career and oeuvre) or *Who-centric* (invested primarily in the long-running series, with its authors as a secondary concern) inevitably shaped my understanding and perception of this particular intersection, this particular moment of meeting between the Doctor and the TARDIS, between *Doctor Who* and Neil Gaiman.

Most specifically, a previous episode of *Doctor Who*, 'The Family of Blood' (series three, episode nine), had struck me immediately as an homage to Gaiman's work, or what I knew of it; even more specifically, a sequence of just over a minute, towards the very end of the programme, seemed to bear the unmistakeable imprint of *Sandman*'s themes, characters, tropes and rhythms. This sequence, in which the Doctor puts four members of the titular family through individual, inventively cosmic punishments, is narrated through a voiceover (from the family's Son of Mine) that effectively transforms the visuals into moving illustrations, reminiscent – to a superhero fan at least – of the dynamic between words and images that drives comic book storytelling.[4]

Aspects of character and genre in the *Doctor Who* sequence also strongly recall *Sandman*'s recurring tropes. From its ninth issue onward – which introduces the protagonist's sister, Death – *Sandman* was, on one level, about a dysfunctional family of demigods, the Endless, who regularly interfere in human affairs across different points of history and culture, taking forms (and dressing in fashions) that allow them to blend in. 'Family of Blood', of course, echoes this theme through its villains,

TALKING TO THE TARDIS

a clan of aliens who forcibly borrow human bodies in 1913; but the Doctor also takes on a new identity in this episode, disguising himself temporarily as a schoolteacher, and his companion Martha as a maid. *Sandman*, like *Doctor Who*, is essentially built around the motif of gods coming to earth, the juxtaposition between everyday and 'eternal', between widescreen epic and small-scale domestic drama, that structures so many stories from the fables of Zeus and his mortal women through Jesus Christ's short life on earth to the twentieth century's Superman, an alien dating Lois Lane, and many of his costumed counterparts.

This closing sequence depicts the Doctor in what some fans call the 'vengeful god' mode; powerful and terrible, but also grimly merciful.[5] The Son's voiceover delivers a payoff: 'And then we discovered why... why this Doctor, who had fought with gods and demons... why he'd run away from us and hidden. He was being *kind*.'

> He wrapped my father in unbreakable chains forged in the heart of a dwarf star. He tricked my mother into the event horizon of a collapsing galaxy, to be imprisoned there forever. He still visits my sister, once a year, every year... I wonder if one day he might forgive her. But there she is, can you see? He trapped her inside a mirror. Every mirror. If ever you look at your reflection and see something move behind you, just for a second, that's her. That's always her. As for me... I was suspended in time, and the Doctor put me to work standing over the fields of England, as their protector. We wanted to live forever, so the Doctor made sure that we did.

Again, note the rhythms of this speech, its rhetoric ('can you see?') and its rhythms ('once a year, every year'), locating it somewhere between the Bible and Grimm's fairy-tales, with a touch of the pseudo-science of pulp science fiction and comic book melodrama; and compare it to key scenes from *Sandman*, such as the climactic appearance of Morpheus as firm but gentle judge and punisher, at the end of the 'Game of You' story-arc.

> The time has come, then. I am here, by the terms of the contract. Who summoned me? Who calls this skerry to its final judgement? Who seeks my boon? [...] Hush now. I need silence from all of you, while I do uncreate this land. It is an old land, and it is time for it to rest.[6]

The Dream-Lord goes on, standing tall and skinny in a black coat with wild hair, and looking not unlike the David Tennant/Matt Smith incarnations of the Doctor:

> ... you played your part in the Cuckoo's deeds also, Barbara. After all, it is your fault that she was bound to this skerry and could not leave it when her time came to fly, after the manner of her kind. [...] As I said, you are trespassers. You came here without my cognizance, nor with my consent. You must pay the price for that.[7]

Just as *Doctor Who* fans would recognise the 'vengeful god' mode from earlier storylines and relish its return, so *Sandman* readers have seen their hero take this tone before, at the end of a previous episode. Chapter 2 of 'A Doll's House' concludes with Morpheus declaring: 'They know the law. My law. And they have wantonly defied it. Did they think they could hide from me? I do not know what game they are playing. But I know this. I am angry... and it's my move.'[8]

This was the framework of expectation and interpretation that I brought to Neil Gaiman's 'The Doctor's Wife': a crossover between two popular narratives and mythologies, and approaches to narrative and mythology (both popular and classical), that had previously come so close to overlapping – most notably, for me, in 'The Family of Blood' – that this explicit intersection seemed ultimately inevitable, perfectly suited, and almost fated. Gaiman's comic book writing and *Doctor Who*, it seemed, were a love match. Somewhat naively, I expected the dominant discourse around Gaiman's episode – the reviews and audience responses – to echo mine. I was wrong. This chapter explores the ways in which I was wrong, and why, and uncovers meaning in my mistake. It examines the dynamic between a powerful 'author-function', to use Foucault's term,[9] and an equally resonant 'text-function'[10] – and analyses what happens when these two forces meet; it recognises that a Gaiman-oriented, *auteurist* reading of 'The Doctor's Wife' is incomplete, but also proposes that a *Who*-centric approach, which foregrounded the text and saw Gaiman in service to the longer-running narrative as a guest interpreter of a larger myth, could only ever tell half the story. In conclusion, it suggests another approach to – and a new term for – this collision of author and text function.

The *Who*-Centric Response

I surveyed 12 reviews of the episode from May 2011, the month of its release. The sample ranged from British broadsheet newspapers (*The Guardian* and *The Independent*), monthly magazines (*SFX*) and major websites (*Digital Spy*) through smaller online forums (*Den of Geek, Tachyon TV*) to dedicated, amateur blogs like *The Daily P.O.P.* and *I'd Rather Be Killing Monsters*. These reviews were supplemented by multiple discussion threads from *Doctor Who Online*, *Gallifrey Base* and the *Neil Gaiman Board*, giving an inevitably selective but, I hope, representative sense of the response to this episode from British fans, journalists and fan-journalists.

One key finding from this sample is that, although Gaiman's first major published works were comic books, with the *Sandman* and its multiple spin-offs constituting his most celebrated (or at least, most sustained) artistic accomplishment, expectations for the author's first *Doctor Who* episodes were framed in relation to other texts, or more general generic terms.

Tim Knight's blog *I'd Rather Be Killing Monsters* is unusual in naming specific comics at all, but typical in its broad sense of Gaiman's cultural credits:

> Neil Gaiman is a geek god, he wrote the incredible *Sandman* comic and countless highly-acclaimed, best-selling novels as well as having a race named after him in *Babylon 5* and several of his tales turned into popular movies.[11]

Digital Spy simply introduces Gaiman as a 'legendary fantasy author';[12] *SFX* describes him as 'the *Stardust* and *Coraline* scribe'.[13] For Neil Perryman at *Tachyon TV*, Gaiman's name has narrow and negative associations – 'I wasn't particularly enthused [...] as far as I am concerned, he's responsible for the worst episode of *Babylon 5* ever made, which is no mean feat'.[14] Rickey Hackett admits to his fandom, but holds it at a distance to ensure objectivity in his piece for *Review the Who* – 'being a fan of Neil Gaiman's work was never going to be all it took to make me enjoy his first episode'[15] – while Tim Knight, despite his enthusiasm for Gaiman as a 'geek god', also foregrounds his own scepticism. 'My experience with "celebrity" (or "stunt") writers and *Doctor Who* hasn't been too great so far – I've made my dislike of Richard Curtis' *Vincent and the Doctor* and Michael Moorcock's *The Coming of the Terraphiles* abundantly clear'.[16]

Dan Martin, writing for the *Guardian*, also strikes a cautious balance.

> I won't pretend to be an expert in Gaiman's work, but his script feels like a masterstroke in bringing his twisted fantasia to the show without ever

smothering it. The patchwork people, the talking planet, the steampunk stylings all felt like vintage Gaiman, but the episode was also steeped in *Who*-ness, in a way that guest writers don't always manage.[17]

Where a fan investment in Gaiman is admitted, then, it is held in check for the benefit of an assumed *Who* fan-readership, to assure fellow members of a shared community that the assessment of this episode is loyal primarily to the on-going, unfolding text, rather than the guest (stunt, celebrity) author.

Among the discussion forums, too, *Who* fandom clearly comes first; those who encountered Gaiman through 'The Doctor's Wife' are guided to further reading by more experienced contributors, but again Gaiman is associated with a broad and vague range of texts across media, rather than identified primarily as a comics author. One poster on *Doctor Who Online* asks 'who is he? What are his works?' and is directed to Gaiman's film and TV credits through his *imdb.com* profile; another reply refers to 'my favorite comic book, *The Sandman*', and a third lists 'his collab with Terry Pratchett on *Good Omens* or (most likely) *Stardust*... he's also written many other awesome books'. 'He's a writer,' another contributor helpfully adds, while one lone voice worries, 'wonder if his book writing can translate into screenplay'.[18]

On *Gallifrey Base*, the references are more knowledgeable but equally scattered, ranging from novels through cinema and short stories to relatively obscure single-issue comics. 'I'm pretty partial to *Signal to Noise*,' one member volunteers, recalling Gaiman's serial for *The Face* magazine in 1989. 'He also wrote a really great *Hellblazer* issue (#27, "Hold Me").' Other contributors have their own favourites:

> The original graphic rendition of *Stardust* is stunning to behold... and by extension, the film is a joy. But *Sandman* and *American Gods* are his best works IMHO.

> If anyone hasn't seen his short film *Statuesque* from Christmas 2009, it's a very nice little silent piece.

Further posts confirm that '*Stardust* is fun, *Coraline* is brilliant,' suggest that 'Conan Doyle/Lovecraft fans may like his short "A Study in Emerald",'[19] advise readers to give their friends 'a copy of *Mr Punch* and watch their world turn upside down,' and proclaim 'You can also put me down as recommending *Anansi Boys* and *American Gods*, and also his short story collections'.[20]

This last is from a user called Bulletproof, who goes on to comment that Gaiman's '*Neverwhere* TV series is an underrated gem, and very reminiscent of the classic [*Doctor Who*] series (he's even said one of its characters was basically his take on the Doctor)'. Bulletproof's suggestion leads to a particularly interesting angle on the Gaiman/*Who* dynamic, which was unexpected from my own perspective as a comic book fan. Rather than positioning Gaiman as a powerful author-figure whose recurring motifs and traits, well-established over 25 years, had already influenced *Doctor Who* (in 'Family of Blood') and were now being brought to bear directly on the series, this online comment reverses the relationship, locating Gaiman in a far humbler role as *Doctor Who* fan, and *Neverwhere* not so much as an early expression of the author's concerns and themes, but as, essentially, *Doctor Who* fanfic.

Bulletproof was not alone in this interpretation. *SFX* praised 'The Doctor's Wife' as 'a big smoochy kiss blown to proper *Who* fans,'[21] while Draven-uk, commenting under the online review, agreed 'it's an ode to the TARDIS and to the most important relationship in the Doctor's life'.[22] Neil Perryman concluded that 'as a love letter to the show, "The Doctor's Wife" will take some beating';[23] Tim Knight agreed that it was 'an incredible love letter to the show's forty-plus year history,'[24] while Suthers, at *Gallifrey Base*, praised Gaiman's 'deep, encyclopaedic knowledge of the series and its history.'[25]

Dr Quinzel, on the *Guardian*'s blog, commended the episode as 'not as Gaiman-esque as some people expected, but that's a good thing. He didn't let his quirks and trademarks overshadow the episode. This wasn't Neil Gaiman putting his stamp on *Doctor Who*, this was just a really, really good episode of *Doctor Who*.'[26] Simon Brew, from *Den of Geek*, assured his readers that 'if there was any doubt that Gaiman was a *Who* devotee, then they must have been eradicated in any sane person's mind.'[27]

A significant strand in the audience response, then, saw 'The Doctor's Wife' as a loving homage from a fan position. Indeed, this interpretation was confirmed by no less an authority than showrunner Steven Moffat, on the *Doctor Who Confidential* that followed the episode.

> It occurred to me, knowing Neil's work [...] that I just thought, this guy's a *Doctor Who* fan. I can tell [...] I can smell it! He must, he loves *Doctor Who*. He's practically writing *Doctor Who* in disguise.[28]

There were further suggestions on *Gallifrey Base* that Gaiman had borrowed ideas (such as the living TARDIS) from a specific author of *Doctor Who* spin-off novels, Lawrence Miles. That Gaiman had directly lifted from Miles was firmly discounted – 'the odds that Neil Gaiman was cribbing ideas from Doctor Who's professional fanfic circuit seem to me basically zero'[29] – but the subsequent debate introduced a new spin on the Gaiman/*Who* dynamic.

'I used to like [Neil Gaiman's] first *Death* miniseries a lot,' suggested Emsworth, 'but if I read it again I'd think it is what Lawrence Miles thinks Neil Gaiman is like.'[30] Contributor Phil Sandifer explained:

> The thing is, the entire tone of Lawrence Miles [...] was basically 'Ooh, let's try to make *Doctor Who* feel more like *Sandman*.' The Virgin and BBC Books reek of Gaiman's influence through and through. Lawrence Miles in particular, much as he slags Gaiman as a cheap Alan Moore imitator [...] is one of the most Gaimanesque writers out there. Neil Gaiman wrote Gaiman-style *Doctor Who*. Unsurprisingly, it sounded like some of the attempts of people to imitate what Gaiman-style Doctor Who might sound like.[31]

These arguments and counter-arguments reveal the relationship between Gaiman and *Doctor Who* to be more complicated than that between powerful author-figure and malleable, impressionable text (to characterise my own original assumption) or influential text and authorial fanfic, as Moffat and many Whovians seemed to be suggesting. While Sandifer concludes that 'the arrow of influence runs unambiguously one way here'[32] – from Gaiman to Miles, and not *vice versa* – the dynamic between Gaiman and *Who* as a whole is better seen in terms of closely-related spheres (of narrative, theme, character and motif) that overlap at the crossover point of 'The Doctor's Wife', but already had a great deal in common, and, arguably, share a common ancestry or cultural DNA. The remainder of this chapter explores that overlap, and seeks to explain its sources.

Overlapping Spheres

I am suggesting, therefore, that 'The Doctor's Wife' is best seen neither as an adaptation of *Doctor Who* conventions to Neil Gaiman's authorial mode, nor as an adaptation of Neil Gaiman's authorial mode to the conventions of *Doctor Who*; rather than a process of influence one way or the other, I suggest that the episode represents a fascinating point of overlap. This overlap can be broken down, in turn, into multiple categories: on the most immediate level, form, genre, and authorship; more broadly, a shared intertextual approach, and most fundamentally, underlying discourses of canon, continuity and mythos.

To deal first with form: Gaiman, in my reading, brings one small but distinct aspect from comics to his *Doctor Who* television script. This is the moment where the TARDIS, embodied as Idris, telepathically implants Rory and Amy with the key to the old console room. Rory is given four words – crimson, eleven, delight, petrichor – which Amy then has to imagine vividly in order to open the door. As she does so, we hear her voice over four images located in her own consciousness, rather than the TARDIS diegesis: a red flag against a blue sky, a birthday cake, Amy's beaming face on her wedding day, and a drop of water hitting dry earth. Online *Who* fans puzzled over this sequence, searching for deeper symbolism, but from my own perspective it reads simply as an importing of comic-book conventions to the screen. As in 'Family of Blood', where Son of Mine's voice-over made the accompanying shots into a vivid, moving illustration, this string of quick shots, with Amy's voice serving as captions, echoes the dynamic of words and pictures on the comic book page.[33] We can readily find examples in Gaiman's comic book work – the first page of *Whatever Happened to the Caped Crusader?*,[34] for instance, offers an enigmatic narration against a montage of unexplained images – and an influence in the 1980s comics of Alan Moore, who originally guided Gaiman into the industry and pioneered this technique of juxtaposed language and image.[35]

Gaiman's comic book work falls largely into the superhero genre, a hybrid of fantasy and pseudo-science; *Sandman* was launched as a horror comic, but evolved into an exploration of folklore, history and mythology, still nominally framed within the DC superhero universe, which clearly intersects, on a generic level, with *Doctor Who*. The evolution of the Doctor, during the Russell T Davies period of Christopher Eccleston and David Tennant, into a 'lonely god' figure, haunted by guilt from the Time War – able to unleash vengeful fury when provoked but ultimately destined to travel in solitude as the last of his kind – brings the character closer to the 'dark' and 'grim' vigilante protagonist that has dominated comics since the 1980s, epitomised most obviously by Frank Miller's

Batman: The Dark Knight Returns and Alan Moore's character Rorschach, from *Watchmen* (both 1986).[36]

This more 'adult' approach to superheroes was motivated by discourses of 'realism'; specifically, Moore and his contemporaries asked, and explored with varying degrees of success, how humans with uncanny powers would function in, and alter, the everyday world. We can identify this trend in Moore's pioneering British series *Miracleman*,[37] which began in 1982 and was later taken over by Gaiman himself; in Moore's later work from *Swamp Thing*[38] through *Watchmen*[39] to *The League of Extraordinary Gentlemen*,[40] and indeed in Gaiman's superhero stories, which tend to frame the spectacular within a mundane, quotidian framework, and introduce us to the miraculous through a relatable viewpoint character. Gaiman's second *Sandman* story arc, 'The Doll's House', initially positions Rose Walker in this everywoman role.[41]

While this approach may seem distinctively 'Gaimanesque' to a comic book reader, it is also, and equally, identifiable as a key trait of new *Who*: Rose Tyler, rather than Rose Walker, here takes the role of the relatable protagonist. Matt Hills terms this the 'intimate epic' – the grafting of small-scale 'emotional realism' onto wide-screen stories of time-travel and alternate worlds – and sees it as evidence of genre hybridity, a fusing of soap opera with science fiction and action adventure:

> Nowhere is this more evident than the conclusion to 'Last of the Time Lords' (3.13) where an SF invasion storyline [...] is followed by Martha Jones' decision to stop travelling with the Doctor in order to get over her unrequited love.[42]

That the ambitious science fiction conceits of 'The Doctor's Wife' – the TARDIS inhabiting a human body while its casing is possessed by a malignant consciousness – are the set-up not for grand spectacle but for emotionally-resonant scenes between Rory and Amy (he accuses her of abandoning him again) and Idris and the Doctor (in a tearful farewell) could be read as typically Gaiman; but they are no less characteristic of *Doctor Who*, in its post-2005 incarnation at least.

The introduction of characters called simply 'Auntie', 'Uncle' and 'Nephew' is also, from a comic book fan perspective, a clear signal of Gaiman's authorship; as noted, *Sandman* is structured around family relationships, with characters who refer to each other regularly as 'Sister' and 'Brother',[43] to the extent that 'The Family of Blood' resonated, coincidentally or not, as an homage. Again, though, the trope can be read back to both the author and the series, as online comments confirm: Tarryn, on *The Daily POP*, suggested that 'As for the odd names of Auntie and Uncle and Nephew, well that's just Neil Gaiman being creepy for you,'[44] while Ovinicus noted that 'the naming of Uncle, Auntie and Nephew stem from all the fantastic names that have cropped up over the years in *Doctor Who*, but remind me in particular of the familiar yet alien names used in *Paradise Towers* and *The Happiness Patrol*'.[45] This second reviewer even uses the names as evidence that 'through and through, Gaiman shows himself to be a TARDIS blue blooded fan'.[46]

On the broader level of authorship, the notion of a named – even a 'celebrity' – guest writer bringing (usually) his own individual slant to an existing text and its heritage, giving the mythos a distinct personal twist while respecting established continuity, is long-established in comics. Once more, while discourses of authorship emerged during the 1960s and 1970s, they reached full force in the mid-1980s with Alan Moore and Frank Miller's revised versions of familiar templates (Batman for Miller, and standard hero archetypes in Moore's *Watchmen*). It was within this culture of named authorship that Gaiman entered the superhero industry, bringing a new slant first to the little-known DC Comics heroine Black Orchid, and then to a vintage, equally-forgotten character, the Sandman. As Gaiman's writing style and recurring concerns became established, his name evolved into a 'function', to use Michel Foucault's term; a trusted brand, carrying certain values and guarantees.[47] By the time he wrote *Whatever Happened to the Caped Crusader?*[48] in 2009, readers were primed to expect certain recognisable tropes and motifs from 'Gaiman's Batman' – as opposed to 'Grant Morrison's Batman' or 'Frank Miller's Batman' – and those expectations were rewarded as Gaiman brought a tale about storytelling, respectful to the history yet offering inventive new takes on it, which concluded by making the Dark Knight narrative into a cross between lullaby and folk myth, told from Bruce Wayne's mother to the infant crime-fighter.

Yet as both fan and fan-academic reports demonstrate, this discourse of authorship is equally active around *Doctor Who*. James Chapman posits that the 2005 series was modelled explicitly on the American model of television authorship, with 'Russell T. Davies as writer-producer in the mould of a [Chris] Carter or a [Joss] Whedon'.[49] Matt Hills proposes a more uncertain dynamic, with Davies as a '(de)materialising *auteur*' and 'the very concept of an authorial "era" [...] an unstable artefact, winking in and out of existence like a TARDIS,' thereby suggesting that *Doctor Who* is read within fandom as 'multi-authored'.[50] The contributors to *Gallifrey Base* clearly identify individual stories from the series (both new and 'classic') in authorial terms, enjoying the personal stamp of Douglas Adams on the unaired episode 'Shada', Richard Curtis on 'Vincent and the Doctor' and Mark Gatiss on 'The Unquiet Dead'. 'I like it,' one fan offered, simply. 'A writer should have a voice.'[51]

In a further parallel, as Hills discusses at length, the new generation of *Who* writers, including Gaiman, grew up as followers of the show. 'Executive producer Russell T. Davies and producer Phil Collinson were card-carrying fans; the actor playing the tenth Doctor was a fan; writers such as Paul Cornell, Mark Gatiss, Steven Moffat, Gareth Roberts and Rob Shearman were all fans...'.[52] Similarly, Gaiman, like many of his contemporaries, had grown up on comic books and been inspired specifically by the work of Alan Moore before following him into the industry, arguably borrowing from the older author's stylistic tricks and traits, and in some cases (such as *Miracleman*) actually inheriting his long-running narratives. Most specifically, the popularity of the 'adult' superhero comic and the rise of the 'graphic novel' in the mid-1980s led to a generation of writers, and a wealth of texts, which were actively mentored or indirectly influenced by Alan Moore; James Chapman suggests that Moore, who had at one point contributed to *Doctor Who Magazine* and was even invited to write for the series, directly inspired certain *Doctor Who* episodes of that decade.[53]

We could, therefore, identify a distinctive shared heritage for both *Who* and Gaiman through the mid-80s work of Alan Moore.[54] However, Moore's authorial influence, while significant, cannot fully account for the overlap between the author and the TV series. Gaiman and *Who* also share an intersection in Douglas Adams,[55] and arguably also both owe a debt to Lucas' *Star Wars* saga, which in turn, of course, poaches from a vast range of ancient mythology and twentieth century popular culture, including Jack Kirby's 'New Gods' superhero titles from the 1970s. To try to pin down a single source for a text and author who have clearly borrowed with abandon from previous stories would be pointless.

Equally, as Hills suggests, finding an explanation for this intertextual poaching and pastiche in the cultural aesthetic of postmodernism is too reductive: 'These interpretations [...] are rather limited. They tell one theoretical story about society, find a version of that same story in the programme, and speculatively conclude that the success of the 2005 series was a result of the alleged similarity.'[56] There is no doubt that 'The Doctor's Wife', from its junkyard location – itself a call-back to the 76 Totter's Lane setting of the first episode, 'An Unearthly Child' – to its patchwork people and its recycled TARDIS console, itself designed by a *Blue Peter* viewer in a further example of fan-creation, could be read as postmodern quotation and homage in the sense proposed originally by Fredric Jameson, with his metaphor of an 'imaginary museum'.[57]

We could, however, follow the theme of recycling to find another common factor in the 'revisionist' comic book and the 'rebooted' TV show culture: like the graphic novel trend that Gaiman joined in the mid-to-late-1980s, the post-2005 *Doctor Who* enters into a dynamic with the past that reworks existing motifs and characters, aiming for a balance between familiarity and novelty. Moore's celebrated description of Frank Miller's *Dark Knight Returns* – 'everything is exactly the same, except for the fact that it's all totally different'[58] – could equally apply to Christopher Eccleston and Billie Piper's first appearance under the *Doctor Who* banner in 2005.

I want to suggest in conclusion however that, while *Doctor Who* and Neil Gaiman were clearly bound up in a network of shared networks, influences and approaches even before they came together explicitly with 'The Doctor's Wife', the text and the author both occupy, and have long occupied, a particular common territory. That territory is the conflicted, rich and shifting arena of canon, continuity and cultural myth.

Continuity and Canon

Gaiman's episode, as the reviewers all recognised and enjoyed, paid tribute to the history of *Doctor Who* from 1963 onwards; both explicitly, through the re-use of the communication cube not seen since 'The War Games' (1969) and the 'Coral' control room from the Eccleston/ Tennant period, and more subtly through lines of dialogue like 'old girl' (recalling Jon Pertwee's relationship with the TARDIS) and the naming of the Corsair according to the Time Lord conventions that gave us the Master, the Valeyard and the War Chief. Its engagement with canon and continuity is what gave the respondents cited above so much pleasure, and led them to see the episode as a 'love-letter' from a fan-author to an equally-devoted and knowledgeable audience. 'It's the kind of story that's wonderfully backwards-compatible with *Who* of old,' concluded reviewer Simon Drew.[59]

But 'The Doctor's Wife' also altered canon, equally subtly: a passing mention of the Corsair's gender-fluid past immediately demonstrated that Time Lords can become Time Ladies – fans recognised this as an authoritative confirmation of a previously-suspected fact – and Idris's retort to the Doctor 'I always took you where you needed to go' rewrote several episodes from the series' history. 'This story told us so much,' one online reviewer enthused, while another called the Idris dialogue 'the most important exchange [...] in the history of *Doctor Who*, ever'.[60]

> The idea of the TARDIS taking the Doctor where he was needed was mentioned back in 'The Gallifrey Chronicles', and it was awesome to see that become 'canon'.[61]

> It was a delight to behold that subtle shifting of our understanding of the legend, with nothing ditched or contradicted.[62]

> For decades we have blithely assumed that the Doctor stole/borrowed his TARDIS from Gallifrey but now we know different [...] it's a subtle but fundamental shift. Until now, we have assumed that the Doctor was the one flicking the switches and pulling the levers, but now it turns out that she's been the one pressing *his* buttons.[63]

This is precisely the pattern through which contemporary comics' continuity operates, as Geoff Klock illustrates through a similar example from *The Dark Knight Returns*:

> When Batman takes a rifle shot to the chest, which any reader assumes would kill him instantly, it reveals metal shielding. Batman says, 'Why do you think I wear a target on my chest – can't armor my head,' and with that one line, a thirty-year mystery dissolves as every reader runs mentally through previous stories, understanding that plate as having always been there. [...] *his* Batman is almost always wounded, sometimes badly, and the Batarang is reconceived as a kind of bat-shaped throwing star that

disarms by slicing into the fore-arm, rather than its former, sillier portrayal as a boomerang that disarms criminals by knocking weapons out of their hands. The strength of Miller's portrayal leaves readers with the impression that all of Batman's fights must have been of this kind, but that they have been reading a watered-down version of the way things 'really happened.'[64]

The strongest version, Klock concludes, 'is retroactively constituted as always already true'.[65] Richard Reynolds confirms this process of addition, revision and rearrangement through reference to T.S. Eliot's 'Tradition and the Individual Talent':

> ...what happens when a new work of art is created is something that happens simultaneously to all the works of art which preceded it. The existing monuments form an ideal order among themselves, which is modified by the introduction of the new (the really new) work of art among them. The existing order is complete before the new work arrives; for order to persist after the supervention of novelty, the whole existing order must be, if ever so slightly, altered...[66]

It is this dynamic process that Gaiman explores, alongside other comic book writers like Morrison, Miller and Moore, within the mythology of DC and Marvel comics, and alongside other screenwriters like Moffat, Davies and Paul Cornell ('The Family of Blood') within the equally rich and complex continuity of *Doctor Who*. As the TV series reaches its 50th anniversary, it is, in chronological and textual terms, at the point *Batman* reached in 1989, five decades after that character's inception: it has an encyclopaedia of past stories, across multiple media, to play with, to tweak, to revisit, revise and re-edit.

More importantly yet, *Doctor Who* has become far more than just a television series; not just because of its audio, cinema, videogame and novelised spin-offs, but because of the role it plays in the popular imagination. *Doctor Who* is, at this point in its history, like Batman in that a non-fan, with little specific knowledge or experience of the primary text, could readily reel off the protagonist's vehicle, props, principal sidekicks and key villains: it has entered the realm of modern mythology. Matt Smith realises this, when in the *Confidential* that follows 'The Doctor's Wife', he asks his co-star, Suranne (Idris) Jones, how she feels about taking on 'such an iconic part and role [...]. She has no idea what she's letting herself in for,' he muses to the camera, and breathes, almost to himself, 'Folklore'.[67]

Any writer engaging with *Doctor Who* now enters a conversation with a 50-year heritage, and – as we have seen – also has the power to change the rules of present-day canon, which in turn shapes the future development of the myth, until another author decisively changes it back. No surprise that Idris initially speaks out of time, confusing her tenses; like Gaiman, she is addressing *Doctor Who* across history.[68]

'The Doctor's Wife', then, is a playful, respectful, affectionate dialogue with the myth of *Doctor Who* that – like many conversations within marriage – remembers earlier adventures and looks forward to others. And it also speaks on another axis, from Gaiman to his fellow fans, as they clearly recognised and appreciated. It was this particular conversation – this aspect of the dialogic network that surrounds the episode – that eluded me on my first viewing. I approached the text from one angle, as a reader versed in Gaiman-as-comic-author, and the response from *Who* fans struck me as unfamiliar and perplexing, a dialogue on a new dimension slightly removed from my own.

Their half of the conversation, however, was also incomplete. Neither a Gaiman-centric nor *Who*-centric approach to 'The Doctor's Wife' – neither a focus that favours the author or one that privileges the text – fully captures the matrix of meanings, of borrowings, in-jokes, friendly debts and affectionate repayments that makes up this meeting. When a resonant author-function meets an encyclopaedic text-function, the result, in perfect keeping with both Gaiman and *Doctor Who*'s playfully celebratory approach to history and narrative, is a family reunion, a massive textual party. 'The Doctor's Wife' is, above all, a marriage. We could call it a meta-function, but we might prefer to name it a *wedding-function*. We have to listen to both sides of the union, and let all the guests speak.

Next Time

It was their first and unique meeting; but just as old foes and former assistants tend to return to the *Doctor Who* text, so Gaiman's path will intersect with the Doctor's again, in the series' 50th year. Even the snatches of publicity, brief interviews and online rumours about Gaiman's Cybermen episode confirm the same sense of intersection. Gaiman reports from a French festival that:

> Steven wrote to me and asked if I wanted to make the Cybermen scary again. I thought back to myself at the age of six or seven, *The Moonbase*, *Tomb of the Cybermen*... I saw them when they were first broadcast. The Cybermen were much scarier than the Daleks, because they didn't make any noise. The Daleks moved around all over the place shouting "Exterminate", etc. With the Cybermen, it's different. You turn around and bam! There they are. It's scary.[69]

While Moffat, in a different time and place, explains:

> Cybermen were always the monsters that scared me the most! Not just because they were an awesome military force, but because sometimes they could be sleek and silver and right behind you without you even knowing.[70]

Two separate interviews, on different dates, but already the voices of *Who* showrunner and guest author overlap with and echo each other. Gaiman's second intervention in the series' mythology is presented by Moffat as a combination of iconic character ('one of the all-time classic monsters returning') and literary author-function ('a script from one of our finest novelists'), while Gaiman sees an opportunity to speak back to his own childhood memories of *Doctor Who*, and to revisit previous episodes, by other authors, starring different Doctors.[71] Gaiman captures perfectly, knowingly, the dynamic between sameness and difference, familiarity and novelty that frames and informs the contemporary adventures of this cultural icon:

> The dialogue is completely different. Just as it is with the various Doctors. But some things don't change: the companion will always be intelligent and brave, and the Doctor will always be funny, annoying and strange, and he will always succeed in getting out of inextricable situations.[72]

And as always, as Gaiman notes, it's about dialogue, to the extent that you forget who said what, and who came up with which idea. The dynamic between the author-function and the unfolding text is always (at least) a two-way conversation.

NOTES

1   See for instance Barthes, Roland, 'The death of the author,' from *Image-Music-Text* (originally Paris, 1968) reprinted in John Caughie (ed.), *Theories of Authorship* (Routledge, 1981), p. 21; Bakhtin, Mikhail M., 'Discourse in

the novel' in M. Holquist (ed.), *The Dialogic Imagination: Four Essays by M.M. Bakhtin* (University of Texas Press, Austin, 1981), p. 272–6, and Kristeva, Julia 'Word, dialogue and novel' in T. Moi (ed.), *The Kristeva Reader* (Blackwell, Oxford, 1981), p. 37.

2   Neil Gaiman and Dave McKean, *Black Orchid*, New York: DC Comics (1988); Neil Gaiman and various artists, *The Books of Magic*, New York: DC Comics (1990–91); Neil Gaiman and various artists, *Sandman*, New York: DC Comics (1989–1996); Neil Gaiman and Andy Kubert, *Whatever Happened to the Caped Crusader?*, New York: DC Comics (2009).

3   Neil Gaiman and Lenny Henry, *Neverwhere*, BBC Television (1996); *Coraline*, dir. Henry Selick (2009); *Stardust*, dir Matthew Vaughn (2007); Neil Gaiman, *American Gods* (London, Headline Review, 2005); Neil Gaiman, *Anansi Boys* (London, Headline Review, 2006); Neil Gaiman, *The Graveyard Book* (London, Bloomsbury, 2009).

4   That narration also draws attention to the process of storytelling itself, another theme deeply embedded in Gaiman's work, from *Violent Cases* through his *Sandman* series to *Whatever Happened to the Caped Crusader?*.

5   See for instance Mills, Catriona *The Circulating Library*, http://circulatingli-brary.net/archives/live-blogging-doctor-who-season-three-the-family-of-blood, accessed 1 June 2013); the term 'vengeful god' was itself coined in the 2007 episode 'Utopia' (series three, episode 11).

6   Gaiman, Neil and McManus, Shawn, et al., *The Sandman: A Game of You* (Titan Books, London, 1993), p. 151.

7   Ibid., p. 164–5.

8   Gaiman, Neil, and Dringenberg, Mike, et al., *The Sandman: The Doll's House* (Titan Books, London, 1990), p. 88.

9   See Foucault, Michel, 'What is an author?' from *Language, Counter-Memory, Practice* (originally Paris, 1969), reprinted in Caughie: *Theories of Authorship*.

10 This is Matt Hills's extrapolation from Foucault: see Hills, Matt, *Triumph of a Time Lord* (I.B.Tauris, London and New York, 2010), p. 140.

11 Knight, Tim, 'Doctor Who: The Doctor's Wife', *I'd Rather Be Killing Monsters* (14 May 2011), available at: http://www.heropress.net/2011/05/doctor-who-doctors-wife.html, accessed 1 June 2013.

12 Jeffrey, Morgan, 'Doctor Who review: The Doctor's Wife', *Digital Spy* (15 May 2011), available at: http://www.digitalspy.co.uk, accessed 1 February 2012.

13 Anon (2011) 'Doctor Who The Doctor's Wife – TV Review', *SFX* (14 May 2011), http://www.sfx.co.uk, accessed 1 February 2012.

14 Perryman, Neil, 'Her Indoors', *Tachyon TV* (14 May 2011), available at: http://tachyon-tv.co.uk/2011/05/her-indoors, accessed 1 February 2012.

15 Hackett, Rickey (2011) '6.4 The Doctor's Wife', *Review The Who* (14 May 2011), available at: http://reviewthewho.wordpress.com, accessed 1 June 2013.

16 Knight: 'Doctor Who'.

17 Martin, Dan (2011) 'Doctor Who: The Doctor's Wife – Series 32, episode 4', *The Guardian TV & Radio Blog* (14 May 2011), available at:

http://www.guardian.co.uk/tv-and-radio/tvandradioblog, accessed 1 June 2013.
18. Various, 'Who is Neil Gaiman?' *Doctor Who Online* (11 May 2011), available at: http://forums.drwho-online.co.uk, accessed 1 June 2013.
19. Note that this specific recommendation frames Gaiman as a playful master of pastiche, skilled at adopting other textual voices.
20. Various, 'The best of Gaiman', *Gallifrey Base* (15 May 2011), available at: http://gallifreybase.com/forum, accessed 1 June 2013.
21. Anon: 'Doctor Who The Doctor's Wife – TV Review'
22. Draven-Uk, 'ode to the TARDIS and the most important relationship...', comment on "Doctor Who 'The Doctor's Wife' – TV Review", *SFX*, http://www.sfx.co.uk/2011/05/14/doctor-who-6-04-%E2%80%9Cthe-doctor%E2%80%99s-wife%E2%80%9D-review/ (15 May 2011).
23. Neil Perryman, 'Her Indoors', *Tachyon TV*, http://tachyon-tv.co.uk/2011/05/her-indoors, 14 May 2011 (accessed February 2012).
24. Knight: 'Doctor Who: The Doctor's Wife'.
25. Suthers, 'Has Neil Gaiman missed his vocation?' *Gallifrey Base*, op. cit.
26. Martin: 'Doctor Who: The Doctor's Wife – Series 32, episode 4'.
27. Brew, Simon 'Doctor Who series 6 episode 4 review: The Doctor's Wife', *Den of Geek* (14 May 2011), available at: http://www.denofgeek.com, accessed 1 June 2012.
28. Moffat, Steven, 'Bigger on the inside', *Doctor Who Confidential* (14 May 2011).
29. Sandifer, Phil, 'Toy Story by Lawrence Miles – will they acknowledge it?' *Gallifrey Base*, http://gallifreybase.com/forum/ (14 May 2011), accessed 1 February 2012.
30. Emsworth, in 'The Best of Gaiman'. *Gallifrey Base*, http://gallifreybase.com/forum, 15 May 2011 (accessed February 2012).
31. Sandifer: 'Toy Story'.
32. Ibid.
33. Although at another level it enacts the principles of cinematic montage proposed by Sergei Eisenstein in the 1920s. In this context, 'petrichor' – the scent of earth after rain – is a synthesis of two ideas (*petra* + *ichor*) and the accompanying shot is a visual illustration, an ideogram, of two distinct concepts combining into a third; juxtaposed 'drop of water' plus 'dry earth' explodes into 'petrichor'. See Sergei Eisentein, 'The dramaturgy of film form' in R. Taylor (ed.), *Selected Writings* (British Film Insitute, London, 1988), p. 164.
34. Neil Gaiman, *Whatever Happened to the Caped Crusader?* (2009).
35. Most obviously in *Watchmen*. The *Doctor Who* episode 'A Good Man Goes to War', subsequently, also uses this technique and vividly evokes the superhero epics of Gaiman's contemporary Grant Morrison, who was also heavily-influenced by Moore's 1980s work.
36. Moore, Gibbons and Higgins: *Watchmen*; Frank Miller, Klaus Janson and Lynn Varley, *Batman: The Dark Knight Returns* (New York, DC Comics, 1986).
37. Alan Moore, Alan Davis and Gary Leach, *Miracleman*, originally in *Warrior*, London: Quality Communications (1982–1984).
38. Alan Moore, Steve Bissette, John Totleben, *Swamp Thing*, New York: DC Comics (1984–1987).

39. Alan Moore, Dave Gibbons and John Higgins, *Watchmen*, New York: DC Comics (1986).
40. Alan Moore and Kevin O'Neill, *The League of Extraordinary Gentlemen*, ABC/Wildstorm/DC Comics/Top Shelf/Knockabout Comics (1999-present).
41. Neil Gaiman and Mike Dringenberg, *Sandman: The Doll's House*, New York: DC Comics (1990).
42. Hills: *Triumph of a Time Lord*, p. 102.
43. Even more explicitly, Idris's whimsical dialogue recalls the verbal meanderings of the youngest sister, Delirium.
44. TarrynM, 'Doctor Who: The Doctor's Wife' (15 May 2011), available at: http://dailypop.wordpress.com, accessed 1 February 2012.
45. Ovinicus, 'Doctor Who: The Doctor's Wife' (15 May 2011), http://ovinicus.blogspot.com, accessed 1 February 2012. *Doctor Who* is, of course, threaded with complex family relationships, from the Doctor's granddaughter Susan Foreman in the first (1963) episode through 'The Doctor's Daughter' (2008) to another wife, River Song (also known as Melody Pond, and daughter of the Doctor's companions). Fans will be well aware of the further twist that the Doctor (David Tennant) married his diegetic 'daughter' played by actress Georgia Moffett, who is in fact the real-life daughter of previous Doctor, Peter Davison.
46. Ibid.
47. Foucault: 'What is an author?', p. 285.
48. Gaiman: *Whatever Happened to the Caped Crusader?*
49. Chapman, James, *Inside the Tardis* (I.B.Tauris, London, 2006), p. 165.
50. Hills: *Triumph of a Time Lord*, p. 26.
51. Various: 'The most individual episode of *DW* ever?' *Gallifrey Base*, op. cit.
52. Hills: *Triumph of a Time Lord*, p. 56.
53. Chapman: *Inside the TARDIS*, p. 167. Online commentator Philip Sandifer confirms Moore's direct influence on the series during the 1980s: 'Much of [Andrew] Cartmel's tenure as script editor can be read straightforwardly as an attempt to do Alan Moore's *Doctor Who*.' See Philip Sandifer, TARDIS Eruditorum, http://tardiseruditorum.blogspot.co.uk/, accessed 10 December 2012.
54. The confusion of tenses in Idris's early conversations, for instance, strongly recalls Moore's temporal play in the dialogue of *Watchmen*'s blue-skinned traveller in time and space, Dr Manhattan.
55. Adams also wrote for *Doctor Who*, most famously the 'lost episode' 'Shada', and Gaiman is author of *Don't Panic*, a guide to Adams's life and work.
56. Hills: *Triumph of a Time Lord*, p. 88.
57. See Jameson, Fredric, 'Postmodernism and consumer society', reprinted in Peter Brooker (ed.) *Modernism/Postmodernism* (Longman, London, 1992), p. 169.
58. Moore, Alan, 'Introduction' to F. Miller and L. Varley, *Batman: The Dark Knight eturns* (Titan Books, London, 1986), n.p.
59. Brew: *Den of Geek*.
60. Catweevil (2011), *SFX*, op. cit.
61. Sentient_Omlette (2011), *Den of Geek*, op. cit.
62. Harries, Simon (2011), *Tachyon TV*, op. cit.

63 Perryman: *Tachyon TV*.
64 Klock, Geoff, *How to Read Superhero Comics* (Continuum, London, 2002), pp. 30–1.
65 Ibid.
66 Eliot, T.S., 'Tradition and the individual talent', *Selected Essays* (Faber, London, 1932), p. 15. Quoted in Reynolds, Richard, *Superheroes* (Batsford, London, 1992), p. 43.
67 Matt Smith, *Doctor Who Confidential*, BBC One (14 May 2011).
68 And indeed like Susan in 'An Unearthly Child'.
69 Leger, Francois, 'Neil Gaiman on making the Cybermen scary again', *Den of Geek* (13 November 2012), available at: http://www.denofgeek.com/tv/doctor-who/23423/doctor-who-neil-gaiman-talks-cybermen, accessed 1 June 2013.
70 Mellor, Louisa, 'Cybermen confirmed for Neil Gaiman episode', *Den of Geek* (7 November 2012) http://www.denofgeek.com/tv/doctor-who/23348/doctor-who-cybermen-confirmed-for-neil-gaiman-episode, accessed 1 June 2013.
71 'Tomb of the Cybermen' (series five, episode one, 1967) was written by Kit Pedler and Gerry Davis, and starred Patrick Troughton.
72 Leger: 'Neil Gaiman'.

II

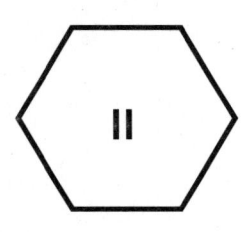

NEW TELEVISION, NEW MEDIA

5

DOCTOR WHO AS PROGRAMME BRAND

Catherine Johnson

BBC Worldwide's website proudly lists *Doctor Who* as one of its 'leading international and multi-format brands' (alongside Lonely Planet, *Top Gear*, *Dancing with the Stars* and BBC Earth).[1] Meanwhile, academic study, particularly since the broadcast of the new series, frequently refers to *Doctor Who* as a brand.[2] Indeed, it could be argued that the history of *Doctor Who* as a text is bound up with the history of television branding. The original *Doctor Who* television series came to an end in 1989. At the same time, the BBC was instigating a five-year plan to position itself as 'the brand-leader' in public service broadcasting.[3] By 2005, when the new *Doctor Who* series was launched, branding had been firmly established as a central strategy in BBC management, extending across the corporation, its channels and key programmes such as *Doctor Who*.[4] But why was *Doctor Who* identified as a key programme brand by the BBC over this period, and what does it mean to understand *Doctor Who* as a brand rather than a television series? This chapter will examine these questions, focusing on asking why branding has become particularly important for the BBC in the development of the new series in 2005. Drawing on interviews and primary industrial documents, it will examine the ways in which branding has been used by the BBC in relation to *Doctor Who* and argue that the development of the series as a brand articulates a broader tension within the corporation between commercial and public service values.

Between 1989 and 2005 the technological, political and economic context within which the BBC was operating changed significantly. With the emergence of new satellite, cable and digital services, the BBC had to compete for viewers with a vastly expanded range of channels and services, both on television and on new platforms, such as the internet and mobile phones. At the same time, these platforms offered new opportunities for the BBC to engage with and serve the British public, activities that were endorsed in government policy over the 1990s and 2000s and that specified the development of digital services as a core objective for the corporation.[5] Yet, the development of new services and content across multiple platforms is a costly enterprise and this, alongside cuts to the licence fee and pressure from successive governments, led the corporation to increase its commercial activities. These pressures of commercialisation and digitalisation make branding a particularly valuable industrial strategy for a number of reasons. First, branding offers a valuable commercial model for the development of television programmes. As McDowell and Batten argue, 'By depicting a program as a *product* and an audience member or advertiser as a *consumer*, most branding concepts can be adapted readily to broadcasting'.[6] As such, branding emerges as a useful tool within an increasingly commercialised broadcasting environment within which programmes are devised and exploited as products to be sold to audiences as consumers. Second, branding functions as a form of product differentiation. While all television programmes are differentiated by name, genre, design, and so on, the development of programmes as brands formalises and emphasises product differentiation. Importantly here, programmes are differentiated not just in aesthetic terms, but also, as we shall go on to see, through elements of 'packaging' and 'design' that can be legally protected by trademark law. As such, programme differentiation becomes not just a matter of distinguishing one series from another, but rather it becomes part of a larger production logic in which programmes function as forms of intellectual property whose difference can be legally protected. Third, through a focus on programmes and products that can be managed as intellectual property, the programme brand becomes a template for the extension of the programme into new products, such as spin-off texts and merchandise. Branding thus emerges as a way of managing a product range developed out of an initial programme. Within the digital era, when the BBC was under pressure to encourage the uptake of digital technologies and to increase its commercial revenue, developing programmes as branded products that could be exploited through trademark and copyright law across a wide range of extensions across multiple media emerged as an important industrial strategy.

Within this industrial context, programmes characterised by longevity, transferability and multiplicity become highly valuable[7]; three characteristics that are particularly applicable to *Doctor Who*. *Doctor Who* has a format that is designed to have story latitude. The ability for the Doctor to regenerate means that the series can withstand actors departing and accommodate significant twists in the narrative, allowing the writers to regularly kill off (and bring back) the central character. Such character latitude is mirrored in the companions who join and leave the Doctor at regular intervals, allowing character relationships to be refreshed and altered over the course of the series. Story latitude also comes in the narrative format, with the TARDIS allowing the characters to travel to infinite worlds across a vast past, present and future. Such story latitude enables the construction of a series that is big enough to justify overseas sales, distribution across multiple platforms and extension onto multiple media. Yet story latitude alone is not enough to generate a strong programme brand. In addition, a programme needs to offer opportunities to be extended onto multiple different forms of media. Such transferability facilitates the development of transmedia expansions and merchandise. From its start, and while perhaps not intentionally at first, *Doctor Who* has been created with iconic images that quickly became defining features of the series. One of the earliest examples of transferability that was exploited by the BBC was the Daleks. Although the corporation initially turned down an offer to sell licences for Dalek-related products,[8] by the mid-1960s the BBC had licensed a wide range of Dalek merchandise including toys, costumes, games, badges, chocolates and soap.[9] The Doctor himself also functions as an iconic character, with the costuming of each Doctor functioning to differentiate and distinguish the character in a manner that could be easily transferred into merchandise, such as posters and action figures.

While transferability is based in part on the creation of iconic images, it is also facilitated by what Sharon Ross has termed an 'aesthetics of multiplicity'[10] in which multiple points of view are inscribed within one series, often accompanied by incomplete or open-ended storylines. Jonathan Bignell describes the way in which the original series was developed to appeal to both children and adults, from the inclusion of teenage companion Susan alongside adults Barbara and Ian (and the Doctor himself) to the construction of narratives combining mystery and imagination with historical and scientific plausibility. In doing so the series 'offered pleasures to both child and adult audiences, and most significantly, each different component could have an appeal that overlapped between child and adult viewers and brought them together in shared experiences of engagement with the programme'.[11] Multiplicity refers, then, not only to audience appeal but also to the differentiated experiences and meanings offered by a programme. Bignell provides an excellent example of this in his discussion of the Daleks in mid-1960s *Doctor Who*. He argues that the Daleks can be understood as offering a point of identification for children, sharing childlike characteristics in their powerful drive to get what they want and their inability to adopt appropriate social codes, such as deference and empathy.[12] At the same time, as objects of fear they also functioned as sites through which children could 'test out their own maturity at coping with troubling emotions'.[13] These possible modes of engagement with the Daleks were extended through the merchandising of these characters, often integrating the characters into social play with siblings or in the playground. As Bignell argues:

> Playing with a toy Dalek extends the possible meanings of the creatures [...], either as representations of the child's own desires or as representations of those forces outside him or her with which the child has to negotiate.[14]

The aesthetics of multiplicity extends the appeal of a series to a range of audience segments (adults and children) but also provides multiple points of identification that can be experienced simultaneously (fear and the desire for power).

While, as Chapman argues, *Doctor Who* was regarded with some derision by programme and policy-makers at the corporation across the 1990s, within the BBC's commercial arm, BBC Worldwide, '*Doctor Who* was a profitable "franchise" that could guarantee steady income through sales of videos, DVDs, books and other licensed merchandising'.[15] Although the 1996 co-production failed to revitalise the series on television, BBC Worldwide continued to expand and exploit the *Doctor Who* franchise, for example, creating a series of audio dramas produced by Big Finish[16] and including a section devoted to the series on its online BBC Cult website that contained archive photographs, production facts and the BBC's first webcast drama serial.[17] Even before its revival in 2005, then, *Doctor Who* was a valuable commercial asset for BBC Worldwide. The worth of *Doctor Who* as a commercial asset lay not only in the original broadcast episodes, but in the series' potential as a franchise that could be extended and exploited across multiple forms, formats and media, frequently innovating with new media forms, such as the webcast drama series in 2003. As such, from 1989 the development of *Doctor Who* as a brand at the BBC can be understood to function within the context of a broader corporate strategy to exploit the series' longevity, transferability and multiplicity in order to increase the BBC's commercial activities and to extend its digital provision. It seems unsurprising, therefore, that the BBC should look towards developing *Doctor Who* as a programme brand in 2005.

However, these textual, political, technological and economic elements need to be understood alongside the activities of specific agents involved in the day-to-day production of cultural artefacts.[18] While it is tempting to think of corporations such as the BBC as operating as rational structures whose strategies and intentions can be easily read, in practice – particularly in such a large organisation as the BBC – the processes involved in the production of a series such as *Doctor Who* are far more messy, complex and potentially contradictory, as decisions are often made on an *ad-hoc* basis in response to issues as they arise, with policy or strategy frequently following on from practice, rather than *vice versa*.[19] As Ian Grutchfield (former Commercial Strategy Manager and Brand Manager, *Doctor Who*, BBC Cymru Wales) claimed in response to a question about where the idea of *Doctor Who* as a brand originated from, and the relationship between the BBC's public service and commercial interests regarding the series:

> Your question is really meaty. It perhaps imagines a clearer planning and thinking process than exists in many creative organisations – it is the creative leaders who drive so much of the entertainment industry, how

they act and motivate is often a lot more important than formal guidelines or systems.[20]

For Ian Grutchfield, the origins of *Doctor Who* as a brand can be traced to the rise of digital and the commercialisation of the BBC, but they also lie in the hands of certain creative agents:

> Within the BBC (public service) there wasn't a strategic decision to manage key brands – it came about more through circumstances and individual people's ideas. For *Doctor Who* it was a commercial director who suggested the scale of *Doctor Who* was becoming so large – from rights and clearances to the needs of co-production and distribution – that it would benefit from having an organised function. In contrast at BBC Worldwide, there was a decision to anoint and appoint certain major properties as global brands, as part of a strategy of driving exploitation and revenue growth.[21]

When asked why the BBC developed certain programmes as brands, Grutchfield explained:

> For [BBC] Worldwide – to make lots of money. For the BBC – because it is what key talent wants. For *Doctor Who*, the concept of managing all activities, whether public service or commercial came from the Showrunner model of management deployed by the two visionaries at its helm – i.e. Russell T Davies writer and executive producer and Julie Gardner, head of drama Wales and executive producer. Russell knew the sort of series he wanted – what he would change and what he would revive of the *Doctor Who* format, Julie Gardner then executed his wishes. Both of them did it with enormous enthusiasm and gusto and creative ideas. They also had big supporters in senior controllers in Wales and in drama – but there wasn't a BBC overall vision to create a massive brand, nor to suddenly resource it. Along the way resources for campaign materials, extra budgets, etc all had to be secured.[22]

For Grutchfield, then, the development of *Doctor Who* as a brand stems from a range of different factors. On the one hand, it was a consequence of the vision of Russell T Davies and Julie Gardner and their attempts to maintain control over the series. Grutchfield's rhetoric in emphasising Davies and Gardner as the creative visionaries behind *Doctor Who* could be seen as part of a broader brand discourse in itself, whereby brand values imbue the very way that employees talk about their work.[23] The positioning of Davies and Gardner in such an authorial position chimes with Matt Hills's argument that the revised *Doctor Who* can be understood as a 'fanbrand'. Hills argues that the emphasis placed on the construction of a cohesive fictional world in the new *Doctor Who* stemmed in part from the movement into official production of fans such as Davies, who brought with them a desire to correct the criticisms of unevenness common to fan engagement with the original series by maintaining control over the series' extensive fictional world.[24] While Davies and Gardner may have managed to command significant control over *Doctor Who* as a transmedia series (supported by senior staff at the BBC), helping to construct a coherent brand vision for the series, the positioning of Davies in particular as 'author' of the series equally contributes to the construction of a specific brand identity for the series as a quality text created by a 'visionary' that could appeal to the fan and non-fan audience.

On the other hand, Grutchfield recognises that Davies and Gardner's work on the series took place within a larger institutional context in which the adoption of branding is seen to be driven by the commercial and practical imperatives of a large transmedia franchise. Here, branding has both an organisational and a commercial role to play. Branding is positioned as a commercial strategy (particularly in relation to the BBC's commercial arm, BBC Worldwide) to manage exploitation of the series so as 'to make lots of money'. However, it is also positioned as an organising 'function' that helps to coordinate the increasingly extensive co-production and distribution deals involved in a series that spreads across platforms and media and is licensed and sold in multiple territories. While it may be tempting to see the adoption of branding as indicative of a broader commercialisation of the BBC and its core programming activities, the picture is more complex than that. As we shall go on to see, branding is used by the BBC to manage both its public service and commercial ambitions around the series. Indeed, I shall go on to argue that understanding *Doctor Who* as a brand makes it increasingly difficult to untangle its commercial and public service values.[25]

One example of the intertwining of commercial and public service values in the development of new *Who* as a brand is the redesign of the series' logo in 2009. The original series of *Doctor Who* had a distinctive and innovative title sequence created by Bernard Lodge by filming and manipulating the 'howlaround' feedback created when pointing a television camera at its own monitor, creating a 'vortex' affect that ended with the programme title. Over the years it became common for new seasons of the series (particularly those with new incarnations of the Doctor) to innovate with new title sequences based around the 'vortex' and create different versions of the series' title.[26] These title logos would often feature on merchandise related to that particular season of the show. In 2009, when the BBC were working on the first season of *Doctor Who* to feature Matt Smith in the title role, they partnered with communications agency Red Bee Media to create a new 'identity' for the series. While in some ways similar to the title redesigns of earlier seasons, the production logic behind this redesign was specifically focused on creating an iconic image that could function both as a central aspect of the title sequence and as a trade-marked sign that could be utilised across a wide range of *Doctor Who* products. Trade marks are the primary legal mechanism through which brands are protected in law. The UK's Intellectual Property Office (the official government body responsible for granting intellectual property rights in the UK) defines a trade mark as 'a sign which can distinguish your goods and services from those of your competitors (you may refer to your trade mark as your "brand"). It can be for example words, logos or a combination of both'.[27] The main function of trade marks is to distinguish goods and services from competitors within the same market and to protect trade-mark owners from competitors. However, the trade in property rights (including copyright as well as trade marks) has become an increasingly central aspect of cultural production. As Celia Lury argues, trade-mark law 'makes it possible for mark owners to exploit new forms of production and exchange'.[28] Product differentiation has long since been a key element of television production, with programmes being distinguished through title sequences and theme tunes that are distinctive for each programme, as well as through specific genre combinations or the use of different creative personnel (stars, writers, directors and so on). However, since the 1990s producers have increasingly developed programmes as intellectual property that can be sold. While the most obvious indication of this might be the rise in format sales (particularly in reality television and game shows),[29] the creation of programme titles as logos is part of the same production logic, producing graphic signs that can be trade marked and then licensed across a range of ancillary merchandise. As such, the development of a new *Doctor Who* logo in 2009 can be seen as part of a broader commercial logic in television design that emerged over the 1990s.

However, the logo was designed with more than just commercial goals in mind. The new logo was based on the letters DW moulded into the iconic shape of the TARDIS with a flashing light above. The design was created to be simple enough that it could be easily reproduced by children doodling on their pencil cases at school, while also carrying strong associations with the series' existing iconic images, such as the TARDIS. As Charlie Mawer (Executive Creative Director, Red Bee Media) describes:

> We felt that *Doctor Who* deserved a logo as iconic as Superman or Batman that could be drawn onto a school pencil case. [...] The logo had to act as a simple branding device across a myriad of products and merchandise as well as acting as a strong mark on the title sequence and trailers themselves.[30]

Mawer's comments point to two aspects of contemporary programme branding. First, the new design of the title sequence was informed by the need to create a logo that could function as a trade-marked branding device across a range of products. At the same time, however, Mawer also hints at another aspect of branding when he refers to creating a design that could be easily appropriated by children. Here the aim of the redesign is to create a logo that is simple, memorable and that allows children to copy and borrow it. In this sense, the intention behind the redesign is in part to encourage participation by the programme's core child audience, and to encourage the forms of participatory culture more commonly (and historically) assigned to fan practice.[31] Indeed, for series 7 in the autumn of 2012, the BBC created different versions of the logo for each episode that incorporated some element of the story: for the Western-inspired episode 'A Town Called Mercy', the background of the logo was changed from silver to a bullet-ridden saloon door, and for 'The Power of Three' the background was composed of the small black boxes that invaded Earth. Mawer's comments remind us that while branding is in part about developing and managing programmes as products that can be commercially differentiated through design and packaging and exploited across multiple media, it is equally concerned with establishing a (sometimes playful) relationship between the branded product and the consumer/audience. Branding aims not only to distinguish a product in a marketplace, but to act as a guarantee of the quality and qualities of that product. As the Intellectual Property Office claims:

> Brands are [...] reputational assets based on powerfully held beliefs; they drive the understanding of value in a product or company, and, perhaps most importantly, customer loyalty.[32]

Red Bee's redesign of the *Doctor Who* logo aimed not only to create a symbol that identified and distinguished the new 'Matt Smith era' for the programme, but also to enhance audience engagement with the series by developing an identity that could be simply replicated, played with and thus integrated into the everyday lives of the series' core (child) audience. Strikingly, when *Doctor Who*'s title sequence was refreshed ahead of the 2013 anniversary year – with a design paying homage to earlier 'howlaround' and 'star-field' effects from across the show's history – the DW TARDIS logo was dropped, seeking to integrate audiences as participatory in commemorating the programme's past rather than, on this occasion, playing with a replicable logo.

The interrelationship between commercial and public service can also be seen in the brand extensions produced around the new series of *Doctor Who*. In June 2009, the BBC launched four PC and Mac games based on the series that could be downloaded in the UK free of charge. The *Doctor Who: Adventure Games* were commissioned by BBC Vision Multiplatform and driven by BBC Wales.[33] The ambition behind the games was to produce 'interactive episodes' that allowed the audience a different form of engagement with the narrative of the show. Importantly, the narrative of the games was intertwined with the narrative of the series. As Piers Wenger (then Head of Drama, BBC Wales and Executive Producer, *Doctor Who*) explained, 'There aren't 13 episodes of *Doctor Who* this year. There are 17 – four of which are interactive. We'll be taking you to places you've only ever dreamed about seeing – including locations impossible to create on television.'[34] The integration of the games with the television series was further ensured through the sharing of key creative talent. Not only did Karen Gillan and Matt Smith voice the characters of Amy Pond and the Doctor in the games, the games were produced by the same team responsible for the television series (Steven Moffat, Piers Wenger and Beth Willis) along with Anwen Aspden from BBC Interactive, video game creator Charles Cecil and independent game developer Sumo Digital, with scripts from writers on *Doctor Who* (Phil Ford and James Moran). The coming together of talent from gaming and television to produce online games that function as part of a broader television narrative represented a new and potentially risky production decision by the BBC. Victoria Jaye (then BBC

Head of Fiction and Entertainment Multiplatform Commissioning) described the process as 'creative alchemy like nothing before, bringing writing talent and games talent together to write narrative, and the learning that has come from that, we've been doing a lot of workshops about what we've found out through that process'.[35] Such creative innovation directly supports the BBC's public purpose to 'stimulate creativity and cultural excellence'. As Simon Nelson (former Controller, Multiplatform and Portfolio Services, BBC Television) claimed of *The Adventure Games*: 'We're hugely proud of *Doctor Who: The Adventure Games*, which will establish new standards in interactive drama and allow families the country over to enjoy *Doctor Who* stories in unique and innovative ways.'[36]

As well as supporting the BBC's public purpose to stimulate new forms of creativity, *The Adventure Games* also addressed its public purpose to 'deliver the benefit of emerging communications technology'. One aim of integrating the games into the narrative of the television series was to encourage a broad audience to try online gaming for the first time. As Jaye argued, 'They really are aimed at taking a big broad audience, three generations of *Who* fans, onto the internet platform and they are aimed at entry level PCs, as well as being compelling enough (we hope) for a loved games player to enjoy in their own right'.[37] Indeed, Simon Nelson goes so far as to argue that the games might enhance computer literacy:

> By aiming these 'interactive episodes' at the broad audience of TV show – unique in British television, in that it encompasses at least three generations – we're aiming to encourage the family to gather round the PC or Mac in the same way they do the television. Driving computer literacy is a keystone of the BBC's public service remit and we expect *Doctor Who: The Adventure Games* to be hugely popular in the homes of Britain this year.[38]

For audiences, the games offered a new way of engaging with the television series, giving them the opportunity to take on the role of the Doctor and his companion Amy, as well as allowing them to interact with the fictional world of *Doctor Who* by, for example, exploring the TARDIS or fighting the Daleks.

Although *The Adventure Games* supported the BBC's public service aims, they also functioned to demonstrate the commercial potential of *Doctor Who*-related computer games. In December 2011 the BBC announced the launch of two new commercial *Doctor Who* games that had been co-developed between BBC Worldwide and commercial games companies, each targeted at a different market. *Doctor Who: The Eternity Clock* was aimed at existing gamers through PlayStation 3 and the new PlayStation Vita handheld and PC platforms. Unlike the previous console games created out of the *Doctor Who* franchise for Nintendo (*Evacuation Earth* on DS and *Return to Earth* on Wii), BBC Worldwide did not just issue a license for the development of *The Eternity Clock*, they co-produced the game, working closely with Supermassive Games as well as drawing on key talent from the series, such as Matt Smith, Alex Kingston (River Song) and Murray Gold (composer). *Doctor Who: Worlds in Time* was also a co-production, this time between BBC Worldwide and Three Rings. This multiplayer online game targeted a broader audience with 'an intriguing narrative for sci-fi followers and serious gamers and stimulating missions for game enthusiasts looking for a quick pick-up-and-play game'.[39] While *Worlds in Time* is free to play, gamers can purchase 'Chronons' to enrich gameplay and enhance their progress through the game. Ian Grutchfield argues that *The Adventure Games* facilitated the development of these commercial games:

> In a way BBC have taken the biggest risk and shown an audience appetite, so now commercial partners can come in and publish. For a long time games companies delivered licences in *Doctor Who* as it is not a major property akin to a multi-territory movie franchise. It is small scale/niche outside of the UK. *The Adventure Games* have shown that the dedicated fan market is passionate and large enough for commercial publishers to take some risks.[40]

These examples demonstrate the complex interrelationship between the commercial and public service aims of the corporation. The development of *The Adventure Games* served the corporation's public service values, particularly its public purposes to stimulate creativity and deliver the benefits of new communications technologies. At the same time, however, they also demonstrated the potential commercial market for *Doctor Who* games and the benefits to both game producers and the BBC of co-producing, rather than licensing, computer games based on the series.

The involvement of the BBC in the creation of the recent *Doctor Who* computer games points to a key difference between the BBC's earlier treatment of *Doctor Who*'s intellectual property and its treatment of *Doctor Who* as a brand in the digital era. Classic pre-digital examples are the *Doctor Who* spin-off films in the 1960s, where the nature of the Doctor as a character was changed from alien to human. This is indicative of the relative lack of coordination in the licensing of the series and the exertion of less control over *Doctor Who* as a franchise in the 1960s and 1970s. This stemmed from the broader institutional context within which such extensions were managed. At this time, the licensing of spin-off films, books and merchandise were not core to the BBC's activities, but peripheral, and often responsive rather than strategic.[41] By contrast, in the 2000s the extension of television programmes onto other media has become a more central strategy for the BBC (as argued above), leading to a greater emphasis on the need to manage and coordinate such activities. As the job description for the BBC role of 'Commercial Strategy Manager' states:

> Leading Intellectual Properties have a complex range of rights and marketing issues and are 'project managed' to maximise added value for the audience and generate revenue to supplement the licence fee. At the same time as maximising new opportunities to make the biggest impact, brands need to be developed in an organised manner true to the BBC's values, approval and integrity.[42]

Here it is apparent that the management of programmes such as *Doctor Who* as intellectual property is not just driven by commercial desires to generate increased revenue from one product/programme, but is also seen as part of a broader strategy of maximising the value of BBC programming for audiences. Similarly, the need to manage brands is not just driven by commercial imperatives, but also by the need to ensure that the range of programme extensions does not undermine the BBC's 'values' and 'integrity'.

From the BBC's point of view, then, the *Doctor Who* brand needs to be managed not only to enhance revenue and audience engagement with the series, but also because the programme and its range of extensions have the potential to have an impact on the 'reputational asset' of the BBC's corporate brand. Indeed, the increased repurposing of content in the digital era makes the range of extensions associated with *Doctor Who* more visible. At any one time, episodes from different seasons of *Doctor Who* might be broadcast in the same week, while viewers can now own the series on DVD or Blu-ray and purchase episodes on demand through iTunes. In addition, online audiences can search for *Doctor Who* merchandise and spin-off series, play *Doctor Who* games, listen to audio stories transmitted last week alongside ones produced years ago, and view clips and behind-the-scenes footage. Increasing media convergence brings together the wide range of different extensions of *Doctor Who*, making any inconsistencies across different texts and products more apparent and evident, but also making the corporation's own expansion and exploitation of the series more visible to the public. This increased visibility comes at the same time that the corporation's activities have come under increasing scrutiny. While successive governments have encouraged the BBC to increase its commercial revenue in order to keep the cost of the licence fee down and provide additional revenue to expand into digital services, at the same time there has been public debate about the potential negative consequences of the corporation's increased commercial activities. Hills gives the example of the BBC's response to a *Doctor Who* fan who was selling knitted Adipose figures on eBay, which became headline news in 2008.[43] The BBC intervened against what it saw as unlicensed exploitation of its brand property (*Doctor Who*), arguing that it needed to police such fan activity in order to protect the brand.

There are two elements to brand protection here. On the one hand, the brand needs to be protected in order to ensure that it retains the distinctiveness necessary to be recognised as a trade mark. On the other hand, the brand needs to be protected in order to ensure that the qualities and values expected from the BBC are retained across all products associated with *Doctor Who*. Yet there are potential contradictions for the BBC here. Brand management at the BBC aims in part to ensure that there is brand congruence, not only across the branded programme (*Doctor Who*) but also with the broader values of the BBC. Such a strategy functions in part to ensure that the commercial exploitation of the series is not at the expense of the corporation's public service values. At the same time, attempting to manage a programme such as *Doctor Who* as a piece of intellectual property can lead to practices that could be seen to undermine the creativity of the series itself – for example, Hills argues that changes to the design of iconic features of the series are driven by the need to generate new merchandise[44] – or the creativity of its fans (such as the BBC attempting to prevent fans from sharing user-generated material based on the series).

At the start of this chapter I asked why *Doctor Who* was identified by the BBC as a key brand, and what it means to understand and examine *Doctor Who* as a brand rather than a television series. I have argued that the development of *Doctor Who* as a brand since the 1990s cannot be attributed to a single factor. The commercialisation of the BBC and the rise of digital services across the television sector created a broader context within which branding offered a useful commercial model for programme development, emphasising the creation of programmes as intellectual properties that could be exploited commercially. While the development of *Doctor Who* as a brand can be understood as an attempt to increase the commercial revenue generated by the series, it was also a response to digitalisation and the desire to produce programmes that could be used to innovate with emerging media (such as the internet, gaming and mobile devices). Within this context, *Doctor Who* was an existing property that had the key characteristics of longevity, transferability and multiplicity to be able to function as a media brand and so generate extensions across a wide range of media. While branding offered an important organisational function used by the BBC to manage and coordinate the increasing range of activities around *Doctor Who*, the development of *Who* as a brand was also shaped by key strategic players at the BBC, such as the commercial director and the re-imagined series' executive producer team (Russell T Davies and Julie Gardner).

While it may be tempting to see the adoption of branding as indicative of a broader commercialisation of the BBC and its core programming activities, I have argued that branding has been used by the BBC to manage both its public service and commercial ambitions for *Doctor Who*. For example, brand expansions such as *The Adventure Games* became a valuable means for the BBC to engage with its audiences in new ways, and fulfil its public service purposes to stimulate new forms of creativity and deliver the benefit of emerging communications technology. At the same time, they demonstrated the potential market for such games, leading to the development of new commercial initiatives by BBC Worldwide. Indeed, central to the BBC's adoption of branding around the series is the attempt to ensure a coordinated approach to the series across all of its activities, both commercial and public service. The rationale for such brand management lies less in the corporation's desire to generate increased commercial revenue from the series and more in the perceived need to control the potential impact of the series (and all of the public service and commercial activity surrounding it) on the reputational asset of the BBC as a corporation. Yet, paradoxically, the attempt to control the series could be seen as undermining the creativity of the series and its audience, both important aspects of the BBC's public service remit. Understanding *Doctor Who* as a brand, therefore, involves exploring and unpacking the tensions and contradictions inherent in the BBC's attempts to manage and reconcile its increasing commercial activity with its core public service remit and identity.

NOTES

1. See http://www.bbcworldwide.com/, accessed 14 October 2012.
2. See Chapman, James, *Inside the TARDIS: The Worlds of Doctor Who* (I.B.Tauris, London and New York, 2006), p. 186, and Hills, Matt, *Triumph of a Time Lord: Regenerating Doctor Who in the Twenty-First Century* (I.B.Tauris, London and New York, 2010), pp. 66–79.
3. BBC, *Annual Report and Accounts 1987–88* (BBC, London, 1988), p. 5.
4. See Johnson, Catherine, *Branding Television* (Routledge, London and New York, 2012).
5. See Steemers, Jeanette, 'Between culture and commerce: the problem of redefining public service broadcasting for the digital age', *Convergence: The International Journal of Research into New Media Technologies* v/3 (1999), pp. 44–66.
6. McDowell, Walter and Batten, Alan, *Branding TV: Principles and Practices* (Focal Press, Burlington and Oxford, 2005), p. 23.
7. Johnson: *Branding Television*.
8. Bignell, Jonathan, 'The child as addressee, viewer and consumer in mid-1960s *Doctor Who*' in D. Butler (ed.), *Time and Relative Dissertations in Space: Critical Perspectives on Doctor Who* (Manchester University Press, Manchester and New York, 2007), p. 52.
9. See http://www.dalek-mania.co.uk/INDEX2.htm, accessed 1 June 2013.
10. Ross, Sharon Marie, *Beyond the Box: Television and the Internet* (Blackwell, Malden and Oxford, 2008), pp. 20–6.
11. Bignell: 'The child as addressee', p. 45.
12. Ibid., p. 49.
13. Ibid., p. 51.
14. Ibid., p. 52.
15. Chapman: *Inside the TARDIS*, p. 186.
16. Hills, Matt, 'Televisuality without television? The Big Finish audios and discourses of "tele-centric" Doctor Who' in D. Butler (ed.), *Time and Relative Dissertations in Space: Critical Perspectives on Doctor Who* (Manchester University Press, Manchester and New York, 2007), pp. 280–95.

17 Perryman, Neil, 'Doctor Who and the convergence of media: A case study in transmedia storytelling', *Convergence: The International Journal of Research into New Media Technologies* xiv/1 (2008), p. 25.
18 This position reiterates de Leeuw's arguments on the importance of the development of a history of television 'which reinstates the role of the individual actor, yet places it into the integrative discourses about television's historical development' concerned with institutions, production, aesthetics, technology and so on. See de Leeuw, Sonja, 'Transnationality in Dutch (Pre) Television: The central role of Erik de Vries' in A. Fickers and C. Johnson (eds), *Transational Television History: A Comparative Approach* (Routledge, London and New York, 2012), p. 50.
19 Jem Stone's (Head of Social Media for Audio and Music at the BBC) 2011 blog about the development of social media at the BBC is an excellent example of this, demonstrating the uneven and often *ad-hoc* development of new initiatives, with formal guidelines often following practice by a number of years. See http://jemstone.wordpress.com/2011/07/13/a-quick-history-of-the-bbc-and-social-media/, accessed 1 June 2013.
20 Interview with the author, 16 January 2012.
21 Interview with the author, 8 November 2010.
22 Ibid.
23 Johnson: *Branding Television*, pp. 20–1.
24 Hills: *Triumph of a Time Lord*.
25 For more on this increasing entanglement of commercial and public service values, see Chapter 11's discussion of *Who*'s 50th anniversary celebrations as a 'hyped, brand anniversary' quite unlike *Doctor Who*'s previous commemorations.
26 See http://www2.tv-ark.org.uk/cult/cult-whomain.html, accessed 1 June 2013.
27 Anon, 'What is a trade mark (or brand)?', *Intellectual Property Office Website* (2011), available at: http://www.ipo.gov.uk/types/tm/t-about/t-whatis.htm, accessed 1 June 2013.
28 Lury, Celia, *Brands: The Logos of the Global Economy* (Routledge, London, 2004), p. 123.
29 See, for example, Moran, Albert (ed.), *TV Formats Worldwide: Localising Global Programs* (Intellect Books, Bristol, 2010).
30 Interview with the author, 5 April 2012.
31 Jenkins, Henry, *Textual Poachers: Television Fans and Participatory Culture* (Routledge, New York and London, 1992).
32 Anon. 'What is a brand?' *Intellectual Property Office Website*, available at: http://www.ipo.gov.uk/types/tm/t-about/t-whatis/t-brands.htm, accessed 1 June 2013.
33 And for more on *The Adventure Games*, see Elizabeth Evans's Chapter 7.
34 Wenger cited in BBC, '*Doctor Who: The Adventure Games*', *Doctor Who Website* (7 April 2010), available online at http://www.bbc.co.uk/doctorwho/dw/news/bulletin_100408_01, accessed 1 June 2013.
35 Interview with the author, 1 June 2010.
36 Cited in BBC: *Doctor Who: The Adventure Games*.
37 Interview with author, 1 June 2010.

38 Cited in BBC: *Doctor Who: The Adventure Games*.
39 BBC, 'BBC Worldwide transports *Doctor Who: Worlds in Time* into commercial launch', *BBC Media Centre* (13 March 2012), available at: http://www.bbc.co.uk/mediacentre/worldwide/130312worldsintime.html, accessed 1 June 2013.
40 Interview with the author, 16 January 2012.
41 For a discussion of the BBC's commercial exploitation in the 1940s and 1950s, see Johnson, Catherine, 'Trading Auntie: the exploitation and protection of intellectual property rights during the BBC's monopoly years', *New Review of Film and Television Studies* vii/4 (2009), pp. 441–58.
42 BBC, 'Commercial Manager Job Specification', 16 October 2005, BBC.
43 Hills: *Triumph of a Time Lord*, pp. 68–9.
44 Ibid., p. 68.

6

ON SPEED
The Ordering of Time and Pace of Action in *Doctor Who*

Andrew O'Day

From its origins in 1963, *Doctor Who* has been a programme about travelling through time and space. By taking narratives from the Russell T Davies and Steven Moffat eras of the BBC Wales series, and contrasting them with the 'classic' series, however, we can see that new *Doctor Who* is characterised by a particularly fast narrative pace. This is especially so in series openers, potentially introducing new audience members to the programme's format for the first time. In investigating pace, we shall see how the Davies and Moffat eras contain a variety of intratextual allusions. However, rather than being a postmodern 'pasting together' of elements of the old series in a type of pastiche – what Fredric Jameson would call 'the complacent play of historical allusion'[1] – at the level of pace something novel is created. I further investigate narratives that directly concern the notion of 'speed' in order to address the pacing and the contexts of contemporary television production. Finally, in contrast to this speeding-up of episodic narratives, the slower, drawn-out nature of the 'story-arc' is also considered.

This chapter, then, will evidently engage in an aesthetic reading of new *Doctor Who*. In his book *TARDISbound: Navigating the Universes of Doctor Who*, Piers Britton begins his chapter on the aesthetics of the programme by asking 'Is *Doctor Who* any good? Is it valuable, aesthetically speaking? Is it art?'[2] He goes on to say that 'To some readers the very idea of characterizing *Doctor Who* as art may seem faintly absurd,' and that 'science-fiction fantasy' is 'a genre which, like the television medium itself, has not historically been much associated with the highbrow or elevated'.[3] 'Academics,' Britton states, 'remain cautious in identifying television fiction [...] as art'.[4] Britton points out that:

> In the recent upsurge of texts on television aesthetics, relatively few scholars focus as unabashedly as Sarah Cardwell on the formal and stylistic merits of a text, which she forthrightly describes as 'artistic achievements'. Most, following the critical norms of cultural studies, at least indirectly take political implications into account.[5]

The purpose of this chapter, however, is not to ask 'Is *Doctor Who* art?' – or even 'Is *Doctor Who* any good? – but rather to argue that the fast-paced aesthetics of the new series may appeal to an audience steeped in postmodern media culture, as well as resonating with current television practices more generally. To do this I shall, for example, compare new *Doctor Who* to the rebooted *Dallas* (not a comparison that has frequently been made by scholars, it has to be said, particularly when telefantasy or cult TV tend to frame engagements with *Who*). By linking TV aesthetics with cross-generic contexts I'm pursuing a television studies that's less interested in legitimating specific programmes (for example *Doctor Who*), and more interested in producing a 'take on the changes of television's present'.[6]

Pace, Speed and Programme Format

Graham Sleight has written about the characteristics of the Russell T Davies era of *Doctor Who*. Sleight identifies the key hallmarks of the era as an emphasis on emotion rather than science fiction; attempts (however unsuccessful) at conveying a grand scale; and, significantly, a faster pace. Sleight writes:

> The speed at which the new series is told is, perhaps, the most predictable change from the classic series [...]. Quite apart from the production values, the old series is simply slower. Exposition, in particular, is almost entirely verbal [...] Davies' remarks on the DVD and podcast commentaries for many of the episodes make it clear that [faster pace...] is a primary goal for him[7]

But there is room for a far more detailed discussion of the ways in which the series exhibits this faster pace. In fact, there are a number of ways in which Russell T Davies's incarnation of *Doctor Who* is fast-paced in its form and in the establishment of format. These can be summed up in five key narrative characteristics:

(i) the span of episodic narratives;
(ii) fast-paced editing and camera work;
(iii) a rapid 'cut to peril';
(iv) narratives beginning *in medias res* in the midst of action; and
(v) the use of technology as a narrative tool.

First, like most American science fiction programmes, *the majority of narratives in the new series are now told in the span of a single episode approximately 45 minutes long*, except for multi-episode narratives and slightly longer episodes such as Christmas specials. This contrasts with the classic show, which was mostly composed of lengthy episodic serials. These typically consisted of 25-minute weekly instalments, lasting for anything from two to 14 weeks. As Trisha Dunleavy has noted, albeit without considering the narrative compression resulting from new *Who*'s adoption of series norms:

> Even though drama's 'series' and 'serial' forms involve quite different narrative structures, these differences making it very unusual for any one programme to oscillate between them, *Doctor Who* has offered a particularly successful demonstration of the potential for some TV dramas to move from one to the other.[8]

Second, Davies's *Who* is also characterized by speed because *editing and camerawork give the feel of a fast pace*. Robin Nelson notes that 'pacey cutting of dynamic images and a strong soundtrack typify the modern drama series,' adding that in today's TV industry climate 'it is perceived to be necessary at the start of any drama to capture the audience [...where] an exceptionally fast-cut sequence precedes the unfolding of the action proper of the episode'.[9] Nelson points to a couple of ways in which this is achieved, using the examples of editing together excerpts of the programme to come and having a title sequence made up of fast-cut action as in *Casualty*.[10] *Doctor Who* does neither of these, though its reimagined 2005 title sequence represented a rushing, whirling time vortex with the TARDIS hanging still in space just for a brief moment, as if to then emphasise the speed with which it hurtled away down the vortex.

It is common, however, for episodes to begin with a quickly paced sequence. After the first intratextual borrowing of an element from the classic series – a shot of space echoing 'Spearhead from Space' (1970)[11] – and a bravura special effects zoom-in to Earth, 'Rose' (2005), for example, springs to life with the sound of an alarm clock and features an opening montage of an ordinary day in Rose Tyler's life including fast-motion images and accompanied by lively music. As Rebecca Levene puts it, this 'economically tell[s] us far more [about Rose and those around her] than any dialogue could have managed in the same amount of time'. Levene argues that, this sequence aside, 'the editing was at times a little too MTV frenetic'.[12] Furthermore, James Chapman has demonstrated that the camera work in 'Rose' dynamically eschews conventional two-character shot/reverse shot dialogue sequences in favour of long tracking shots.[13]

Third, in new *Who* there is *a prompt cut to peril*. As executive producer Julie Gardner explains, 'I remember watching six-part stories and four-part stories and thinking, "you could never do that now." You have to cut to the jeopardy much faster.'[14] Gardner's comment indicates the importance of changing industrial and production contexts – highlighting the transformative relationship between 'new' and 'classic' series – yet we can explore pace further by comparing individual instances from Davies's *Who* with end-of-episode cliff-hanger moments from the classic series. 'Spearhead from Space' (1970), which similarly involves an attack on Earth by the Nestene Consciousness using 'plastic dummies', takes time to first introduce us to the new format of the third Doctor exiled to Earth. By contrast, in under two-and-a-half minutes into 'Rose' we are presented with a staple scene of the horror genre.[15] Rose descends in a lift to the basement (typically a place of secluded horror), calls out for someone, gets no reassuring response, and moves into a dimly-lit space with the door closing behind her. The viewer sees the menace (here the 'plastic dummies') before Rose does, and witnesses them moving towards her, accompanied by haunting music. While there were suspended enigmas within episodes of the original *Doctor Who* series – where Roland Barthes's (2000) notion of 'the hermeneutic code' was in play[16] – this scene of Rose in peril could almost have been a cliff-hanger in classic *Doctor Who*. For instance, the shot of 'plastic dummies' raising their arms to strike Rose visually echoes that of the Cybermen raising their arms to strike Peri at the end of part one of 'Attack of the Cybermen' (1985).

Yet in 'Rose' the situation is not deferred by a week: it is immediately resolved by the first emergence of the Doctor under five-and-a-half minutes into the episode, shouting at Rose to 'Run!'. Director Keith Boak explains that Davies 'was very keen [...] that this should be a really fast-paced show' and that 'the Doctor is a fast-paced man [...] an action man, a man of "doing" [whose] life runs at a pace of knots'.[17] The way in which scenes resemble old-school episode endings can be seen elsewhere, such as in 'Dalek' (2005). Approaching eight minutes into the episode, the Dalek's threat to exterminate the Doctor while he's locked in a room with it lead him to bang desperately on the door for help. This has echoes of 'Remembrance of the Daleks' (1988), where at the end of part one there is a Dalek point-of-view shot, and then a close-up of the Dalek exterminator stick followed by one of the Doctor's fearful expression. However, the Dalek's cries in 'Dalek' can generate little suspense without the deferral of an episode ending. In short, new *Doctor Who*'s narratives seemingly lack gaps and punctuation, instead moving swiftly from problem to resolution. Rapid cuts to peril are partnered with equally pacey leaps to safety.

Fourth, in the Davies era *some narratives begin* in medias res *('in the midst of things')* with the Doctor already embroiled in the action. Two of the principal notions in narrative theory are that all narrative takes place over time and that all narratives are constructed and arranged in particular ways to have certain effects.[18] All fictional narratives create worlds, something that is especially true of television science fiction, and the rules of these narrative worlds must be explicated to viewers. TV narratives beginning *in medias res* are commonly starting-points that see a change to the established programme format. But such structure is also detectable in episodes like 'Rose' and 'Bad Wolf' (2005).[19] In 'Rose', as Scott Allan Woodard states, 'we [...] blunder into the Doctor's world in the midst of one of his adventures,' while Robert Franks notes that 'it feels like we've been dropped in mid-way through Episode 3 of a classic series story. Everything moves so quickly that hopefully the audience won't notice that the other two and a half episodes are missing'.[20] The difference in pace between 'classic' and 'new' *Doctor Who* is well illustrated by the viewing experiences of older fans. This group is aware of the intratextual, postmodern referencing of elements from the classic series together with something distinctly new in the delivery of each episode's narrative speed.

Compare, for example, the very different opening episodes of 1963 and 2005. In the original opening episode 'An Unearthly Child' (1963), we are gradually introduced to the narrative rules of the *Doctor Who* universe. These rules must be explained, while at the same time the Doctor's companions are introduced, thus giving viewers characters to identity with. That these characters are ordinary and have no knowledge of the rules of the fictional world is important, since we share their position of ignorance, requiring the narrative to explicate things. But 'An Unearthly Child' is in many respects a stand-alone episode – for which a separate pilot was made – where the set-up occurs *before* rather than during the main adventure. As John Tulloch and Manuel Alvarado note, there is an emphasis on mystery as two schoolteachers follow pupil Susan Foreman 'home' and the narrative of discovery is largely one of talk.[21] Time is taken to introduce us to Susan's grandfather, the alien yet humanoid Doctor and his spacecraft. The TARDIS materialises at the scene of the subsequent adventure – on a rocky landscape – only at the very end of episode one. Since *Doctor Who* was a set of serials, with each new serial made possible by the transporting device of the TARDIS, this ending marks the programme's move into the terrain of the serial following its first episode.

In 'Rose', however, the TARDIS is already stationed at the scene of the adventure, and is called to our attention as Rose runs outside the department store where she works. This narrative sequencing differs greatly from 'An Unearthly Child', and indeed from 'Spearhead from Space', as the emphasis is placed squarely on action. 'Rose' is perhaps slightly more reminiscent of 'Remembrance of the Daleks', which also begins *in medias res* (an experiment attempted earlier in 1978's 'The Invasion of Time') with the TARDIS already stationed at the scene of the adventure, and with the Doctor epistemologically ahead of both companion (Ace) and viewer. This was part of then script-editor Andrew Cartmel's narrative strategy to create a darker and more manipulative Doctor. Unlike 'Remembrance of the Daleks', however, in 'Rose' the titular companion learns about the TARDIS while under attack by the 'plastic dummy' version of her boyfriend Mickey. Furthermore, after stepping inside the vast Police Box, Rose returns outside and races around the small outer shell in disbelief, intratextually echoing the scene of Chang Lee doing the same in the TV movie (1996). What is most important, though, is that all of the setting-up of *Doctor Who*'s narrative world occurs *during* the main adventure here; it is only at the end of the episode that Rose races into the TARDIS to join the Doctor on his travels. The notion of *in medias res* is akin to a form of editing. To say that a narrative begins *in medias res* assumes that prior events have been edited out when the narrative commences, and as such new *Who* is marked by an emphasis on immersive duration – being caught up in the whirl of an adventure's events – rather than gradual exposition and scene-setting.

This faster narrative pace is also apparent in the introductions of Donna Noble and Martha Jones. At the end of 'Doomsday' (2006), Rose is separated from the Doctor, who is then faced with Donna's materialisation on board the TARDIS in her bridal dress. Russell T Davies has said that:

> ... right from the start of Series Two, we knew that we had to write out Rose Tyler, and introduce a new companion – to use that opportunity to show the new audience the full, proper format of *Doctor Who* [...] that life changes, the TARDIS changes, that the Doctor remains constant while his fellow travellers come and go.[22]

There is no time for the Doctor to mourn the loss of Rose[23] even though 'The Runaway Bride' and episodes of the third series display emotional realism, featuring on-going mentions of the character before her eventual return. The 2006 Christmas special is characterised by pace and action, with Donna giving the show 'a blast of energy'.[24] As Donna declines the Doctor's offer to travel with him at the end of the episode, however, we are presented with a new companion: Martha Jones. As with Rose, in 'Smith and Jones' (2007) we are swiftly introduced to Martha's family as she talks to them one by one on her mobile phone. Moreover, as Stephen James Walker notes, 'the fact that the Doctor is already posing as a hospital patient [where Martha is training] when the story begins means that he is thrown straight into the action without any tiresome preliminaries'.[25] And when Donna returns in the fourth series opener, 'Partners in Crime' (2008), a scene of Donna walking down the street echoes Martha's introduction. This episode similarly begins *in medias res* with Donna investigating Adipose Industries in her hunt for the Doctor, and their reunification happens in the thick of the action, again stressing immersive duration, with emotional plot beats integrated into action-adventure.

Finally among my five key narrative characteristics, representations of technology are vital to the establishment and functioning of *Doctor Who*'s science-fictional format. In the classic series, the set-up for many serials included lengthy opening TARDIS scenes. However, these are generally rejected in the current format.[26] Such scenes are typical, for example, of season 22 of classic *Who* where a 45-minute episode is almost treated as a 25-minute one, with time stretched out as opposed to condensed. The TARDIS has always been able to instantly materialise in different times and places, meaning the Doctor and his companions are 'foreigners' having to learn about situations as they enter into them. As such, the TARDIS is an important narrative tool. However, the special characteristics of the TARDIS do not guarantee a particular narrative speed. Indeed, for Russell T Davies's Doctor, it is instead tools such as the sonic screwdriver and 'psychic paper' that are used as devices to bring the Doctor into, and also progress him through, *narratives with speed*.[27]

Other technologies are utilised with similar effect. While the mobile phone, for example, is used by Rose and Martha to call their mothers from the future in 'The End of the World' (2005) and '42' (2007), respectively, it is used by Mickey to contact Rose and bring her and the Doctor into the action in 'School Reunion' (2006). It is also used by Martha to contact the Doctor in 'The Sontaran Stratagem' (2008) bringing him back to Earth. The internet is often called upon to provide information, as in 'Rose' or '42', much as it is in everyday life. Moreover, these newer (arguably) postmodern technologies create a sense of immediacy much like the TARDIS itself, and are often used to increase the pace of narratives. Technology, then, whether real like the internet, science-fictional like the TARDIS, or even 'magical' like the psychic paper, provides important narrative tools throughout new *Doctor Who*, allowing its narratives to progress with speed. Having introduced the major narrative characteristics of new *Who*'s pace, I will now move on to consider how speed – and sometimes its dramatic obstruction or delay – is thematically present in a number of stories.

Against the Clock or Stuck in a Jam: Narratives with Speed

Narratives are carefully arranged; they are plotted. They usually begin with an inciting incident, which is often worked out in some fashion by the end. Tzvetan Todorov argues that narratives commonly begin with a state of equilibrium, then involve a disrupting disequilibrium, and ultimately conclude with a new state of equilibrium.[28] This pattern is only partly replicated in most *Doctor Who* narratives, from both the classic and contemporary series. As a time traveller, the Doctor frequently arrives in a time and space where an initial equilibrium has already been disrupted and so he must act to bring about a new equilibrium – moving with speed, given the current form of the programme.

Todorov's narrative pattern where disequilibrium gives way to equilibrium, which he commented on in relation to literary texts, is particularly appropriate to the television series form. While individual episodes may delay narrative progression, there will always be a return to the more or less stable format. Highlighting this, Len Masterman calls attention to the notion of 'narrative prediction', arguing that because of the ordered nature of TV formats we can predict what will happen in television series.[29] Moreover, Brian Stableford notes, in relation to telefantasy specifically, that despite the series being an open narrative, each episode will move towards a resolution, and the characters will return to equilibrium,[30] a point also stressed by Henry Jenkins.[31] *Doctor Who*, to an extent, fits in with what Nelson calls 'the single narrative action-adventure series, the plot of which is goal-orientated'. Drawing on Vladimir Propp, Nelson argues that 'in the problem/resolution narrative model, the story follows a circuitous route to the inevitable solution of a problem posed to the central characters,' the paradigm of which is the detective story.[32] In BBC Wales's *Doctor Who*, this must be achieved with greater speed and in individual storylines/episodes compared to the multi-episode serials of classic *Who* with their extended run-time. Speed is a notion that runs through new *Doctor Who* not only in the compression of its storytelling, but also sometimes thematically.

In the first season episode 'The End of the World', for example, the Doctor must pass a number of obstacles in order to raise a heat shield. This must be achieved before everyone present on Platform One is incinerated. And in 'Dalek', as the Dalek ascends through the museum, a shield must be speedily closed to prevent the monster's advance. This means that Rose must pass a set point with haste, something which she fails to do. The lone Dalek is here shown as threatening due to the fact that it can elevate up stairs, an idea introduced in 'Remembrance of the Daleks'. Indeed, CGI monsters in the series are often associated with (unnatural) speed, like the flying Daleks in 'The Parting of the Ways' (2005) and later Dalek stories, the Slitheen in 'World War Three' (2005), and the Lazarus monster from 'The Lazarus Experiment' (2007), to name just a few.

However, speed is more obviously and thematically central to the third season episode '42' (2007). The title itself is a playful reversal of the action-thriller series *24*, and the episode is told roughly in real-time, where the Doctor has only 42 minutes to prevent a spaceship from crashing into the sun.[33] Additional pressure is created in this race against the clock because the Doctor, Martha, and the crew face several obstacles. Martha and crewmember Riley, for example, must answer a series of questions in order to gain access to the control room, while the Doctor tells Martha to 'keep moving as fast as you can'. Urgency (balanced with a little comedy) is also stressed by Martha's reaction when she rings her mother for an answer to a question only to be told to 'wait a minute'. The pressure and pace are further increased by an infected, murderous crewmember who dispatches victims by placing his hands on their heads and apparently boiling them, echoing the episode one cliff-hanger to 'Pyramids of Mars' (1975).

In '42', however, the narrative again continues without a week's deferral. While there is a slower moment when Martha and Riley are jettisoned in a pod towards the sun – first silent, then punctuated by romantic music – and when Martha takes 'time' to call her mother to tell her she loves her, this is soon replaced by speed and dramatic music.[34] Pace is further stressed by the image of a digital clock (used 19 times in all) accompanied by the on-board computer stating the time until impact. Indeed, the use of this clock becomes more frequent towards the end of the narrative; it is used seven times in the last five minutes of jeopardy to create an even more heightened sense of pressure. The narrative is resolved when it transpires that particles have been taken from a sun, which is alive, and must be returned. This alludes to the classic series story 'Planet of Evil' (1975), where antimatter was taken aboard a spaceship, meaning that it could not escape the planet.[35] What marks '42' out as radically different is its playful use of temporality, especially its real-time conceit. This thematising device, making *Doctor Who* almost purely *about time*, was never contemplated in the original series, where narrative time was spread out over many weeks of television time.

Narratives in new *Who* can also operate through a deliberate *lack* of pace and speed, however, such as in 'Gridlock' (2007). In a dystopian future that owes much to films such as *Blade Runner* (1982), motorists are caught in an unceasing traffic-jam beneath the city of New New York.[36] This contrasts with images seen on a screen near the start of the episode, showing the open spaces of New New York, as well as scenes of the upper-level from the beginning of the previous year's episode 'New Earth' (2006). In this earlier episode, the Doctor and Rose lie on the grass on a beautiful day while vehicles fly past in the open air. In 'Gridlock' the only way for motorists to supposedly break free of the traffic jam is to occupy the fast lane – the very lowest level – in a vehicle containing three passengers. For vehicles with less than three passengers there is an automated system: the wheel will 'lock' if an attempt is made to descend into the fast-lane.

In order to access the fast lane a male–female couple, Milo and Cheen, abduct Martha. The Doctor races after her and, on reaching the motorway, joins a vehicle on the slow-lane, contrasting starkly with the prior speed of the chase. Here the Doctor learns that the feline driver Brannigan and his partner Valerie have been on the motorway for 12 years, while another couple have been in their vehicle for no less than 23 years. Martha's abductors face an additional problem trying to access the fast lane: they find the junction closed and consider doing a 'loop' until they can proceed forward. However, communication from another vehicle reveals that the junction is permanently closed and that they are actually permanently 'stuck'. Far worse than this, the monstrous crab-like Macra, living at the depths of the city, slaughter those using the fast lane. Once they reach the fast lane the only thing Martha and her abductors can do to prevent this fate is to turn 'everything off', therefore bringing the vehicle to a complete state of stasis. Despite this, the engines can only remain 'off' for minutes before the air runs out.

'Gridlock' provides a particularly interesting case study of pace because the state of disequilibrium central to the narrative (noted by Todorov) is associated with stasis. This loop of traffic – the gridlock – is never-ending, and stands against narrative progression. But as it must, the episode progresses towards a resolution – one that quite literally involves moving forwards as the traffic jam ends. As with other *Doctor Who* narratives, there is movement from disequilibrium to equilibrium brought about by the Doctor's intervention: people are freed and he is reunited with his companion. Unable to move forwards in a linear fashion through the traffic, the Doctor instead moves downwards from the bottom of each car in an attempt to reach Martha at the lowest level. Russell T Davies constructs many of his narratives on vertical planes – as in 'New Earth' (2006), for example – and such a move is significant in 'Gridlock'.[37] While the occupants of every car remain in a state of stasis, each turning in their seats to see the Doctor arriving through the top of the vehicle before exiting through its floor, the Doctor is a doer, a man of action.[38] But it is the near-instantaneous transport through teleportation that really speeds up the narrative, taking the Doctor to the scene of a now-deceased Senate, from where the episode can be swiftly concluded.

Consequently, when the Doctor eventually opens the roof to the motorway he provides literal and metaphoric space in which the motorists, including those with Martha, can move. Thus at the narrative's end all trapped motorists can move upwards and forwards into the symbolically bright sky of New New York. Since there is no emergency assistance available for the motorists from their own world, the Doctor must take action and become the enabler of narrative progression, thereby living up to his title as 'one who saves others'. Moreover, the fact that the Doctor's face occupies all the screens in the motorists' vehicles while he rescues them is important. The use of broadcasts is commonly associated with narrative control and the redirection of the story. The screens, which had previously broadcast recycled news from the automated Sally Calypso, allow the Doctor to fulfil a narrative role; to 'author' a new stable situation with 'authority'. The Doctor provides emergency assistance, dictating with glee that the motorists must ascend and escape the traffic jam's monotony.

The direction and production of 'Gridlock' – the *mise-en-scène* of the episode – reinforce a notion of stasis, again highlighting the Doctor's pace as a character. His life is lived at 'full-throttle', but

ON SPEED

interrupted by the near-immobile traffic jam. We see the Doctor entering the lay-by of the motorway as the camera moves out to provide an establishing shot of lanes of stationary vehicles. Later, when Brannigan's wife tells him that they are moving, the camera framing remains static and we are presented with a shot of the vehicles moving and then stopping within the limited area of the television frame, making them feel boxed-in and trapped. Furthermore, a repeated shot composition adds to the feeling of stasis. Since Martha and the Doctor are trapped in their respective vehicles for a time, there is a repeated triangular pattern in many of the shots, interspersed with close-ups. Brannigan and his wife are presented on the far left- and right-hand sides of the frame in the driver and passenger seats, respectively, while the Doctor occupies the centre. A similar pattern can be observed in Martha's car, right down to the gender of those at the far left and right sides of the frame, with Martha occupying the central position. Significantly, at the end of the episode when the Doctor appears on Brannigan's vehicle screen, he is again presented in the centre of this triangle but reflected in it (as was Sally Calypso earlier). He is therefore able to move the narrative forwards as he is no longer physically trapped in the vehicle.

Sound and music also contribute to the pace and rhythm of the motorway. The sound of horns is commonly associated with the traffic jam, and these sound out at several points during the episode. Emphatic music is used as the Doctor gives chase to Martha's abductors, and there are also marked shifts between lively and solemn, slow-paced music at times. For example, the sober motorists' hymn is replaced by more up-tempo non-diegetic music as the Doctor makes his own way down to the fast lane to rescue Martha. Similarly, the striking soundtrack that accompanies the Macra's attack on Martha's vehicle is replaced solely by dialogue when the system is shut off, and in turn replaced by dramatic music when the system is restarted and the Doctor instructs the cars to ascend.

'Gridlock' therefore repeatedly emphasises the pace of the Doctor as the central character driving the narrative onwards. For a while he is trapped on the slow path until he can save Martha and the motorists. When the Doctor is again able to speak to Martha, he says, 'It's been quite a while since I saw you, Martha Jones,' although in terms of television time, i.e. episode run-time, it has not been very long at all. The form and format of new *Who* dictates that a situation characterised by lack of speed must, before long, give way to a speedy resolution.

Thus far my examples have all been taken from Russell T Davies's time as showrunner. But this raises a puzzle: are new *Who*'s pacey narrative characteristics a matter of authorial agency – in which case we might expect Steven Moffat's tenure to ring the changes – or are they more significantly delimited by TV industry contexts and common-sense, meaning we'd expect narrative speed to remain crucial after the show's 2010 rebranding and partial reboot.

Steven Moffat and Pace

When Steven Moffat took over as executive producer of *Doctor Who* he inherited the form of the series, and many of the narratives of his era are also told in single 45-minute episodes. The title of the first episode of the Moffat era, 'The Eleventh Hour' (2010), which was indeed an hour in length, played with the notion that this was the first episode of Matt Smith's 11th Doctor, and with the point that the Doctor was racing against the clock to save the Earth from eradication. This he naturally managed to do by the end of the episode. But Moffat's *Who* plays with the time-travelling format of the series more than any other era in the programme's long history, and this also influences episodes written by others on his watch.

Waiting is a key theme that Moffat introduces in 'The Eleventh Hour' and resurrects in the series five finale 'The Big Bang' (2010) – young Amelia Pond must, like Reinette in 'The Girl in the Fireplace' (2006), take the slow path and (unknowingly – or so we assume) wait until adulthood for the Doctor to return to her. Similarly, Rory the Centurion must guard the Pandorica, with Amy within, from the beginning of British history through to the present-day. However, in television time the viewer is immediately transported to the next significant narrative event: it is seemingly characters that wait, not audiences. The series six episode, 'The Girl Who Waited' (2011), centrally draws on this motif, although written by Tom MacRae rather than Steven Moffat. Here, the Doctor and Rory move forwards in time to find that Amy, who has been separated from them, has taken the slow path and aged drastically, becoming an embittered woman as a result of her isolation. This comes as a shock to the television viewer, for whom no time at all has passed, and Amy's ageing represents a narrative disequilibrium that must be restored to the format's *status quo* within 45 minutes.

Unlike Davies, however, Moffat's play with time creates a disorientating effect, and he has spoken about the need for viewers to fully concentrate on what is going on in his narratives.[39] This can be seen in 'The Girl in the Fireplace', which begins *in medias res*, and in 'Blink' (2007), as well as in the introductions of Oswin/Clara that radically disrupt or re-orient *Who*'s format by introducing a new lead actress playing not one companion character, but rather a sequence of inter-linked versions. Challenging the typical assumption that lead characters must survive narrative events, Moffat kills off Oswin and Clara, converting what would usually be a moment of narrative equilibrium into disequilibrium (and *vice versa*). Even while playing baroque storytelling games, the showrunner still maintains a keen narrative pace: 'Asylum of the Daleks' (2012) boasts a convenient transmat via which the Doctor, Amy and Rory can instantaneously escape from the Dalek Asylum, while the narrative economy of 'The Snowmen' (2012) includes a dissolve from Clara's fresh gravestone in 1892 to its time-worn, present-day version, as well as a jump from Simeon's childhood to '50 years later'. It could even be suggested that Moffat delights in creating wild juxtapositions and narrative leaps in time and space, with 'The Wedding of River Song' (2011) taking this authorial predilection to one logical extreme (all of time collapsing together), and 'The Big Bang' offering up another diegetic shock-cut via its '1,894 years later...' caption.

Two-parters such as 'The Pandorica Opens'/'The Big Bang' can spread out stories, meaning that hypothetically there could be a slower pace. The second episode of a Moffat two-parter, however, often begins in a completely different time and space to where part one has left off. For instance, 'Day of the Moon' begins with a (relatively paltry by Moffat's standards) '5 months later' caption, and a fast-moving shot of Amy being chased by men in vehicles, accompanied by lively music. There are a montage of scenes of the regular companions under threat and 'dying' before being resurrected, just as 'The Pandorica Opens' (2010) and 'A Good Man Goes to War' (2011) similarly feature montages of characters in different times and spaces in order to contribute to Moffat's story-arcs, of which more below.

The Need for Narrative Speed: Putting *Who* in Context

New *Who* is recognisable to viewers of the classic series because it intratextually references many well-established elements of the original programme. Despite that, the narrative speed of contemporary *Doctor Who* is very different to classic series' adventures. In this respect *Doctor Who* represents an interesting case study in the changing face of television and broadcasting contexts. For example, on a micro-narrative level, edited sequences such as that at the beginning of 'Rose' were not technically possible for the producers of 'An Unearthly Child' back in 1963. At this level, the time and space of story telling has been technologically compacted. Another context underpinning new *Who*'s fast pace is the fact that we are able to instantly access a variety of programmes in an increasing multi-channel environment. Nelson writes that 'Given the increasing competition between channels for viewers' attention, it is [...] necessary to capture the audience',[40] accustomed to the fast pace of other programmes. It has therefore become even more important to maintain what Klaus Bruhn Jensen calls 'channel flow', where viewers remain with one channel, as opposed to 'viewer flow', aided by the remote-control, where viewers are free to change and move between channels.[41] And given today's accelerated media culture of 24/7 news, real-time Twitter trends,[42] on-demand television and always-on digital fandom, audiences may now be more accustomed to instant rather than deferred gratification. Indeed, while a larger audience study would be needed to be of any real use, it is interesting to note that in a *Doctor Who Magazine* feature interviewing a class of school pupils, one stated 'a week is way too long to find out what happens next!', while another pupil noted that she was just getting into an episode ('The End of the World') when it finished, highlighting that the pace of the new series may still be too fast for some.[43]

On a macro-narrative level, however, a more sustained and drawn-out quality is introduced through the series-long 'story arc', showing how modern *Doctor Who*'s 45-minute episodes again mirror American science fiction television and its dominant forms.[44] Nelson contrasts goal-orientated 'single narrative action-adventure series' with soap operas, where 'stories do not reach narrative closure at the end of an episode'.[45] *Doctor Who* now contains elements of both, as was established by the 'Bad Wolf' story arc in 2005 and seen, for instance, in the Master storyline of 2007 where there was indeed an ellipsis of one year between 'The Sound of Drums' and 'Last of the Time Lords' to add to the epic feel.[46] Classic *Who*, by contrast, only occasionally featured linked stories over the course of a season, again signalling that the BBC Wales's production operates in a changed TV industry context.

Russell T Davies's story-arcs are both science fictional *and* have the emotional quality of soaps, concentrating on the companion's family and their relationship with the Doctor. Steven Moffat's story-arcs also schematically fuse domestic and galactic dimensions, whether focusing on Amy's baby and the Silence, or the Doctor and River Song's marriage. While most episodic narratives move at a fast pace, there is not only more time for development in two-part stories, but also over each series as a whole. Flashbacks have become a recurrent feature of the new series, where episodes connect back to past events. Nevertheless, Russell T Davies has asserted that because only approximately 10 per cent of the audience are devoted to watching the programme every single week, the series must not be 'too continuous and mythology-heavy' and that 'each episode should work in its own right'.[47] However, indicating that there is some scope for authorial agency on this ground (albeit within TV industry contexts), the Moffat era has relied heavily on the story-arc, such as in the revelation that River Song is Amy Pond's daughter Melody. Moffat's *Who* has also deployed narrative misdirection, for example implying that a story is a stand-alone, episodic drama only to then strongly pull it back into story-arc territory. 'Let's Kill Hitler' used this strategy; the title suggested a particular type of time-travel story, seeming to move in a completely different direction from River Song's revelation at the end of 'A Good Man Goes to War', and promising a self-contained 45-minute narrative about the notorious historical figure. Yet in the event, Hitler turns out to be a marginal character in the narrative – locked away in a cupboard by Rory – while the 'new', original character of Mels regenerates into none other than a pre-River Song (Alex Kingston) version of Melody Pond. Narrative expectations and forms can thus be deliberately played off against one another – what seems, to the audience, to be a fast-paced, frenetic instalment of an episodic series can be transformed into an incremental, story-arc serial. Moffat's *Who* moves 'from one to the other' even more radically than Trisha Dunleavy's account permits, doing so within the span of a single episode rather than across a new/classic *Doctor Who* comparison *tout court*.

That the faster pace of *Doctor Who* is not unique can be observed by looking at other programmes. Sleight suggests that 'editing in film and television is faster and faster,' but without considering any actual programmes.[48] The remake of *Survivors* (BBC, 2008, 2010) echoed new *Who*, and specifically Russell T Davies's *Doctor Who*. Unlike *Doctor Who*, *Survivors* is a modern remake (of Terry Nation's original), rather than a reboot (carrying on the story), and a serial, rather than featuring separate episodic narratives. However, like *Doctor Who*, *Survivors* was produced by BBC Wales and it duplicates new *Who*'s fast-paced storytelling. Akin to the rushing time vortex and whizzing TARDIS, *Survivors*' title sequence also emphasises speed, this time with people and vehicles presented in fast-motion to indicate the rapid spread of a virus. Indeed, the shot of people in fast-motion, reminiscent of the pacey opening montage from 'Rose', is repeated in *Survivors*' first episode proper. Very quickly, we are introduced to the main characters and come to possess all the information that we need about *Survivors*' diegesis. There is also a marked use of ellipsis with captions such as '2 Days Later' appearing on screen, increasing the pace yet further.

Venturing outside telefantasy, we might also consider a more recent 'remake', this time from the United States: that of the soap opera *Dallas* (TNT, 2012). Unlike *Doctor Who*, the original series of *Dallas* was composed entirely of roughly 45-minute episodes. With the exception of the first five-part mini-series in 1978 and the first part of the initial full-length season (which were both episodic in nature), however, storylines tended to stretch out across the entirety of a season, which could be anything between 22 and 31 episodes, depending on how well *Dallas* was doing in the United States ratings at the time. While there are obviously key differences between the genres of *Doctor Who* and *Dallas*, the reboot of *Dallas* does share some cross-generic features with the return of the world's longest-running science fiction programme. Both have been brought back by new showrunners (Russell T Davies in the case of *Doctor Who* and Cynthia Cidre in the case of *Dallas*); and both are continuations of their original series, remaining faithful to the original while bringing it up-to-date. TNT's first season of *Dallas*, for instance, plays on nostalgia for the original series with the inclusion of many of its actors, while simultaneously centring on a new generation of Ewings. But journalist Danielle Turchiano says of *Dallas*, still made in 45-minute segments and still offering continuous, serialised stories:

The original *Dallas* [...] was a master at dragging out emotional arcs to keep the internal romantic and other family tension going for episode after episode, season after season. But the original *Dallas* started airing on a major television network in the 1970s, at a time when soap operas were successful for slow-burning story arcs. Today, though, the television audience expects reveals much faster. It is not enough for a season finale [...] to feature a game-changing cliffhanger, but individual episodes must, as well [...]. Cidre acknowledged that there is pressure to tell stories faster these days so the audience doesn't get so far ahead of the characters they start to disbelieve the characters couldn't catch on on their own...[49]

Conclusion

This chapter began by looking at how pace is established in Russell T Davies's *Doctor Who* largely by form and through the introduction of format. I went on to look at episodes that thematise the notion of speed, standing as representative examples of how the Doctor now commonly resolves situations within a tight television timeframe. I then looked at how Steven Moffat plays with time in similar and reconfigured ways. Furthermore, I have hypothesised reasons for new *Who*'s speed, marrying a more textually-based aesthetic approach with a contextually oriented one by placing the programme in its broadcasting contexts. Since *Doctor Who* has a long-standing history, it is appropriate to consider how the new series both intratextually alludes to, and is characterised by difference from, the classic series. One of these new dimensions is *Doctor Who*'s pace, which continues to hurtle forward as the BBC Wales show continues its journeys through time and space.[50]

NOTES

1 Jameson, Fredric, 'The politics of theory: ideological positions in the Postmodernist debate' in J. Storey (ed.) *An Introduction to Cultural Theory and Popular Culture* (Prentice Hall, London, 1997), p.184. For a wider discussion also see Jameson, Fredric, 'Postmodernism, or the cultural logic of late capitalism', in D. Kellner and G. Meenakshi Durham (eds), *Media and Cultural Studies: Keywords* (Blackwell, Oxford, 2001).
2 Britton, Piers D., *TARDISbound: Navigating the Universes of Doctor Who* (I.B.Tauris, London and New York, 2011), p.146.
3 Ibid.
4 Britton: *TARDISbound*, p. 147.
5 Britton: *TARDISbound*, p. 149.

6. Newman, Michael Z. and Levine, Elana, *Legitimating Television: Media Convergence and Cultural Status* (Routledge, New York and London, 2012), p.171.
7. Sleight, Graham, 'The big picture show: Russell T Davies' writing for *Doctor Who*', in S. Bradshaw, A. Keen and G. Sleight (eds), *The Unsilent Library: Essays on the Russell T Davies Era of the New Doctor Who* (Science Fiction Foundation, Chippenham, 2011), pp.22-3.
8. Dunleavy, Trisha, *Television Drama: Form, Agency, Innovation* (Palgrave Macmillan, Basingstoke and New York, 2009), p. 65.
9. Nelson, Robin, *TV Drama in Transition: Forms, Values and Cultural Change* (Macmillan, Basingstoke, 1997), p. 36.
10. Ibid.
11. Lyon, Shaun J., *Second Flight: The Unofficial and Unauthorised Guide to Doctor Who 2006* (Telos, Tolworth, 2006), p. 130.
12. Levene, Rebecca, 'After-image: Rose' *Doctor Who Magazine* 355 (2005), p. 57.
13. Chapman, James, *Inside the TARDIS: The Worlds of Doctor Who* (I.B.Tauris, London, 2006), pp. 192-3.
14. Cook, Benjamin, 'Run', *Doctor Who Magazine* 355 (2005), p. 14.
15. Times are calculated including the opening title sequence and, where relevant, the pre-credits sequence.
16. Barthes, Roland, *S/Z* (Blackwell, Oxford, 2000), pp. 19–30. See also Bignell, Jonathan and O'Day, Andrew, *Terry Nation* (University of Manchester Press, Manchester, 2004), p. 87.
17. Cook, Benjamin, 'Gardner's world', *Doctor Who Magazine* 354 (2005), p. 15.
18. Kozloff, Sarah, 'Narrative theory and television' in R. Allen (ed.), *Channels of Discourse, Reassembled: Television and Contemporary Criticism* (Routledge, London, 1992), pp. 67–100.
19. Lyon, Shaun J., *Back to the Vortex: The Unofficial and Unauthorised Guide to Doctor Who 2005* (Telos, Tolworth, 2005), p. 365.
20. Lyon: *Back to the Vortex*, p. 222.
21. Tulloch, John and Alvarado, Manuel, *Doctor Who: The Unfolding Text* (Macmillan, Basingstoke, 1983), pp. 22–31.
22. Davies, Russell T, 'Companion piece', *Doctor Who Magazine* 373 (2006), p. 14.
23. Cook, Benjamin, 'TV preview: 2006 Christmas special – The Runaway Bride', *Doctor Who Magazine* 377 (2007), p. 18.
24. Cook: 'TV preview: 2006 Christmas special', p. 19.
25. Walker, Stephen James, *Third Dimension: The Unofficial and Unauthorised Guide to Doctor Who 2007* (Telos, Tolworth, 2007), p. 119.
26. Chapman: *Inside the TARDIS*, p. 192.
27. *Doctor Who Confidential*: 'River Runs Deep', 7 June 2008.
28. Todorov, Tzvetan, 'The grammar of narratives', in R. Howard (ed.), *The Poetics of Prose* (Cornell University Press, Ithaca, 1977), p.111.
29. Masterman, Len, *Teaching the Media* (Routledge, London, 1985), p. 177.
30. Stableford, Brian, *The Sociology of Science Fiction* (Borgo, San Bernadino, 1987), p. 325.

31 Jenkins, Henry, *Textual Poachers: Television Fans and Participatory Culture* (Routledge, London, 1992), p. 99.
32 Nelson: *TV Drama in Transition*, p. 33.
33 Walker: *Third Dimension*, p. 186.
34 Owen, Dave, 'After-image: 42', *Doctor Who Magazine* 384 (2007), pp. 61.
35 Walker: *Third Dimension*, p. 183.
36 Ibid., p. 140.
37 *Doctor Who Confidential*: 'Are We There Yet?', 14 April 2007.
38 Walker: *Third Dimension*, p. 140.
39 Quoted in Millard, Rosie, 'Best job in the universe', *Radio Times* 4-10 June 2011, p.19.
40 Nelson: *TV Drama in Transition*, p. 36.
41 Bruhn Jensen, Karl, 'Reception as flow' in J. Corner and S. Harvey (eds), *Television Times: A Reader* (Arnold, London, 1996), p. 189.
42 See Chapter 8 on Twitter's 'presentism'.
43 Wyman, Mark, 'Class of 2005', *Doctor Who Magazine* 361 (2005), p. 17.
44 Chapman: *Inside the TARDIS*, p. 194.
45 Nelson: *TV Drama in Transition*, p. 33.
46 For more on these, theorized narratively as 'implied story arcs', see Hills, Matt, 'Absent epic, implied story arcs, and variation on a narrative theme: *Doctor Who* (2005-) as cult/mainstream television' in P. Harrigan and N. Wardrip-Fruin (eds), *Third Person: Authoring and Exploring Vast Narratives* (MIT Press, Massachusetts, 2009), pp.333–42.
47 Cook, Benjamin, 'Leader of the gang', *Doctor Who Magazine* 386 (2007), p. 13.
48 Sleight: 'The big picture show', p. 22.
49 Turchiano, Danielle, 'Cynthia Cidre reveals "Dallas" season finale – and season two! – secrets', 8 August 2012, available online at www.examiner.com/article/cynthia-cidre-reveals-dallas-season-finale-and-season-two-secrets, accessed 1 June 2013.
50 I am grateful to Professor Jonathan Bignell for suggesting some valuable secondary sources for this chapter and for his advice concerning certain points, and to Tim Harris for providing some much needed archival material.

7

LEARNING WITH THE DOCTOR
Pedagogic Strategies in Transmedia *Doctor Who*

Elizabeth Evans

Remember, Remember the Fifth of November,
Gunpowder, treason and plot.
I see no reason, why gunpowder treason,
Should ever be forgot.

At the close of the 11th Doctor's first season, the BBC launched *Doctor Who: The Adventure Games*, a series of third-person action-adventure games. Four initial games ('City of the Daleks', 'Blood of the Cybermen', 'TARDIS' and 'Shadows of the Vashta Nerada') were released between June and December 2010 via the BBC website, with 'The Gunpowder Plot' being released on Halloween the following year. Gaming has long been a part of the transmedia *Doctor Who*, with game-style content, ranging from television-based interactive episodes and Flash games to jigsaw puzzles and quizzes, being regularly released since the series re-launch in 2005.[1] *The Adventure Games*, however, gained a higher profile than previous transmedia elements, being positioned as 'interactive episodes',[2] advertised extensively after the television episode broadcasts, written by series personnel, and voiced by lead actors Matt Smith, Karen Gillan and Arthur Darvill. With 'The Gunpowder Plot', this profile saw the combination of two of the BBC's core purposes: to educate and entertain.

This chapter will explore how this final game was integrated with a number of pedagogic strategies that explicitly positioned it as a classroom tool. Significantly, however, 'The Gunpowder Plot' is not a purely educational game; it was not produced by an educational establishment solely for engagement within schools. The educational components of the game are intertwined with the fictional and entertainment-focused position of *Doctor Who* as a core BBC programme brand, bridging the corporation's public service and commercial concerns.[3] In exploring how historical knowledge is built into the game and into the game's marketing and distribution, I will examine how 'The Gunpowder Plot' was given particular resonance within the BBC's broader public service remit to simultaneously serve specialised and general audiences. This chapter does not seek to determine how successful the game is in teaching the gunpowder plot and its historical context. Instead it will explore the strategies employed by the BBC and game producers Sumo Digital (media companies not solely – or even primarily – focused on educational material) to encourage learning and consider why such strategies were made more explicit in association with the gaming, rather than the televisual, texts of *Doctor Who*. In part, this relates to the status of the game as a transmedia extension of the core television series, rather than being the central text itself. However, as the final section will explore, the nature of the game actually allows for a certain amount of failure in its pedagogic aims, something that relates to both the nature of gaming and the broader industrial context from which the game emerges.

Remember, Remember the Fifth of November: *Doctor Who* and History

'The Gunpowder Plot' focuses on one of the most enduring events in British history, and one that is still celebrated annually. On 5 November 1605, a group of Catholic rebels planted 36 kegs of dynamite underneath the Houses of Parliament, intent on blowing up the House of Lords and the protestant King James I, who was due to attend the opening of Parliament that evening. The plot failed when a letter warning Lord Monteagle to avoid Parliament was passed to the King. The Palace of Westminster was searched and one of the plotters, Guido 'Guy' Fawkes, caught. Fawkes's capture led to the unravelling of the conspiracy and the arrests of other members of the group. Fawkes has become the figure most readily associated with the event in British folk culture, with the annual 5 November celebration being referred to as either bonfire night or Guy Fawkes night and a key component of it being the construction of effigies, or 'Guys'.

In the *Doctor Who* version of events, the TARDIS lands in London on the day of the plot after crashing with an alien ship. The crash causes a series of lesions in the space–time continuum that the Doctor determines must be closed in order to save London. He, Amy and Rory venture out into the streets of London in order to find the ship that has crashed and close each lesion. At this point the game narrative follows two parallel strands, intercutting between them with the player switching avatars between the Doctor, Amy and Rory. In the first, Amy and Rory stumble into a planning meeting for the plot to blow up Parliament and assassinate King James I, a plot that is being encouraged by Lady Winters, a mysterious woman with glowing green eyes. This woman is revealed to be a Rutan from the crashed ship who is seeking a 'Doomsday weapon' that will end the Rutan/Sontaran war and aims to use the explosion of Parliament to launch her ship and return home. Shortly after, a Sontaran army arrives in order to claim the Doomsday weapon for themselves and destroy the Rutans. Two young boys, Barnaby and Charlie, become embroiled in Lady Winters' plot and the player must, respectively, interrogate and rescue them. In the second narrative, the Doctor infiltrates the plotters' group, aiding leader Robert Catesby, Guy Fawkes and Thomas Percy with key tasks necessary for the successful completion of their plot. Both stories converge at the Houses of Parliament, where the Doctor temporarily resolves the Rutan/Sontaran conflict before locking Guy Fawkes in a room underneath the Houses of Parliament, ensuring that he is caught and arrested.

As with historically-focused episodes of the *Doctor Who* television series such as 'The Crusade' (1965) or, more recently, 'The Fires of Pompeii' (2008), 'The Gunpowder Plot' combines real past events with the hyperdiegesis of the series, integrating alien races (and conflicts) into significant moments in human history. Daniel O'Mahony describes this historical storytelling technique as 'pseudo-history': 'In these stories, the historical period has either been invaded by a science-fictional presence before the Doctor shows up [...] or turns out to be a fabrication mocked up by the villains for their own dubious purposes'.[4] The Doctor must interfere to ensure that such moments continue as 'history' remembers it, in other words with the same ultimate outcome that the audience is aware of from outside of the series. Although minor alterations to history occur (for instance when the tenth Doctor saves a family from the destruction in Pompeii), large well-documented events must be allowed to happen unimpeded.[5] In the case of 'The Gunpowder Plot', the Doctor must simultaneously help the plotters so they complete their preparations correctly, and prevent them from being successful where history records they were not. Although the presence of the Doctor and aliens immediately adds an element of fantasy to the historical reality of the plot, the ultimate historical ideology of the series, that history must be allowed to the continue as it is remembered, privileges as 'accurate' a portrayal of events as possible. As such then, the historical ideology of *Doctor Who* provides a diegetic space where the generally perceived reality of historical events can be explored to enable greater understanding.

The educational potential of television has long been established,[6] with education forming a significant part of the BBC's public service remit since its very beginning. The oft-repeated Reithian idiom, on which the BBC's role has been based, 'to inform, educate and entertain' foregrounds the corporation's pedagogic function from its outset. For much of the corporation's history, its formal educational remit has emerged through dedicated television programming such as BBC Schools (1957–) and the BBC Learning Zone (BBC 2, 1995–), which align with the National Curriculum. As already discussed, the televisual text of *Doctor Who* has often dealt with historical events within its episodes, with its earliest serials even following an '(elusive) educational brief'.[7] That brief rapidly disappeared in terms of the television episodes.[8] The increased exploitation of transmedia online extensions by the series, however, provides a space away from the core television episodes that can be used to step back into a more explicitly educational area. This aligns with the BBC's growing focus on the pedagogic potential of digital content, generally, and videogames specifically. Georgina Born recounts the centrality to the BBC, in the early 2000s, of creating 'an online digital curriculum for all schools to replace traditional schools broadcasting'.[9] The 2006 Charter review officially brought digital services under the BBC's remit, aligning the development of such services with the corporation's other responsibilities, including, of course, educating and entertaining.

The BBC's televisual and digital educational services predominantly involve content that is deliberately created for a purely formal learning-focused audience. The corporation's online 'Bitesize' service, for instance, closely follows the National Curriculum and exam structure set by the Department for Education. Unusually, 'The Gunpowder Plot' integrates the BBC's educational pedigree with its entertainment programme brands. On the one hand, 'The Gunpowder Plot', along with the other *Adventure Games*, serves arguably as any game does to teach gaming literacy, including hand–eye coordination, puzzle solving, strategic thinking and spatial and visual abilities.[10] On the other hand, as discussed above, it also exploits the series' central premise, of a character who can travel in time and space, and historical ideology to teach elements of British history. Kurt D. Squire has explored how mass market strategy games such as the *Civilisation* series (MicroProse/Hasbro, 1991–) can be used to enhance history education, arguing that '[s]imulation games allow players to participate in virtual social systems and to adopt perspectives that they normally may never have access to'.[11] This context, of games that straddle an educational and mass audience, is the key to the commissioning, promotional and structuring principles behind 'The Gunpowder Plot'.

Gunpowder, Treason and Plot: *The Gunpowder Plot*'s Formal Pedagogic Strategies

'The Gunpowder Plot's' status as a learning tool emerging from an entertainment environment was apparent from its inception, as a co-commission between Victoria Jaye (Head of IPTV and TV Online Content, BBC Vision) and Saul Nassé (BBC Learning). This continued throughout its promotion. BBC Learning hosted a launch event in York (where Guy Fawkes was born) and invited local schoolchildren and their teachers to play the game. An edited video of the launch became part of the game's online promotional material and clearly worked to construct the game as a simultaneously entertaining and useful alternative to traditional teaching methods. It showed children playing the game in pairs, exclaiming it as 'awesome' compared to 'boring' lessons, while teachers commented on its value as a classroom tool to help children learn 'without realising it'.[12] Footage of a group quiz provided clear evidence of the kinds of historical facts that children could learn from playing the game before the children used that knowledge to defend against an attack from the Silents and a Sontaran. The game's twin functions, as entertainment but also as educational, were the clear focus of its promotion and continued after the game's launch. When the game won a BAFTA Cymru award its co-production status with BBC Wales Interactive and Learning was heavily emphasised.[13]

This twin function continued throughout the game's structure and the extratextual material around it. Alongside the game's release, the BBC produced a series of 'Teachers' Resource Packs' that provided tasks and materials for integrating the game into the classroom and positioning it as a tool for formal learning. Three learning 'approaches' were devised, each aimed at a different level of the National Curriculum. 'Doctor's Detectives' was aimed at children aged five to seven (Key Stage 1), 'Deep Cover Time Agents' at children aged seven to 11 (Key Stage 2) and 'TARDIS Media Team' at children aged 11 to 14 (late Key Stage 2 and Key Stage 3). Each of these approaches positioned the children within the *Doctor Who* diegesis, with letters from the Doctor setting tasks and knowledge collection being positioned as central to the Doctor, Amy and Rory's ability to survive seventeenth century London and ensure that history happens as it should. Although these packs were accessed via the School area of the BBC website, a hyperlink to them was prominently placed on the game download page, extending the connection between the game and education that was established in the promotional materials.

Combining entertainment with explicitly educational content sets the game apart from its televisual counterpart. The BBC website has long contained a large amount of material on historical events, and so more details on those events depicted in the television series can also be found online. That online content was firmly entrenched in the BBC History portion of the site, however, only accessible via links from the programme's webpage, and there was little attempt to make a direct connection between the events in the series and non-diegetic information about them. A clear separation was made between the television episodes and any potential historical knowledge that may be connected with them, a move that mitigates the risk involved in merging entertainment and educational content. Daniel O'Mahony argues that explicitly historical episodes of the *Doctor Who* television series have had problems ensuring audience engagement. He discusses two historical serials from the programme's first series, 'Marco Polo' (1964) and 'The Aztecs' (1964), and identifies their emphasis on imparting knowledge at the expense of story as highly problematic: 'Both stories are pocked with historical details, of varying degrees of relevance to the unfolding story but pertinent to *Doctor Who*'s early (elusive) educational brief.'[14] He goes on to argue that such moments 'act as distancing device[s] in a story that makes compromises with its popular fiction status purely because the alternative would be to make *Doctor Who* a kind of time-travelogue'.[15] In discussing the disappearance of historically educational episodes from the television series, he argues, 'the lesson learned was that the audience of *Doctor Who* liked to be entertained rather than stretched'.[16] Recent 'pseudo-historicals' of the television series similarly provide little information on past events beyond the main facts: Pompeii was destroyed by Mount Vesuvius erupting; Vincent Van Gogh committed suicide. Any educational content in the core television episodes is side-lined in favour of maintaining an engaging entertainment experience.[17]

'The Gunpowder Plot', however, placed education and the Teachers' Resource Packs as a central part of its identity. Although positioned outside of the core *Doctor Who* online space, and so potentially ignored or missed, the hyperlink was nonetheless prominently placed on the main game download page. Teachers' Resource Packs were created in direct connection with the game's narrative and explicitly designed for use in conjunction with gameplay. This, in turn, is essential to the game's pedagogic function. Unlike television, which can be viewed communally and (with videotape and DVD) stopped to allow for further consideration of its content,[18] videogames can have significant logistical issues for use in the classroom. *The Adventure Games* are single-player games and so, although it is possible to watch someone else play, there is little sense of large-scale communal engagement. At the same time, games do not have a fixed duration in the way that films and television programmes do; the input required from the player means that individual players are likely to finish at different times. The Teachers' Resource Packs subsequently work to transform the game into a practical classroom tool, following Kurt D. Squire's assertion that, 'the educational value of the game-playing experiences comes not from just the game itself, but from the creative coupling of educational media with effective pedagogy to engage students in meaningful practices'.[19] Indeed, several of the tasks set for older children require further research beyond the boundaries of the game, asking the children to gather information on the plague, or seventeenth century beliefs about witchcraft from other sources. The Teachers' Resource Pack explicitly positions the game within a broader educational setting, not replacing more traditional pedagogic strategies, but offering an alternative enhancement of them.

The game's broad pedagogic scheme follows a constructivist tradition of learning by using a virtual environment to allow students to 'experience' something that is otherwise impossible. This follows the potential for video games to create what Paul Shaffer, Kurt D. Squire, Richard Halverson and John Paul Gee call 'situated understanding':

> In virtual worlds, learners experience the concrete realities that words and symbols describe. Through such experiences, across multiple contexts, learners can understand complex concepts without losing the connection between abstract ideas and the real problems they can be used to solve.[20]

The ability for games to virtually place the student within an environment and gather information through non-expositional means emerges through the specific ways in which 'The Gunpowder Plot' positions and reveals historical information. The Teachers' Resource Packs focus this 'situated understanding' around four specific historical themes. Two relate specifically to the events of the Gunpowder Plot: 'The Plot' and 'Crime and Punishment'. The other two relate to the social and political history of London in the reign of James I, with an emphasis on issues that would be directly relatable to young children: 'London in 1605' and 'Childhood'.[21] By analysing how these themes appear both through the game and are then brought into the classroom via the Resource Packs, it becomes possible to produce a taxonomy of the three distinct learning strategies employed within the game – narrative learning, 'found' learning, and ambient learning – each of which relates to specific forms of gameplay.

Narrative learning

By far the most common and significant way in which 'The Gunpowder Plot' integrates historical learning into its gameplay occurs in moments where historical knowledge is either required in order for the player to proceed in the game, or is provided to the player through other actions required to complete each task. Primarily, these involve interactions with non-playable characters based on historical figures or archetypes. The game features three of the plotters (Catesby, Fawkes and Percy), an apothecary (Alice Flowers), a town crier, two young homeless boys (Barnaby and Charlie) and 'Black Rod', a character who is unnamed and only identified via his parliamentary role.[22] Each of these characters has a significant role within the gameplay. Some set tasks for the player, as when the plotters ask the Doctor for help with three tasks. Others represent a task in and of themselves, for instance towards the end of the game when the Doctor must convince Black Rod that he is loyal to the crown in order to find the hidden Doomsday weapon. At the same time, however, the presence of these characters also provides the conduit for learning historical information about them. The plotters provide information about the involvement of King Phillip of Spain in their plans, while Black Rod teaches the player about his role in government, the wider context of the threats towards King James I, and the workings of Parliament.

Many of the tasks within the Teachers' Resource Packs focus on moments of narrative learning. This occurs most significantly in terms of learning about the Plot itself, something that is perhaps unsurprising given the game's core narrative. Several of the game's tasks require the player to either learn or impart knowledge about the Plot. For instance, the player must aide the plotters by performing a number of tasks based on the group's preparation and imbued with facts about the Plot, such as finding a sleeping draft for Princess Elizabeth, who the plotters planned to place on the throne, or the Parliamentary seal that will allow them access to the Houses of Parliament. Later, they must earn the trust of Black Rod in order to gain his help with defeating the Sontarans, something that is only achieved through having knowledge of the Monteagle letter. In both cases, knowledge of the real Plot is integrated with core gameplay tasks. Elsewhere, conversations with non-playable characters that take place within individual tasks contain historical information. At one point, for instance, Amy has a conversation with an apothecary, Alice Flowers, in order to get an anti-Plague posy that will prevent the young boy Barnaby running away from her. This conversation and Amy's subsequent talk with Barnaby also serves to recount details about the Plague and its possible treatments. Often the Resource Packs tell teachers to focus on specific moments such as these. The plotters' tasks game and conversation with Black Rod feature in the 'Deep Cover Time Agents' and 'Doctor's Detectives' packs for 'The Plot', for instance. This points towards a focused engagement with the game that privileges knowledge as much as achievement or the completion of in-game tasks.

'Found' learning

This second strategy ties closely to a secondary gameplay format that *The Adventure Games* utilise more generally. Each game in the series is predominantly a goal-oriented three-dimensional platform-style game in which the player moves an avatar around a virtual space and completes tasks that further a relatively linear narrative. Simultaneously the games also recreate collecting-style games, such as themed trading cards, that are popular among young children. While moving around the space, certain items become highlighted by a coloured glow. Although some (highlighted in blue) are key items to be picked up in order to complete a task or puzzle, others (highlighted in purple) are 'facts'. When selected, a pop-up window appears, providing a few short paragraphs explaining what the item is. In an earlier *Adventure Game*, 'TARDIS', these facts form a crucial part of the gameplay, allowing the player to gather enough information about the narrative history of *Doctor Who* to pass a quiz that ends the game if failed. Within 'The Gunpowder Plot' these facts provide information on a range of items from a gibbet, or the importing of potatoes, to the role of Princess Elizabeth in the Plot as well as information about events from past *Doctor Who* episodes or games.

This particular strategy relates to what James Paul Gee calls the 'discovery principle' in which '[o]vert telling is kept to a well-thought-out minimum, allowing ample opportunity for the learner to experiment and make discoveries'.[23] Although more overt learning strategies occur through narrative learning, here it is down to the player to explore and discover knowledge hidden within the virtual environment. Found learning appears throughout the Teachers' Resource Packs in various ways. Many of the tasks set through the different packs focus around historical objects uncovered by the player's exploration of the game environment. Tasks examining childhood games are explored via objects such the whip and top, football and nine men's Morris board,[24] for instance, or food and drink are identified via cabbage, beer, potatoes and a fork and spoon.[25] In addition to providing a series of tasks for students to complete, the packs also include pictures of key characters and settings, plus printouts of the various historical object 'facts' that the player can collect throughout the game. These facts are then used as jumping-off points for discussions and tasks throughout each of the learning themes, with the Resource Packs calling attention to particular items that may be physically dispersed throughout the game, but are thematically connected.

Ambient learning

The third strategy evident in the game is perhaps the loosest and most implicit of the three, and relates to knowledge gained throughout the game without any particular action on the part of the player or in-game characters. This relates to James Paul Gee's concepts of literacy via 'semiotic domains', which he describes as 'any set of practices that recruits one or more modalities (e.g., oral or written language, images, equations, symbols, sounds, gestures, graphs, artifacts, etc.) to communicate distinctive types of meanings'.[26] Videogames function as such because the player must be competent in many different 'literacies', including language, movement and visual images. Learning in 'The Gunpowder Plot' not only occurs through language (the dialogue of on-screen characters, or the text screen that pops up when finding an object) but also through the images that populate the game engine. All characters other than the Doctor, Amy and Rory are dressed in costumes befitting a 1605 setting; the game world reconstructs a small subsection of the buildings and streets of Jacobean London with a style of architecture fitting the period, and so gives the player a visual impression of what London looked like; as the player shifts between locations (London Bridge, The Houses of Parliament and Tyburn) they do so via a map, which shows the geographical location of each area within 1605 London. At any moment, such historical knowledge is being imparted in the background of tasks. It is not the focus of the player's attention, but remains present nonetheless.

The second way ambient learning happens is through how certain social characteristics concerning Jacobean England emerge out of cumulative references within the gameplay, none of which serve an overtly pedagogic or gameplay purpose individually, but which work collectively to imply general beliefs. There are several allusions to a more supernatural belief system, for example with the lesions being referred to as 'sorcery' and the Sontarans as 'devils', and a collective fear of the Plague is built up in the responses of several in-game characters. Such ambient learning does not directly impart historical facts, but instead builds up over the course of the game to imply the general physical and social historical setting.

Within the Teachers' Resource Packs, ambient learning is associated primarily with more contextual subjects. Some tasks involve students having to synthesise information contained within multiple conversations, for instance one task asks students to 'recap on conversations from the game between the Doctor and the Plotters, and Rory and Black Rod, which discuss Catholics'.[27] Both of these conversations have other primary foci in revealing the details of the Plot and the Sontaran involvement in it. Knowledge about the illegality of Catholicism is therefore imparted in pieces alongside more explicit forms of educational exposition and gameplay. Other tasks call for attention to be paid to the game's setting and environment:

> The children should also look closely at the dress of the different characters that appear in the game.[28]

> The students should look closely at the different buildings shown within the game [and] identify common characteristics of the different buildings including the timber framing, windows and the overhanging first floor.[29]

Again, knowledge is found through looking at modes within the 'semiotic domain' that are not directly related to gameplay. The clothes that characters are wearing or the architecture of seventeenth century buildings are things that the player picks up on while their attention is focused elsewhere.

Combining narrative, found and ambient learning

These learning strategies are not mutually exclusive, of course. While some of the classroom tasks focus on one specific learning strategy, others deliberately merge multiple approaches, requiring students to combine knowledge-gathering through narrative, found and ambient means. The second mission in the 'Deep Cover Time Agents: Childhood' pack, for instance, says that:

> ... the Historical Objects of the Black Rat, Chamber Pot, Well, Leeches and Deadly Nightshade should be investigated and discussed. Students should also be encouraged to recap on conversations from the game with the Town Crier and Alive Flowers which discuss health and medicine.[30]

Here, students are required to simultaneously collect facts by finding objects and interpret game events and characters within a knowledge-gathering context. Similarly in a 'TARDIS Media Team' task for the same theme, the pack states that: 'The attire of the characters from the game should be used a starting point for research into clothing of the period. Additional research can be carried out by examining the Historical Objects of Breeches and Swaddling Cloth,'[31] combining both found and ambient learning strategies. Learning is therefore integrated throughout the game in multiple, interconnected ways. As the following section will explore, however, these strategies are far from straightforward.

I See No Reason Why Gunpowder Treason Should Ever Be Forgot: Embracing the Non-Educational Audience

The BBC's turn towards gaming texts as a space to integrate their fictional programme brands with more overtly pedagogic strategies is perhaps understandable, given both the 'interactive' nature of engagement with videogames and the wider connotations that such engagement encourages. Despite finding valuable use in classrooms, 'one-way' media such as television suffer from negative connotations that more freely associate computers with learning and education.[32] The value of videogames' 'situated understanding' lies in the player *doing* something and *participating* in the virtual world.[33] Such participation relies on the agency inherent in the 'mechanical measure of inputting controls or commands in order to influence on-screen action' that is central to videogames.[34] As de Freitas and Griffiths argue:

> ... convergence is also placing a greater emphasis upon the learner, putting the learner into a position where they can produce and actively interact with content generation [...]. The learner as producer of content is to a great extent one of the major shifts in the process of digitisation and convergent media forms.[35]

Although I do not wish to deny the agency television viewers have over their viewing experience, the mechanical input required by game texts creates a different relationship between player and content. The player has the ability to shape the narrative content to a greater degree than the television viewer. However, the player agency inherent within such associations between gaming and learning also has the potential to benefit a media institution that must not only consider an educational audience, but also a broader, non-educational one. Greater agency necessarily involves the ability to choose *not* to do something; this shift to 'learner as producer' has the additional feature of allowing the player to *not* learn. A closer examination of the ways in which the above learning strategies are built into the game demonstrates how, despite the necessary inclusion of some historical knowledge, that inclusion is limited.

The game employs a form of 'selective ignorance' when it comes to the way it presents historical knowledge: although a certain amount is required to complete the game, much of it is easily ignored. The strategy of found learning is the most obvious example of this. The player does not need to look at any of the items that are highlighted throughout the game. Taking the time to read them significantly slows down gameplay, whereas a cursory hover of the pointer icon over them reveals their name and whether they are relevant to the current task. If they are not essential to the gameplay, the player can simply pass them by. The ease with which found learning can be actively ignored is evident in the Teachers' Resource Packs, which reproduce items' images and the short paragraphs of text that accompany them. Any item that is particularly pertinent to a task can therefore be examined outside of the game structure, even if individual students have accidentally or deliberately missed it. Equally, the knowledge contained within ambient learning (architecture, clothing, geography) may not be consciously 'ignorable', but its very nature means that it does not overly impede the progression of the game. It does not require a pause in the narrative and can be taken in without the player paying any devoted attention to it; although it cannot be ignored as such, it is relatively unobtrusive.

The way in which knowledge is imparted or potentially ignored via narrative learning demonstrates this selective ignorance in a more conscious way. As discussed above, some knowledge of the Plot and its context is required to successfully complete the game. However, there are three key conversation sequences where narrative learning can easily be bypassed in favour of a quicker, more seamless gameplay experience: the player's conversation with Barnaby about the Jacobean school system, the discussion with Black Rod about the functioning of Parliament, and the conversation with the plotters about the Plot and their roles in it. In each conversation the player must go through a certain amount of set dialogue in order to be able to move on. In the case of the three plotters, for instance, players are given three tasks that form the next part of the game. They must therefore play through the part of the conversation that relates to these tasks. The player is then given the option to continue the conversation or exit immediately and carry on with the given tasks. An outline of the Doctor's conversation with Robert Catesby, which demonstrates this, can be seen in *Figure 1* below. The player is initially given four options: The Task; Yourself (which is then replaced with 'What is your role?); 'What is the Plan?' (then replaced with 'Why are you doing this?'); and Exit.

This first option provides the player with necessary information on what to do next, i.e. prepare a sleeping draught. At the same time he or she is told that the plotters plan to replace James I as monarch. However, the information about who that replacement will be (James's Catholic daughter Elizabeth) is contained within an optional screen that the player does not need to access in order to proceed.[36] Similarly, the nuances of the plotters' characters, their individual roles within the plot, and their motivations for taking part (for instance that Catesby was involved in a failed rebellion against Elizabeth I and lost all his wealth because of it) can be ignored in favour of simply focusing on the tasks set. A similar approach is taken in the conversations with Barnaby and Black Rod. While the player must follow a certain amount of each conversation, he or she quickly reaches a point where they are given the option of ignoring any further information and continuing with the goal-oriented game.

LEARNING WITH THE DOCTOR

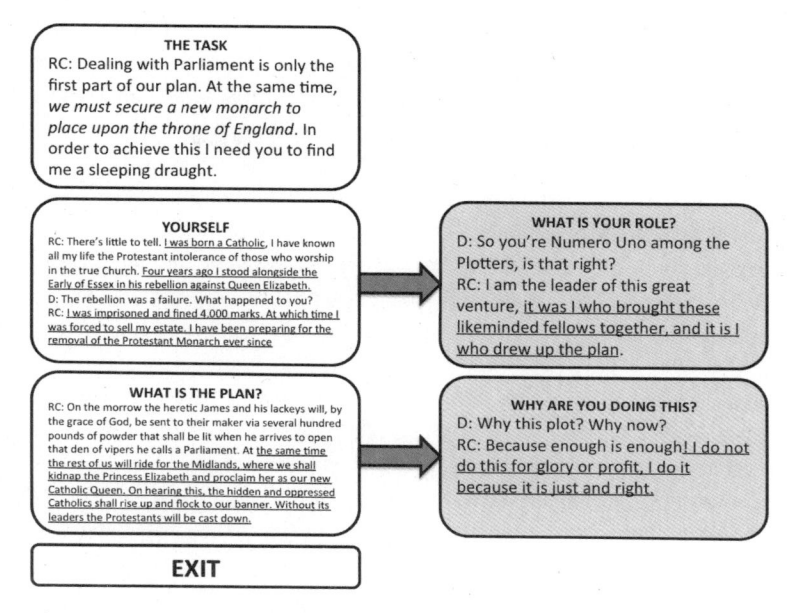

THE TASK
RC: Dealing with Parliament is only the first part of our plan. At the same time, *we must secure a new monarch to place upon the throne of England*. In order to achieve this I need you to find me a sleeping draught.

YOURSELF
RC: There's little to tell. *I was born a Catholic*, I have known all my life the Protestant intolerance of those who worship in the true Church. <u>Four years ago I stood alongside the Early of Essex in his rebellion against Queen Elizabeth.</u>
D: The rebellion was a failure. What happened to you?
RC: <u>I was imprisoned and fined 4,000 marks. At which time I was forced to sell my estate. I have been preparing for the removal of the Protestant Monarch ever since</u>

WHAT IS YOUR ROLE?
D: So you're Numero Uno among the Plotters, is that right?
RC: I am the leader of this great venture, <u>it was I who brought these likeminded fellows together, and it is I who drew up the plan.</u>

WHAT IS THE PLAN?
RC: On the morrow the *heretic James and his lackeys will, by the grace of God, be sent to their maker via several hundred pounds of powder that shall be lit when he arrives to open that den of vipers he calls a Parliament*. At <u>the same time the rest of us will ride for the Midlands, where we shall kidnap the Princess Elizabeth and proclaim her as our new Catholic Queen. On hearing this, the hidden and oppressed Catholics shall rise up and flock to our banner. Without its leaders the Protestants will be cast down.</u>

WHY ARE YOU DOING THIS?
D: Why this plot? Why now?
RC: Because enough is enough! <u>I do not do this for glory or profit, I do it because it is just and right.</u>

EXIT

Fig 1. Flow diagram showing conversation between the Doctor and Robert Catesby in which information that the player must uncover about the plot is italicised and optional information is underlined.

To a certain extent, this approach of 'selective ignorance' allows the game's educational status to apply to a range of age groups. In the 'Doctor's Detectives: Crime and Punishment' Resources Pack, aimed primarily at ages five to seven but also potentially useful for older age groups, a task on the punishments for high treason reads: 'If appropriate for the student's age and abilities, use the Historical Objects of the Gibbet, Rack and Wattled Hurdle to discuss what would happen to the Plotters after they were caught and found guilty of High Treason'.[37] Here, the ability to choose which objects to highlight and which to ignore allows teachers to tailor the specific tasks to the most suitable age group.

At the same time, however, the ability for the player to ignore more overtly educational aspects of the game also helps to broaden its appeal beyond the classroom. One of the BBC's foundational contradictions is, as Georgina Born argues, that it must 'offer mass-appeal programmes, but it must also serve minority audiences and those unattractive to advertisers, who are under-served by commercial television'.[38] The educational audience and *Doctor Who* firmly sit across this dual public service–commercial role. Explicitly educational content has traditionally been seen as non-commercial and only found on the BBC and fellow public service broadcaster Channel 4, through their Schools series. In contrast, the popularity of *Doctor Who* as a TV series means that any associated content will likely find a larger, more general audience. In addition, the series' position within the BBC's slate of programmes is specifically one of cross-audience appeal. As Jonathan Bignell argues, '*Doctor Who* was conceived, scheduled and advertised to address mixed adult and child audiences'.[39] Despite being part-commissioned by the BBC's educational department, the game must still serve a broader audience, especially given the high-profile nature of *Who* as a flagship, mass-audience brand. It is here that pedagogic aims of 'The Gunpowder Plot' become potentially problematic, and hence a strategy of 'selective ignorance' is extremely useful for the BBC, allowing the temporary unification of niche educational players and mass entertainment gamers.

As already discussed, there are potential risks with emphasising educational elements within the television series itself,[40] for example alienating the broader audience that seeks out *Doctor Who* for entertainment in an attempt to reach a specialised educational audience. However, 'The Gunpowder Plot' – and the agency and variability inherent within its gameplay – opens up the potential for bringing in more explicit historical detail without necessarily sacrificing story elements or turning off the non-educational audience. By exploiting the control that the player has over what he or she does or hears, the game allows multiple experiences that may focus on educational content or on the overarching narrative and science fiction elements.

Conclusion

The educational potential of 'The Gunpowder Plot' was clearly a core element of its commissioning and promotion. This centrality continues throughout the structure of its narrative and gameplay, with multiple forms of gaming combining with multiple pedagogic strategies. The paradoxical nature of the BBC's remit as both public service and commercial, however, requires it to acknowledge more than the educational audience, especially for one of its most popular entertainment brands. This need is reflected in the game's approach of allowing educational elements to selectively become secondary to its entertainment focus. In doing so, the game is able to cater for the specialised educational audience without alienating those who value *Doctor Who* for purely entertainment purposes. Unlike a television episode and its preferred readings, this new transmedia dimension of *Who* means that players can choose whether they wish to learn with the Doctor or not.

NOTES

1. See Perryman, Neil, '*Doctor Who* and the convergence of media: A case study in transmedia storytelling', *Convergence* xiv/1 (2008), pp. 21–39; Evans, Elizabeth, *Transmedia Television: Audiences, New Media and Daily Life* (Routledge, London, 2011).
2. Evans, Elizabeth, 'The evolving ecosystem: Interview with Victoria Jaye' in P. Grainge (ed.), *Ephemeral Media: Transitory Screen Culture from Television to YouTube* (BFI Publishing, London, 2011), p. 111.
3. See Catherine Johnson's chapter in this volume.
4. O'Mahony, Daniel, '"Now how is that wolf able to impersonate a grandmother?" History, pseudo-history and genre in *Doctor Who*' in D. Butler (ed.), *Time and Relative Dissertations in Space: Critical Perspectives on Doctor Who* (Manchester University Press, Manchester, 2007), p. 57.
5. This ideology is explicitly stated in 'The Gunpowder Plot' when the Doctor tells Lady Winters: 'The King won't die. Parliament won't be destroyed. I won't have you hijacking the Gunpowder Plot, messing up the timeline and robbing kids of four hundred years of Bonfire nights.'
6. See, for example, Messenger Davies, Máire, *Television is Good for your Kids* (Hilary Shipman, London, 1989); and Nancy A. Jennings et al., 'Educational television as mediated literacy environments for preschoolers', *Learning, Media and Technology*, xxxiv/3 (2009), pp. 229–42.
7. O'Mahony: 'Now how is that wolf able to impersonate a grandmother?', p. 61.
8. Ibid.
9. Born, Georgina, *Uncertain Vision: Birt, Dyke and the Reinvention of the BBC* (Secker & Warburg, London, 2006), p. 475.
10. As with most videogames, a key part of the game's opening stages is teaching the player how to move the avatar around the virtual space and how to interact with on-screen characters and objects. For a summary of the skills developed via videogame playing, see Bottino, Rosa Maria and Ott, Michela, 'Mind games, reasoning skills, and the primary school curriculum', *Learning, Media and Technology*, xxxi/4 (2006), p. 360.
11. Squire, Kurt D., 'Replaying history: Learning world history through playing *Civilisation III*', (2004), p. 55, PhD thesis submitted to Indiana University, available at: http://website.education.wisc.edu/kdsquire/REPLAYING_HISTORY.doc, accessed 1 June 2013.

12 BBC, 'Roll out the barrels' video (2011), available at: http://www.bbc.co.uk/doctorwho/dw/videos/p.0lq1rk, accessed 1 June 2013.
13 BBC, BAFTA success for *Doctor Who: The Gunpowder Plot*, 1 October 2012, available at: http://www.bbc.co.uk/blogs/doctorwho/articles/BAFTA-Success-for-Doctor-Who-The-Gunpowder-Plot, accessed 18/10/12.
14 O'Mahony: 'Now how is that wolf able to impersonate a grandmother?', p. 61.
15 Ibid.
16 O'Mahony: 'Now how is that wolf able to impersonate a grandmother?', p. 84.
17 A similar attitude can be seen in the BBC's scheduling strategy for educational television, which has historically been hidden either during the day or between 2am and 6am, when programmes would not disrupt the general audience.
18 See Messenger Davies: *Television is Good for your Kids*, p. 120.
19 Squire, Kurt D., 'Cultural framing of computer/video games', *Games Studies* i/2 (2002), available at: http://gamestudies.org/0102/squire/, accessed 1 June 2013.
20 Shaffer, David Williamson et al., 'Video games and the future of learning' (2004), p. 4–5, available at: http://www.academiccolab.org/resources/gappspaper1.pdf, accessed 1 June 2013; see also de Freitas, Sara L., 'Using games and simulations for supporting learning', *Learning, Media and Technology* xxxi/4 (2006), p. 344; and Michael, David R. and Chen, Sandra L., *Serious Games: Games that Educate, Train and Inform* (Tomson Course Technology, Boston, 2005), p. 137.
21 To a certain extent, the game also serves to teach players about the history of *Doctor Who* as a series, for example in explaining the background to the Sontaran–Rutan war, or how to exploit the Sontaran's weak spot at the back of their necks.
22 Black Rod, or the Gentleman Usher of the Black Rod, is 'responsible for security, controlling access to and maintaining order within the House [of Lords] and its precincts' (www.parliament.uk).
23 Gee, James Paul, *What Videos Games Have to Teach Us about Learning and Literacy* (Palgrave Macmillan, New York and Basingstoke, 2003), p. 211.
24 'Doctor's Detectives', p. 10.
25 'Deep Cover Time Agents', p. 5.
26 Gee: *What Videos Games Have to Teach Us*, p. 18.
27 'Deep Cover Time Agents: Crime and Punishment', p. 4.
28 'Deep Cover Time Agents: Childhood, Mission 1'.
29 'Doctor's Detectives: London in 1605', p. 4.
30 'Deep Cover Time Agents: Childhood, Mission 2', p. 6
31 'TARDIS Media Team: Childhood', p. 4.
32 See Evans: *Transmedia Television*, p. 95; and Seiter, Ellen, *Television and New Media Audiences* (Clarendon Press, Oxford, 1999), p. 120.
33 Shaffer et al: 'Video games and the future of learning', p. 5.
34 Newman, James, 'In search of the videogame player', *New Media and Society* iv/3 (2002), p. 409.

35 de Freitas, Sara L. and Griffiths, Mark, 'The convergence of gaming practices with other media forms: What potential for learning? A review of the literature', *Learning, Media and Technology* xxxiii/1 (2008), p. 15.
36 This information is also contained in a 'found' portrait of Princess Elizabeth and a later cut-scene.
37 'Doctor's Detectives: Crime and Punishment', p. 7.
38 Born: *Uncertain Vision*, p. 54.
39 Bignell, Jonathan, 'The child as addressee, viewer and consumer in mid-1960s *Doctor Who*' in D. Butler (ed.), *Time and Relative Dissertations in Space: Critical Perspectives on Doctor Who* (Manchester Universitiy Press, Manchester, 2007), p. 43.
40 O'Mahony: 'Now how is that wolf able to impersonate a grandmother?'

8

TWEETING THE TARDIS
Interaction, Liveness and Social Media in *Doctor Who* Fandom

Rebecca Williams

Studies of television audiences and their relationships with producers have often focused on online fan communities, considering how fans communicate with writers, producers, or stars of favourite media texts. Until the recent Steven Moffat era of *Doctor Who*, however, this was not a common strategy of those involved in the production of the BBC series; the previous head writer and producer, Russell T Davies, was not an active participant in online discussions with fans. However, Steven Moffat's participation, not on online fora but rather on the micro-blogging website Twitter, opened up a new dimension of fan participation and contact. Building on prior work on audiences' social media practices,[1] this chapter first examines the uses fans make of Twitter through interaction with Steven Moffat. Taking the period between the 2011 Christmas special and February 2012 as its focus, the chapter considers comments made to and by Steven Moffat on Twitter and how these contribute to a sense of 'ambient intimacy' for fans.[2] It analyses all tweets made by Moffat in this

TWEETING THE TARDIS

period as well as any posts he retweeted and messages that he explicitly replied to. In so doing it draws on work that suggests that 'Twitter demonstrates the transformation of "celebrity" from a personal quality linked to fame to a set of practices that circulate through modern social media'.[3] Second, the chapter examines the importance of live-tweeting to fan engagement. Live-tweeting has typically been considered in relation to the viewing of television programmes since:

> Social media is recreating a pseudo 'group viewing' experience of television. [...] Although television viewers aren't communicating directly with each other while they are viewing, the use of hash tags and re–tweets suggests that although users aren't directly interacting with specific individuals, they want to be part of a larger group.[4]

However, this chapter examines live-tweeting not to explore viewer responses to new episodes of *Doctor Who* but to consider the tweets of those attending a related event, the Official *Doctor Who* Convention in Cardiff in 2012. Examining tweets from attendees, the chapter considers how this creates a 'pseudo group experience' of event participation, both for other attendees and for those who are not able to attend at all. The chapter thus brings together emerging academic work on live-tweeting with consideration of the importance of fan events, exploring the dynamics between online and offline social spaces. It considers dimensions of fandom in the era of new *Who*, and the broader ways in which Twitter interactions can further our understandings of online fandom in the era of social media.

Researching Fandom on Twitter

Twitter is a social networking site (SNS) that allows users to post messages or 'tweets' of 140 characters or fewer to their 'followers'; those who have subscribed to receive their tweets in the 'feeds' on their account homepages. Twitter has a range of unique practices and features that distinguish it from other SNSs such as Facebook, Pinterest, Tumblr, and the older MySpace:

> Built on a restricted set of features including public timeline messages and private direct messages, it has evolved rapidly through user innovation with the retweet (RT) reply (@) and hashtag (#) [...] being introduced by consensus and community behaviour.[5]

Audience scholars have been concerned with how Twitter allows us to 'explore the medium's potential for our understanding of media audiences, their relationships to media products and the relationships between media audiences and those involved in producing the media'.[6] I will expand upon these ideas, contributing to existing understandings of fan/producer interactions[7] and analysing how Twitter intensifies the importance of 'liveness' within fandom.

As with all empirical research, there are limits to conducting research on Twitter. First, there is an issue of sample size, since there is an abundance of data generated by Twitter's labyrinth of tweeting, retweeting and linking. Concerns about the 'welter of opinions, fan expression and debate'[8] generated by online research are magnified when researching Twitter, forcing the researcher to be selective about which tweets to analyse. The method used here to record @steven_moffat's tweets between December 2011 and February 2012 involved access by scrolling through individual users' prior tweets. Due to Moffat's relatively low level of Twitter activity, there were only 34 tweets or replies to examine. As well as this limited corpus, other users' tweets posted during the *Doctor Who* convention were accessed the day after the event, allowing the researcher to save and record these before they became too difficult to search for. This second snapshot (presumably of general fan activity) included all tweets made by or addressed to the official convention Twitter account @DWconvention or using the hashtag #dwconvention. There were substantially more tweets from this sample, which totalled 289 pages' worth of messages to analyse. Since Twitter is a public site and all tweets used here can be freely accessed, tweeters are identified by their real Twitter usernames and all tweets are presented unedited for spelling or grammar in order to best capture the user's expressions and Twitter's unique mode of conversation.

Disclosure and Distance: Steven Moffat and Fandom on Twitter

From Henry Jenkins' study of fan campaigns in the 1970s and 1980s[9] to more recent analysis of discussions on blogs,[10] fan/producer interaction has been a key focus of fan studies. However, the advent of SNSs and their ability to allow media personnel to talk directly to fans is perhaps changing these types of communication. Television showrunners can use sites such as Twitter to encourage viewers and '[w]ith this sort of behaviour, often done in conjunction with answering fan questions or offering insights into the production of the series, showrunners directly facilitate fan community'.[11] During his tenure on Twitter, and given his status as Executive Producer of *Doctor Who*, @steven_moffat received many tweets per day from other Twitter users. I am most interested here in the moments where he interacted with and responded to these tweets, and where a conversation ensued. Twitter is an ideal outlet for producers to be accessible and to talk to fans, often by replying to them through Twitter's @ function since 'Famous people mention fans to perform connection and availability, give back to loyal followers, and manage their popularity'.[12]

Moffat's availability on Twitter often allowed such a sense of 'connection and availability' to be created. For example, he tweeted once on Christmas day in 2011:

> @steven_moffat: In case no one's mentioned it – Doctor Who, 7pm, BBC 1. And a merry Christmas to all of you at home!
> (25 December 2011)

The post works within the industrial context of promoting his show but he also offers a more personal festive greeting to those following him, building a feeling of closeness and intimacy through a shared acknowledgement of an important occasion.[13] Here, the fan is offered a connection to Moffat through the shared greeting and the impression that he is 'just like the fans', experiencing his Christmas in the same way as his followers. A feeling of shared community is created, as it is elsewhere online, offering a 'sense of shared space, rituals of shared practices, and exchange of social support'.[14] At the same time, Moffat paraphrases an infamous piece of *Doctor Who* dialogue from 1965's 'The Feast of Steven' – broadcast on Christmas Day that year – where the first Doctor (William Hartnell) wishes viewers 'a happy Christmas to all of you at home!'.[15] Moffat is therefore also sharing a fannish in-joke, and displaying his fan knowledge – making him 'just like the fans' in this sense, as well as through seasonal sociality.

However, while Moffat and the fans may seem to have had an equal relationship, both being similarly able to tweet at each other, there were often different motivations for tweeting. Indeed,

Celebrity practitioners use public acknowledgment, in the form of @replies, to connect with others [...]. Fans @reply to famous people not only in the hope of receiving a reply, but to display a relationship, whether positive or negative. If fans receive @replies back, they function as a mark of status and are publicized within the fan community.[16]

One example from 12 February 2012 demonstrates such an exchange when a Twitter user accuses Moffat of favouring his series *Sherlock* over *Doctor Who*:

> @steven_moffat: @FrankieTaylor94 Sorry you think that, but NO. I am completely passionate about BOTH of them.
>
> @FrankieTaylor94: @steven_moffat As am I, and will always be a whovian. It's only because your standards are so high in my books. Look forward to next series!
>
> @FrankieTaylor94: Can't sleep because I think I've offended my hero @steven_moffat LOL I'm such a geek:')

Moffat was quick to correct the poster here, reinforcing his producerly commitment to both shows. The tweeter promptly backtracked, proclaiming their long-standing fandom of *Doctor Who*. She then posts another tweet, containing an @ to Moffat to ensure that he will see it, and describes her regret at potentially offending him. This exchange demonstrates how celebrity interactions operate on Twitter since 'celebrity practice necessitates viewing followers as fans. Performing celebrity requires that this asymmetrical status is recognized by others. Fans show deference, creating mutual recognition of the status imbalance between practitioner and fan.'[17] The original challenge to @steven_moffat appears to lack the appropriate deference characteristic of the fan/producer hierarchy. This is, however, reinstated by the subsequent tweets regarding the poster's fandom and their flattery regarding the 'high standards' of programming that Moffat produces. Although this exchange is not entirely positive, the fan is accorded the status and 'subcultural capital'[18] of receiving a reply from her hero; an occurrence that remains relatively rare for fans on Twitter. Indeed, this echoes Chin and Hills's observation that '[a]cknowledgement from these "insiders", be it through a direct response to a posted comment, or indirect reference to fans' views, elevates the symbolic capital of the fans concerned'.[19]

In addition to sometimes replying to fans themselves, and akin to his 'happy Christmas to all of you at home!' tweet, Moffat also performatively positions himself very much as a fan of *Doctor Who*:

> @steven_moffat: Just bumped into Matt Smith – didn't ask for his autograph, but it was a struggle. #onceafan
> (27 December 2011)

While this tweet is clearly tongue-in-cheek, it offers a sense of Moffat's self-identification through playful use of the hashtag demonstrating his fandom.[20] However, this tweet also reinforces Moffat's insider status: he has access to Matt Smith and is able to interact with him, an opportunity that most fans clearly do not get. Moffat is thus both a fan and an insider; he may be 'fan-like', but the fan/producer relationship remains a notably unequal one. This feeling of being 'inside' the industry and the associated 'status imbalance between practitioner and fan'[21] was frequently demonstrated when Moffat tweeted at, mentioned, or retweeted comments from other celebrities. These included his *Sherlock* co-writer Mark Gatiss, his producer wife Sue Vertue and other celebrities such as the actor Simon Pegg. He also welcomed *Doctor Who*-related figures to Twitter, including actresses Louise Jameson and Sophia Myles, and actor John Simm who played the Master. In the latter two cases he did so again via *Doctor Who* references:

> @steven_moffat: Right EVERYBODY who follows me, go and follow @SophiaMyles – spin that fireplace. NOW. I'll explain later. Or not.
> (11 January 2012)

> @steven_moffat: The Master is among us – @john_simm
> (9 January 2012)

The tweet about Sophia Myles references one of Moffat's own episodes 'Girl in the Fireplace', written while Russell T Davies was the head writer. Mentioning 'The Master' was a more general *Who*-reference, but both seem designed to suggest a subcultural knowledge of the show and both work to produce a connection with followers. The assumption here is that Moffat's followers will know that John Simm is the Master and that they will 'get' Moffat's more cryptic 'fireplace' reference. Moffat was performing a service for his fan-followers by introducing them to other people they may wish to follow. However, he was also establishing a form of subcultural capital that fan-followers should share via their recognition of his references to characters, stories, and actors. In another instance, Moffat applauded the abilities of previous showrunner Russell T Davies in response to a question regarding whether it was he or Davies who wrote the scene when the tenth Doctor (David Tennant) regenerated into the 11th, Matt Smith:

> @PatrickAureus @steven_moffat Did you really write that scene, or is that a myth?
> (1 January 2012)

> @steven_moffat @PatrickAurerus I really wrote it – just the post-regeneration bit, with Matt. Up to that was Russell (all the good stuff, as usual.)
> (1 January 2012)

However, there are risks in this type of instantaneous interaction where fans and producers may forcefully diverge in their opinions, and the unfiltered nature of tweets can mean that 'interactions [...] become antagonistic and lead to points of fissure or dispute'.[22] There is therefore a balance to be maintained between reciprocity/conversation and the potential risk that showrunners might encounter dissent or even trolling. Indeed, Moffat's relationship with *Who* fans has not always been positive. In 2011, he launched an angry riposte to those who posted spoilers online commenting, 'can you imagine how much I hate them [...]. It's only fans who do this – or they call themselves fans – I wish they could go and be fans of something else!'.[23] While Moffat was rarely so openly hostile on Twitter, he did use the site to address criticisms. In January 2012 he chose to respond to accusations of hostility to fans:

> @Adam20mbPodcast: @steven_moffat sometimes seems quite hostile towards fans, does he not realise that some of us actually quite like his era of #drwho ?
> (9 January 2012)

> @steven_moffat: @Adam20mbPodcast I'm not REMOTELY hostile. I block people for being rude or threatening, and think I'm entitled to. I'm nice to the nice.
> (9 January 2012)

Here, Moffat addresses such claims directly without the mediation of an interviewer or a publicist, cognisant of the notion that there has been a 'shift in traditional understanding of "celebrity management" from a highly controlled and regulated institutional model to one in which performers and personalities actively address and interact with fans'.[24] In selecting this particular post to engage with, though, Moffat also accorded a certain level of status to its author, despite the negative inference it contained. Such 'recognition of fans [...] particularly those mentioned by "name", elevates their position as expert readers of the text (possessing fan symbolic capital)'.[25] In the hierarchy of cultural, social and symbolic fan capital, any acknowledgement from a showrunner can accord status and value.

Finally, it must be acknowledged that Moffat is a professional producer, working within a media industry, and thus his comments and interactions need to be understood in this context. Examples of his reticence to reply to tweets demonstrate how he is 'bound by codes of professionalism not to reveal anything that might damage his career path'.[26] This can be seen in tweets from February 2012, where he is alerted to fake tweets that have circulated and been attributed to him. He posts:

> @steven_moffat: I hear there are some faked tweets from me circulating. Not offended, understand it was humorously intended but I would prefer it to stop
> (3 February 2012)

> @steven_moffat: Clarifying: not offended by content or presence of fake tweets – just don't want to end up with yet another quote I never said
> (4 February 2012)

These tweets offer both disapproval of fake messages and a warding off of critique via flattery though claiming (twice) that he is not offended and that he understands the comedic intent of the tweets. Elsewhere, Moffat used Twitter to comment on inaccurate stories about *Doctor Who*, such as claims that actor Matt Smith would be leaving the show in 2012:

> @steven_moffat: @BriggsNicholas Be selectively quoting in order to turn into a story. Bless them!
> (27 January 2012)

> @steven_moffat: All that stuff about Matt leaving – here's what he ACTUALLY said: http://goo.gl/RSpsf
> (26 January 2012)

Here, Moffat enacts his authorship and privileged knowledge of the show to close down meaning and prevent speculation over Smith's position on the show. Much like producers who discredit fans' interpretation of narrative events,[27] Moffat also debunked media reports regarding the show, 'reinforcing [his] agency and power over the textual realm'.[28] Given the 'info-war that's been symbolically fought between the fans and producers of NuWho',[29] it is perhaps unsurprising that Moffat would choose to engage so proactively with both fans and the media via Twitter.

The often fraught relationship between Moffat and those on Twitter came to a head in September 2012, however, when he left the site and deactivated his Twitter account. While Moffat himself offered no explanation and simply vanished from Twitter, his departure followed a period of negative and often offensive tweets, along with his query:

> @steven_moffat Forgive my ignorance – is there a way to limit who can follow you and Tweet you?
> (Date unknown)

The general fan consensus was that the negativity often prevalent on Twitter had finally outweighed any pleasures of fan interaction for Moffat, since 'many fans who are unhappy with the direction Moffat has taken the show have used Twitter as a means to be insulting and rude to the man even to the point of telling him he has failed as a show runner'.[30] There was some attempt at explanation via Moffat's wife, producer Sue Vertue, who tweeted that

> @suevertue For all asking @*steven_moffat* is well and currently having a family lunch but he's got a huge amount on and twitter was proving a distraction.
> (9 September 2012)

She later mentioned that:

> @suvertue Obviously the new @*stevenmoffat* is an imposter and not The Moff. It's just these sort of idiots that ruin Twitter for the majority of users.
> (9 September 2012)[31]

Thus while the official party line regarding Moffat's departure is that he is too busy to participate on Twitter, Vertue's second comment clearly demonstrates rather more vitriolic feelings regarding Twitter. Showrunners leaving Twitter is not unprecedented; as Myles McNutt has noted, *Sons of Anarchy*'s showrunner Kurt Sutter deactivated his Twitter account after unfavourable media coverage of some of his comments.[32] Although Sutter eventually returned to Twitter, at the time of writing Moffat's account remains deactivated. Such examples indicate that the parameters of Twitter interaction with both fans and the wider media are still in the process of being negotiated by showrunners.

In many ways, Steven Moffat's presence on Twitter was fairly typical of the fan/producer relationship as this is now played out between showrunners and fans of a range of television programmes. He was able to maintain a sense of closeness and intimacy with fans while also using Twitter as a platform to correct anomalous press stories, or to berate fans who challenged him. Inequalities in fan/producer relationships that have long been inherent are still present, however, in the age of social media. Interactions between Moffat and *Who* fans did not take place on a level playing field. When needed, Moffat was able to pull rank and use his official position to withhold information, tease viewers, or display his own elevated levels of symbolic capital by referring to his relationships with figures such as Matt Smith. Social media offers a new platform for fan/producer interaction, but it has clearly not eradicated the inequalities present with older forms of computer-mediated communication, such as message boards.

Another of Twitter's key aspects is the real-time commentary it enables. Such a notion of 'just-in-time fandom' – posting while an episode is airing – is not new, and was identifiable among fans on fora and message boards where specific fans posted to reflect 'the "timeliness" and responsiveness of their devotion'.[33] With the increase in mobile phone technologies, and constant internet access for many viewers, however, the ability to tweet alongside events on-screen is becoming ever more prevalent: 'A recent study from marketing agency Digital Clarity found that 80% of under-25s used a second screen to communicate with friends while watching TV and 72% used Twitter, Facebook or a mobile app to comment on shows'.[34] Given this, it is to the phenomenon of live-tweeting that I will now turn.

'No-One Gets You Closer': Live-Tweeting the Official *Doctor Who* Convention

Twitter 'exaggerates "presentism": the belief that only things that are happening now are what matters',[35] and is a space where 'a day ago is a long time; a month ago is ancient history'.[36] The importance of presentism is highlighted in Ruth Deller's work on TV audiences since:

> ... tweeting during television watching [...] largely requires TV [...] be watched at the time of broadcast, in the presence of other Twitter users. As such, the notion of 'liveness' becomes important to consider in the way Twitter discussion of programming operates.[37]

For some fans this has become a key part of their interaction with favoured shows. For example, during the screening of the 2011 Christmas episode of *Doctor Who* (entitled 'The Doctor, The Widow, and the Wardrobe'), fans tweeted about the episode using a range of hashtags to follow conversations as they happened, or tweeted directly at Steven Moffat as the episode aired. Such interactions indicate an expectation of co-presence and the assumption that he would both be watching the episode and logged onto Twitter during this period. Rather than focusing on the live-tweeting of TV shows, here I want to extrapolate from existing academic work to instead consider tweets posted by those attending the Official *Doctor Who* Convention in March 2012.

The event took place over two days and was held in Cardiff's Wales Millennium Centre, near the site of the '*Doctor Who* Experience' that opened in the city in summer 2012.[38] It was the first official convention centred on the BBC Wales' series, and offered the chance to meet the then current stars Matt Smith (the 11th Doctor), Karen Gillan (Amy Pond) and Arthur Darvill (Rory Williams), as well as Steven Moffat. Since tickets to the event were limited, and were also relatively costly at £99 per day, many fans were unable to attend. Many of those who did so posted their comments on Twitter throughout the day, however, offering a form of live-tweeting that was based around experiencing a live event, rather than a TV episode:

> @lilpippi Eee! Back at the Millennium Centre waiting for our coach to the TARDIS !! :D @DWConvention
> (25 March 2012)
>
> @drwhofan_194 Nearly at the @DWConvention now! On our way into Cardiff:) #excited
> (25 March 2012)

It has been argued that sharing responses while watching television offers a way for fans to build community since 'viewers are sharing their viewing experiences in real–time through computer–mediated communication, which creates a pseudo–communal viewing experience even though they are not co-located'.[39] Tweets from convention attendees demonstrate a similar pseudo-community, allowing a sense of belonging and shared experience. Many fans who could not attend hoped that those present would have an enjoyable time, but also that they would disseminate or distribute traces of the auratic experience of being there:

> @karengillanfan To all you lovely people who are at the @dwconvention today – have lots of fun!!! Wish I was there too:)
> (26 March 2012)

> @PINKTROID Impatiently awaiting @DWConvention photos. Tweet away Convention goers, tweet away. :) DWCUK #DoctorWho #TheUltimateWhovian! :D
> (24 March 2012)

Factual updates from the event also emerged via Twitter, especially regarding the final episodes featuring Amy Pond and Rory Williams. Such information was frequently retweeted online, with fans sharing this knowledge via their news feeds:

> *@DoctorWhoChile* RT @dwconvention: .@CaroSkinner today confirmed that the last episode with the Ponds will be set in New York
> (24 March 2012)

> @GettingShirty Wanna see, wanna see!! RT @DWConvention: Wow. Just caught an amazing glimpse of series 7 at the Uncut panel! Wait was that a Dalek!?! #dwcuk
> (24 March 2012)

In addition to mundane tweets regarding queuing, lunch and so on, or more general information, fans posted tweets regarding their experiences of meeting stars and production personnel, often including specific details of their interactions. Examples included:

> *@ellesG81* http://twitpic.com/90qkm4 day one @DWConvention – been on tardis and had juice & a cake with a real cyberman..tomorrow is all about the Dr!!
> (25 March 2012)

In some cases, the perceived intimacy gained via physical interaction is reinforced through Twitter conversations, with fans keen to display their subcultural capital and carry it into the online realm. For example, one fan posted about sharing chocolate with an actor and interacting with Nicholas Briggs, who provides the voice of the Daleks:

> @pavedwithgold1 Had such a fantastic weekend. @DWConvention has been awesome. Shared a kitkat with Mark Sheppard and got called darling by @BriggsNicholas.
> (25 March 2012)

On the following day, Briggs responds:

> @BriggsNicholas @pavedwithgold1 @DWConvention That's right, darling.
> (26 March 2012)

Here, subcultural capital and status accrued by meeting *Doctor Who* stars are cemented when the artiste wittily continues interacting on Twitter. This slippage from offline co-presence (however momentary or otherwise) to online recognition is implicit in a large number of thank-you tweets posted at stars who attended the convention:

> @Lytelalix @DWConvention @steven_moffat @RattyBurvil Thank you thank you thank you for a truely wonderful weekend, it was a blast
> (26 March 2012)

> @Sockmonkeyukcom A fab weekend with @hanzypanzy118 @dwconvention Thankyou @steven_moffat hello sweetie ;) #dwcuk
> (25 March 2012)

The use of direct address implies a connection between fan and actor/producer, but these fans can lay claim to a stronger link since they have now met and engaged with celebrities in a face-to-face setting. This is not to suggest that 'real-life' interactions are any more authentic or meaningful than those that take place online. However, SNSs allow subcultural capital to be carried or, in some cases converted, between online and offline spaces, transforming capital accrued at live events into online symbolic capital.

Indeed, attendance at fan events and the prestige associated with liveness and 'being there' is evidenced in a range of fandoms, including football, music, and cult media. Such hierarchies of access 'separate fans by amount of fan participation – those who attend conventions and other organized events versus those who do not'.[40] In his discussion of horror fandom, Hills argues that:

> Embodied interactions are the key to generating and sustaining high levels of subcultural capital, since the fan can say 'I was there', or they can relay to other fans – the relevant beholders for this fan status – their experiences of gaining access to horror filmmakers and/or preview prints.[41]

The importance of physical embodiment is equally clear in tweets regarding the Official *Doctor Who* Convention. While tweets were often informative, allowing those who were not present some sense of insider knowledge, there is also a clear hierarchy at work. By sharing their experience of the event, fans who were physically present occupied a privileged position within the Twitter community of fan-followers who read the #dwconvention feed or the tweets of individual users. Attendance contributes to forms of fan capital and status, since 'being able to say you were there translates into symbolic capital in the appropriate cultural contexts'.[42] As a result, there are countless examples of fans expressing their frustration, upset and jealousy at being unable to make it to Cardiff for the event. For some, this is purely related to their lack of physical proximity:

> @Shire_Patrol looking at all the videos of the @DWConvention on tumblr and am so disappointed that India can't even be slightly close to Cardiff #RAGE
> (26 March 2012)

> @erinpelicano Looking at the photos from @DWConvention Makes me want to go even more! But I can't, because I live in America :'(
> (25 March 2012)

> @Vodkexcrypo I wish I was at the @DWConvention Why I have to live on the other side of the planet!! Dx
> (24 March 2012)

Complaints regarding exclusion from fan events due to geography are also relatively common within a range of fandoms.[43] For some, however, missing out on a fan experience seems to be even more keenly felt. Although one cannot fully gauge the seriousness with which emotional expressions are made online, the performance of affect itself is of interest:

> @BlueBoxDreamer @DWConvention The awkwardness of physically crying for an hour over how much i want to be at the doctor who convention right now.
> (25 March 2012)

> @RosalindBull @DWConvention Wishing everyone a Doctorlishious weekend. So jealous of those who are going I might be sick! Love you Matt!!!
> (24 March 2012)

For other tweeters, the disappointment of non-attendance is mitigated by retreat into alternative expressions of their fandom, including watching episodes or making a commitment to attend the next event:

> @that_unicyclist Couldn't get to @DWConvention this year so I may have to drown my sorrows in [*Doctor Who* episode] Doomsday and [*Sherlock* episode] Reichenbach until next year. Boo.
> (25 March 2012)

The disappointment of 'not being there' is testament to the affective attachments fans have to *Doctor Who* as well as demonstrating the potential threat to subcultural, social and symbolic capital that non-attendance might pose. Indeed, 'festivals/conventions provide the opportunity for fans to viscerally experience the accumulation of subcultural capital. [...] Subcultural capital becomes very directly embodied and objectified in the case of the festival or convention.'[44] Being excluded from accumulation of such forms of capital often forces fans to defend their fan status via declarations of powerful emotional attachment or reiterations of their fan knowledge and intensity of devotion.

Of course, those who cannot attend also risk falling 'out of time with [...] spatio-temporal rhythm' by 'falling out of [Twitter's] mutually reinforcing spheres of anticipation and speculation'.[45] This can occur when fans are unable to watch an episode as it airs, but also when they are late to discussion about live events, for example missing #dwsr ('*Doctor Who* set report') tweets used by fans to share real-time information about location filming. While discussing events as they happen can be a pleasurable part of fandom, for some this is not an option. Fans may attempt to join real-time conversation in the hours or days after an event has taken place, but the sense of community engendered by live-tweeting will not be available to them since they are not operating in the correct time-frame. Furthermore, they cannot be party to the spontaneous hashtags or trends that spring up around events as they unfold. For instance, convention attendees post questions or observations about random happenings at the convention that rely on 'being there' and getting the reference. One example is the sighting of a Dalek in fancy dress, which relies on insider knowledge and mutual recognition:

> @RealPeasant @DWConvention Did you see the Sport Relief Dalek outside with his medal and water cannon (er, pistol)?
> (25 March 2012)

> @DiHard11 There was a Dalek running around. I must find it and stop it!!!! @DWConvention
> (25 March 2012)

While fans at home can follow tweets revealing information about storylines or encounters with actors with little need to be physically present (since their accumulated subcultural capital allows them to appreciate such messages), their social and symbolic capital are not sufficient to enable them to understand and respond to meanings that call upon physical attendance. Twitter discussions often use 'markers of communality' that work to enforce 'an imagined "we" or "us".'[46] The tweeter who is late to the party is therefore excluded from such communality, suggesting that the downside of timeliness and immediacy discussed in relation to earlier online spaces, such as forums and discussion boards, may be even more pronounced in the maelstrom of Twitter's presentism.

Conclusion

As this chapter has demonstrated, the Moffat era of *Doctor Who* has yielded changes in the way in which the showrunner interacts with fans.[47] While there were of course fan/producer interactions in the Russell T Davies era, these rarely utilised social media. Through his presence on Twitter, for a time, Steven Moffat provided a new avenue of fan access. However, as his Twitter departure demonstrates, '[b]y putting their reputations on the line – and online – showrunners open the door to potential rewards (viewer loyalty, new viewers, professional transparency), but [...] they also face definite risk'.[48]

Twitter's emphasis upon liveness adds a further dimension, since viewers can not only share conversations with each other (or with Moffat) as they watch episodes airing, but also when fans attend *Doctor Who*-related events. This 'consciousness of a shared temporal dimension'[49] allows fans to feel a heightened sense of community and intimacy but, as with prior examples of 'just-in-time fandom',[50] risks excluding those who do not engage with tweets as they are posted. While posting about events can be a way to encourage a level of shared interest, information and community, the hierarchies of access, knowledge and subcultural capital engendered by participation in fan events are perpetuated by Twitter's immediacy and its ability to rapidly convert offline fan capital and status into online recognition.

It must be acknowledged that not all fans of Moffat-era *Doctor Who* interact in this way. Many still post on more typical message boards or on Facebook groups. Many more might agree with Steven Moffat's argument that 'you have to pay attention [to *Doctor Who*...] you certainly can't watch it when you are tweeting. You have to sit down and focus.'[51] However, as social network sites like Twitter begin to shape how we watch television and how we interact with other fans and media producers, research into fandom clearly needs to take such sites into account. Moffat's use of Twitter may not have entirely revolutionized *Doctor Who* fandom, but it has certainly had an impact. Once notably described as an 'unfolding text',[52] *Doctor Who* in the Twitterverse starts to become an always *unfolding event* marked by fans' social media-intensified presentism, valorisation of liveness, and desired interaction with the show's various personnel.[53] For all those interested in *Who* fans, or in media audiences more broadly, the developments discussed here provide compelling evidence as to how 'new media [...] complicates the dynamics between celebrity practitioners [and producers], their audiences, and those who occupy spaces in-between'.[54]

NOTES

1. Deller, Ruth, 'Twittering on: Audience research and participation using Twitter', *Participations* viii/1 (2011), available at: http://www.participations.org/Volume%208/Issue%201/deller.htm, accessed 1 June 2013.
2. Thompson, Clive, 'I'm so totally, digitally close to you', *The New York Times Magazine*, 7 September 2008, p. 42.
3. Marwick, Alice and boyd, danah, 'To see and be seen: Celebrity practice on Twitter', *Convergence* xvii/2 (2011), p.156.
4. Wohn, D. Yvette and Na, Eun–Kyung, 'Tweeting about TV: Sharing television viewing experiences via social media message streams', *First Monday* xvi/3 (2011), available at: http://firstmonday.org/htbin/cgiwrap/bin/ojs/index.php/fm/article/viewArticle/3368/2779, accessed 1 June 2013.
5. Dann, Stephen, 'Twitter content classification,' *First Monday* xv/12 (2010), available at: http://firstmonday.org/htbin/cgiwrap/bin/ojs/index.php/fm/article/view/2745/2681, accessed 1 June 2013.
6. Deller: 'Twittering on'.
7. See Williams, Rebecca, 'Good *Neighbours*?: Fan/producer relationships and the broadcasting field', *Continuum: Journal of Media & Cultural Studies* xxiv/2 (2010), pp. 179–89.
8. Hills, Matt, *Fan Cultures* (Routledge, London, 2002), p. 174.
9. Jenkins, Henry, *Textual Poachers* (Routledge, London, 1992).
10. Chin, Bertha and Hills, Matt, 'Restricted confessions? Blogging, subcultural celebrity and the management of producer-fan proximity', *Social Semiotics* xviii/2 (2008), pp. 253–72.
11. McNutt, Myles, 'Tweets of anarchy: Showrunners on Twitter', *Antenna*, 17 September 2010, available at: http://blog.commarts.wisc.edu/2010/09/17/tweets-of-anarchy-showrunners-on-twitter/, accessed 1 June 2013.
12. Marwick and boyd: 'To see and be seen', p.145.
13. Ibid., p.140.
14. Baym, Nancy, *Personal Connections in the Digital Age* (Polity, Cambridge, 2010), p.86.
15. See Howe, David J. and Walker, Stephen James, *Doctor Who: The Television Companion* (BBC Worldwide, London, 1998), p.76.
16. Marwick and boyd: 'To see and be seen', p.145
17. Ibid., p.144.
18. Thornton, Sarah, *Club Cultures* (Polity, Cambridge, 1995).
19. Chin and Hills: 'Restricted confessions', p.258.
20. See Hills, Matt and Williams, Rebecca, 'It's all my interpretation: Reading Spike through the "subcultural celebrity" of James Marsters', *European Journal of Cultural Studies* viii/3 (2005), pp. 345–65.
21. Marwick and boyd: 'To see and be seen', p.144.
22. Williams: 'Good *Neighbours*?', p. 280.
23. Hills, Matt, 'A showrunner goes to war: *Doctor Who* and the almost fans?', *Antenna*, 6 June 2011, available at: http://blog.commarts.wisc.e-

du/2011/06/06/a-showrunner-goes-to-war-doctor-who-and-the-almost-fans/, accessed 1 June 2013.
24 Marwick and boyd: 'To see and be seen', p. 139.
25 Chin and Hills: 'Restricted confessions', p. 259.
26 Ibid., p. 267.
27 See Williams: 'Good *Neighbours*?'
28 Johnson, Derek, 'Inviting audiences in', *New Review of Film and Television Studies* v/1 (2007), p. 77.
29 Hills: 'A showrunner goes to war'.
30 Kay, Janice, 'Steven Moffat deletes Twitter account', *Science Fiction.com*, 10 September 2012, available at: http://sciencefiction.com/2012/09/10/steven-moffat-deletes-twitter-account/, accessed 1 June 2013.
31 The @stevenmoffat account that Vertue refers to was not created as a result of the departure of the real Moffat and was, in fact, a previously established fake account.
32 McNutt, Myles, 'The rise and fall of @Sutterink: Showrunners [off] Twitter III', *Antenna*, 14 August 2011, available at: http://blog.commarts.wisc.edu/2011/08/14/the-rise-and-fall-of-sutterink-showrunners-off-twitter-iii/, accessed 1 June 2013.
33 Hills: *Fan Cultures*, p. 178.
34 Wakefield, Jane, 'Tweeting with the telly on', *BBC News*, 23 March 2011, available at: http://www.bbc.co.uk/news/technology-12809388, accessed 1 June 2013.
35 Gruzd, Anatoliy, Wellman, Barry, and Takhteyev, Yuri, 'Imagining Twitter as an imagined community', *American Behavioral Scientist* lv/10 (2011), p. 1303.
36 Ibid.
37 Deller: 'Twittering on'.
38 For more on the '*Doctor Who* Experience' based at Porth Teigr, see the next Chapter.
39 Wohn and Na: 'Tweeting about TV'.
40 Macdonald, Andrea, 'Uncertain utopia: Science fiction media fandom and computer mediated communication' in C. Harris and A. Alexander (eds), *Theorizing Fandom: Fans, Subculture and Identity* (Hampton Press, New Jersey, 1998), p. 137.
41 Hills, Matt, 'Attending horror film festivals and conventions: Liveness, subcultural capital and "flesh-and-blood genre communities"' in I. Conrich (ed.) *Horror Zone: The Cultural Experience of Contemporary Horror Cinema* (I.B.Tauris, London and New York, 2009), p.87.
42 Auslander, Philip, *Liveness: Performance In A Mediatized Culture* (Routledge, London and New York, 1999), p.158.
43 See Kalviknes-Bore, Inger-Lise and Williams, Rebecca, 'Transnational Twilighters: A *Twilight* fan community in Norway', in M. A. Click, J. Stevens Aubrey, and E. Behm-Morawitz (eds), *Bitten by Twilight: Youth Culture, Media and the Vampire Franchise* (Peter Lang, New York, 2010).
44 Hills: 'Attending horror film festivals and conventions', p. 91.
45 Hills: *Fan Cultures*, p. 176.
46 Deller: 'Twittering on'.

47 And for a related study of Twitter use surrounding *Torchwood: Miracle Day*, see Porter, Lynnette, *The Doctor Who Franchise: American Influence, Fan Culture and the Spinoffs* (McFarland, Jefferson, 2012), pp.132–47.
48 McNutt: 'Tweets of anarchy'.
49 Gruzd et al: 'Imagining Twitter as imagined community', p.1303.
50 Hills: *Fan Cultures*, p.178.
51 Moffat, Steven quoted in Rosie Millard, 'Best job in the universe', *Radio Times* 4–10 June 2011, p.19.
52 Tulloch, John and Alvarado, Manuel, *Doctor Who: The Unfolding Text* (Macmillan, Basingstoke, 1983).
53 See Bennett, Peter, Kendall, Alex and McDougall, Julian, *After the Media: Culture and Identity in the 21st Century* (Routledge, London, 2011), p.161 for an argument regarding the shift 'from text to event'.
54 Marwick and boyd: 'To see and be seen' p. 156

III

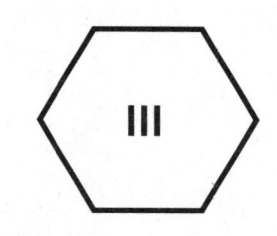

NEW SPACES AND TIMES

9
THE '*DOCTOR WHO* EXPERIENCE' (2012–) AND THE COMMODIFICATION OF CARDIFF BAY

Melissa Beattie

C ardiff is indisputably the home of *Doctor Who*. The series is filmed on location in and around the city as well as at the new BBC Studios in Cardiff Bay. Just next door, the brand new '*Doctor Who* Experience' has brought the Doctor home, making Cardiff the perfect choice for a *Doctor Who* themed break, ideal for fans of any age.[1]

Though filming locations for *Doctor Who* (and its spin-off series *Torchwood* and *The Sarah Jane Adventures*) dot the landscapes of Cardiff and its South Wales environs, it is the now-regenerated area of Cardiff Bay that has become most associated with new *Who*. Although there is a great deal that could be said about the integration – and imposition – of *Doctor Who* onto the area, this chapter will focus on the '*Doctor Who* Experience'. I shall examine issues of city branding, urban regeneration, fan tourism, and commodification of the fan experience, beginning with a discussion of current theory on what has recently been termed city or 'destination branding'.[2] I shall then integrate fan studies' work on cult geography and the impact of commodification, before finally considering how fans and the *'Doctor Who* Experience' work cooperatively to reinforce Cardiff Bay's dominant, commercial meanings.

To begin with, however, I shall give a *précis* of the 'Experience' itself. In fact, there is a slightly longer history of *Doctor Who* exhibitions in Cardiff Bay;[3] the *'Doctor Who* Experience' is the second long-term exhibit, replacing the 'Up Close' exhibition that had been housed in the nearby Red Dragon Centre (from December 2005 to March 2011).[4] This exhibition (as opposed to the 'Experience') was one of several run by a company called Experience Design, based out of Shepperton Studios, rather than being directly run by the BBC.[5] It was a small facility and in its first incarnation (December 2005 to October 2008) was much like a traditional museum with its displays and structure. The second incarnation (October 2008 to March 2011) was slightly larger and featured an interactive element: a green-screen upon which visitors could, on a monitor, see themselves inserted into a shot of the TARDIS materialising. From personal observation, both versions took between 20 and 30 minutes to walk through from the reception area to the gift shop. The shop itself featured a variety of merchandise relating to *Doctor Who*, its spin-off series *Torchwood* (2006–) and *The Sarah Jane Adventures* (2007–2011) along with a small number of other BBC series (such as *Merlin* 2007–2012). These items, though grouped conveniently close to the exhibition, were not exclusive to the shop.

The ultimate closure of the 'Up Close' exhibition in favour of the 'Experience' – initially located in London rather than Cardiff – was covered in the local press, with manager Gareth Jones saying:

> It is damaging to the economy of Wales and the economy of Cardiff. We thought that (BBC Worldwide) would have respect and regard for their fans. It does seem that this decision has been made in a way that is not very compassionate towards Cardiff. If you want to see wee kids crying then you ought to come down to the Red Dragon this Easter because they will come down here to an empty shell.[6]

BBC Worldwide, however, stated that they had '... consulted with the city council for the past two years regarding our plans and we are confident that the attraction's features, size and location will draw many

THE '*DOCTOR WHO* EXPERIENCE' (2012–)

more fans to the Welsh capital from across the UK'.[7] Thus it is clear that the exhibition and the 'Experience' were (and are) positioned as tourist draws. Despite the manager of the former seeming to focus upon the feelings of fans, and BBC Worldwide putting matters in more economic terms, both have clearly co-opted and commodified fan activity, something I'll explore across this chapter.

The '*Doctor Who* Experience' itself is a large, purpose-built facility that houses a number of props from both classic and new *Doctor Who*. It is owned by Cardiff County Council but rented and run by BBC Worldwide, and it was built upon open ground that had been used during a confrontation between the tenth Doctor (David Tennant) and the Master (John Simm) in 'The End of Time, Part One'. The collection had previously been housed in London at Earl's Court through to February 2012, but was moved to Cardiff once the new facility was completed and officially opened in June of 2012.

The 'Experience' itself is divided into different parts. The reception and café area feature exhibits from the third Doctor (Jon Pertwee) era (the yellow roadster 'Bessie') and a Dalek from the 11th Doctor (Matt Smith) episode 'Victory of the Daleks'. Also displayed are multiple copies of the Van Gogh painting of the TARDIS, as seen in 'Vincent and the Doctor'; poster prints of the same image are also available in the gift shop. Though the café is open to the public, access to the second section of the 'Experience' is tightly controlled. Having purchased tickets, small groups are escorted into a viewing room to see a short compilation of clips that sets up the interactive portion of the visit. This is designed to create the sense that viewers can walk through the screen, and get 'inside' *Doctor Who*'s diegesis: it begins with spectatorship only in order to emphasise how 'ordinary' TV viewing will be transformed and worked-over by the installations, events, and physical spaces that are to come. *Visitors thus enter the 'Experience' three times*, and they are made acutely aware of crossing various thresholds: first when they come into the building, second when they are ushered into the viewing room, and ultimately when they cross through the screen, imaginatively 'inhabiting the world'[8] of new *Who*.

In a clever bit of self-reflexivity, the first room after this symbolic transition purports to be a museum storeroom on the Starship UK ('The Beast Below') housing a number of 'artefacts', which are props from the series that are introduced by an info node as seen in the tenth Doctor episode 'Silence in the Library'. This sequence is interrupted by the 11th

Doctor, who breaks in via viewscreen and directly addresses assembled visitors, or – in his slightly disappointed words – 'shoppers'. Visitors are then led through a series of rooms (and past a series of enemies), 'helping' the Doctor land, find and reclaim his TARDIS and escape from a second Pandorica. Throughout this adventure, pre-recorded material of the Doctor constantly hails visitors, encouraging them in their use of the TARDIS joystick controls and warning them of 'dangers'. The 'hands-on' joysticks in the replica TARDIS control room further reinforce an illusion of interactivity, given that this experience is, of course, a pre-determined, reproducible and automated series of incidents. It combines visitors' progress through physical space with filmed inserts, and culminates in a three-dimensional sequence clearly intended to offer a climactic spectacle, yet which also symbolically returns the *Doctor Who* 'inhabitant' to the status of viewer, thus managing and marking his or her return to the 'ordinary' realm of *Who* watching/fandom.

Once the walk-through ends, visitors enter a two-tiered exhibition space. This section is much like a traditional museum in that visitors are not allowed to physically interact with the objects at all, in order to preserve them from damage, and instead they are grouped into displays. The items present during my visit on 6 December 2012 included costumes from all 11 doctors and from all modern companions, including Sarah Jane Smith (Elisabeth Sladen), as well as props from multiple eras and two displays charting the 'evolution' of costumes for the Sontarans and Cybermen. Also present were replicas of two TARDIS control rooms, that of the ninth (Christopher Eccleston) and tenth Doctors, and that of the fourth through seventh Doctors (Tom Baker, Peter Davison, Colin Baker and Sylvester McCoy). There are also informational displays and short films on sound design and music, as well as production design; the former features an interactive element allowing sounds to be played by pressing various buttons on the display wall. A green-screen is available for visitors as with the 'Up Close' exhibition, but at the 'Experience' you must additionally pay for a photograph to be taken. At the 'Up Close' exhibition, everyone walked through the green-screen section as part of the visitors' pathway, rather than as an optional extra. The final section of the 'Experience' is the 'little shop'. This gift shop does feature exclusive items licensed by BBC Worldwide, including replicas of the fourth Doctor's scarf and the tenth Doctor's jacket. Once a visitor walks through this section, he or she finds themselves back at the reception/café area.

While the 'Up Close' exhibition was run by an external agency in a retail area near (but not in) the show's main filming areas, and was predominantly made up of a small series of displays, the 'Experience' is directly run by BBC Worldwide, combines an interactive facility with a more display-based area, is located within sight of the Roath Lock Studios where the series is currently produced, and is not only within the main location shooting area but is literally sited on a former filming location. The 'Experience' shop also sells exclusive merchandise, whereas the exhibition shop did not. Thus, what we can say is that the closure of the 'Up Close' exhibition in favour of the 'Experience' shows the BBC exercising more control over its brand and its commercial interactions with fans. It is also worth noting that the website for the 'Up Close' exhibition has been deleted, further erasing it in favour of the 'Experience'.

The 'Experience' is, of course, part of a greater tourist–industrial complex, itself a part of a heavily-promoted section of Cardiff. There are two aspects to this integration. First there is the general interrelation of city and programme brands, and second there are specific interactions between the programme-branded Cardiff Bay and Doctor Who's (fan) audiences, both fan tourists and what Hills terms 'fan-residents'.[9] Tackling the interrelationship between city and programme, where 'Cardiff has been the home of Doctor Who since 2005',[10] I will begin with a discussion of destination branding, drawn from business/tourism studies and focusing upon capital cities specifically.

The Semiotic Thickness of Cardiff

The city of Cardiff is the youngest capital in Europe, having been proclaimed the Welsh capital in 1955 and becoming the seat of the Welsh Assembly in 1999. The fact that it is a capital city is important in that, as Robert Maitland points out, European capital cities all share

> ...economic and political centrality in national life [... given] their controlling function in administration and organisation of territory; and providing the site of national political, economic and cultural facilities and heritage. As a result, they are home to buildings and spaces that symbolise national identity and power and historical narratives, and attract the interest of both citizens and visitors.[11]

This means that the very fact of the city being a national capital gives it a certain level of cultural and symbolic capital that is further expressed, maintained and reinforced by the image or brand that local and national governments wish to project. Branding the capital as a tourist destination further creates a need for a positive image to be presented. Graham Hankinson points out that the most enduring elements of a city's brand relate to history, heritage and culture, as they are so pervasive in arts and history education that they can outlast any negative event or publicity. In the case of Cardiff, being both a young capital and a city attempting to revitalise and reinvent itself, I would argue that associating itself with a successful, globally-known British icon is a way of binding these brands together. In so doing, this not only translates the economic, cultural and symbolic capital of BBC Wales' *Doctor Who* onto the city, but also creates an association with the city for anyone who watches the series, especially its fans. John Hannigan discusses this in the context of so-called 'fantasy cities'; he points out that these are sometimes seen as an economic panacea for depressed downtown areas. Although the entirety of Cardiff Bay has not been completely commodified with regard to *Doctor Who*, the promotion and foregrounding of the series (and *Torchwood*, where Cardiff almost always appears as itself in the diegesis) corresponds with what Hannigan notes is the norm in the UK's 'fantasy cities', where community influence is confined to image-making by the corporate partner.[12] Hannigan's concern is predominantly that these fantasy cities are 'undemocratic', in that private corporations control the use of public space, thus commodifying it. The fact that, in this case, the corporate partner is the commercial arm of the public service BBC does complicate the issue, but one could argue that in this instance both partners, Cardiff City Council and BBC Worldwide, have a vested interest in promoting the city brand. The relationship is, therefore, to some extent symbiotic.

This symbiosis also implies that *Doctor Who* is being officially integrated into the landscape and heritage of the area. This is important to note, as the whole of Cardiff Bay is and has been in a state of flux since the turn of the century. The area, originally known as Tiger Bay, was dockland that fell into disrepair after the shipping boom faded, leaving a multicultural, socioeconomically impoverished population that was considered unsafe by the mostly-white Anglophone government.[13] It needed to be 'regenerated' in order to represent and maintain the sort of image that was desired for the city, and that was thought to be conducive for investment.[14] These docklands were hence developed into the glossy waterfront visible today, featuring both the old and new Assembly buildings, the Millennium Centre, the dining and shopping area Mermaid Quay, and five-star St David's hotel and spa, as well as various blocks of luxury flats. All in all, Cardiff Bay presents itself as a modern and prosperous urban environment, completely eradicating any sign of its impoverished past. Even the few scattered nautical monuments have a connection to Cardiff that is tenuous at best.[15] The only cultural centre that relates at all to the area's past is located in Butetown, to the northwest of the area, and this is neither highly visible nor well signposted.[16] In short, it is unlikely that a casual visitor to this area would have any idea of its pre-millennial past.

Complicating matters further is the location upon which both the 'Experience' and the nearby BBC Wales Drama Village have been constructed. Part of an overall development of 'waste ground', the area has been named Porth Teigr – Welsh for Tiger Bay (see *Figure 1*).

As can be seen in *Figure 1*, nowhere in the informational text is there any mention of either the past history of the docklands or even that the area used to be known as Tiger Bay. One could also argue that the use of the Welsh term is an attempt to connect the landscape, including Roath Lock Studios and the '*Doctor Who* Experience', to Welsh heritage (something often linguistically-based),[17] and to insulate it against any 'unsavoury' past associations linked to Tiger Bay. Welshness, of course, is a complex concept in and of itself, featuring multiple iterations,[18] but, as the Anglophone South East has been politically- and socially-dominant since the nineteenth century, economically successful, Welsh-made Anglophone *Doctor Who* supports the particular iteration of Welsh identity that Cardiff wishes to express; prosperous and modern, even

Fig. 1. Display boards on the path to the *Doctor Who* Experience.

though it completely ignores much of its own past. This is very much a case, I would argue, of officially 'forgetting' unpleasant or problematic parts of history in favour of remembering only what is useful for the particular image one wants to project.[19]

The other side of this symbiotic relationship is that it grants to *Doctor Who* (and, by extension, everything produced at the Drama Village) a connection to Wales. As noted above, Cardiff is a young capital trying to avoid the stereotypical representations often forced upon it, and so aims to re-present itself as a modern, trendy city ripe for investment. Therefore, while the likes of Porth Teigr's development erase 'unhelpful' portions of the past, they simultaneously create a new present by tying into television texts, fandom, and the '*Doctor Who* Experience'. *Doctor Who* is a flagship programme with a global reach that is, at the same time, inextricably bound to the United Kingdom; by promoting Cardiff as the 'home' of the series, the desired city brand (that of modern, glossy and successful) can be reinforced. *Doctor Who* is perhaps also given an on-brand quirk of eccentricity by this regional association: the fact that it is not based in London – as might be expected, and as was historically the case – reinforces its capacity to stand out as 'different', especially in the United States marketplace.

This relationship between city and programme brand brings me now to interactions between the Cardiff/*Who* symbiosis, of which the 'Experience' is a large part, and fandom. Fan visitors can include both those fans living in Cardiff (Hills's 'fan residents') and those who travel to see the city (fan tourists). As Robert Maitland points out, however, the line between tourist and resident is not always clear-cut, especially in the case of capital cities; residents often engage in tourist practices when visiting areas that are not part of their normal routine.[20] As Cardiff Bay is a centre for shopping, dining, governmental business, and cultural activities, apart from those who work in the area or who reside in its luxury flats, the Bay is not necessarily a routine place for residents to visit. As such, the area is predominantly a tourist zone, or 'tourist bubble',[21] something that has a number of implications. Tourist bubbles confine tourism and its associated economic gain to one main area. The image of the city then becomes significantly skewed towards that semiotically generated in and by the bubble; a sort of synecdoche noted by Maitland.[22] In the case of Cardiff, this excludes not only Tiger Bay's multicultural, economically-deprived past but also the city's present-day impoverished areas. Due to such absences, the semiotic thickness of Cardiff (Bay) is in danger of being whittled away.

Cult Geography and Fan Cooperation

The creation of this tourist bubble also has implications for how fan audiences interact with 'cult geography', in other words publicly-accessible locations where *Doctor Who* has been filmed.[23] Since the series returned in 2005, Cardiff has become a common destination for *Who* fans. Multiple websites feature lists and maps of filming locations (for example Doctor Who: The Locations Guide and Visit Cardiff)[24] in order to aid the research often undertaken by cult media fans engaging in fan tourism. Unlike Vancouver, say, where tour companies have specialised in location tours since the *X-Files* filmed there, there is only one (London-based) company that runs bus tours in Cardiff, Brit Movie Tours, which began doing so in 2010.[25] Up until that point, tours had been a predominantly fan-generated affair, although the BBC released a free, web-distributed tour guide in August 2012 featuring the voice of Arthur Darvill[26] (Rory Williams), and the 'Up Close' exhibition carried maps that were sold for 20p. The 'Experience' also offers a tour map – albeit in the back of its significantly more expensive brochure – which is captioned 'The Experience Continues... A guide to *Doctor Who* filming locations in and around Cardiff Bay'. Decisions as to which sites to visit and interact with, however, remain up to the fans themselves. Having said that, I would argue that the 'Experience' alters fans' agency in relation to cult geography, even while giving the appearance of greater access.

In order to explain this, I must first discuss typical fan interactions with the text of *Doctor Who*. While the degree to which a text, its producers, or its fans create meaning is of course open to argument,[27] as noted by both Hills and Beattie,[28] fans' projection of diegetic space into relevant real-world sites often anchors their interpretation of filming locations. This supports the affective play that fans engage in when visiting locations, as they knowingly blur the boundaries between physical and diegetic space. This playful reading of geography can be carried out predominantly by fans (for example the memorial dedicated to *Torchwood* character Ianto Jones, which was ultimately incorporated into Mermaid Quay[29]) or by a combination of fans and authorities (governmental, *Doctor Who*-related, or both). If these readings are opposed, then counter-histories develop.[30] But if the preferred reading of the authorities is more-or-less shared by fans, then cult geography can be somewhat incorporated into official meanings surrounding a cultural site – in this case helping to erase Cardiff Bay's impoverished past and relegating it to the status of oppositional counter-history.

In addition to denying (metaphorical) access to the Bay's past, commodification also channels and controls present-day access for fans. Both the BBC's recorded tour of filming locations and the Brit Movie Tours's package follow set routes in a set order, offering either Arthur Darvill's voice as a guide, or both a physical tour-guide and transportation.[31] This is a very different experience to walking around Cardiff on one's own (or with other fans); although there may be a certain degree of hierarchy in fan-based groups (such as a fan-resident or frequent fan-tourist being relied upon for directions), in most cases interpretation from 'above' would not occur. Fan-based tours also call for far less economic capital than professional commercial events, while even the BBC's fan (public) service tour requires an mp3 player or other audio device.

Furthermore, in addition to commodified cult geography placing constraints upon fans' movements, the 'Experience' only sells a specific, limited form of access. Despite being next door to Roath Lock Studios, and implicitly trading on its symbolic closeness to *Doctor Who*'s real-world production, the 'Experience' plays on 'the auratic expectations that a media location conventionally has'[32] for fans while generally offering nearness-without-access. The BBC Drama Village itself, despite being visible from publicly-accessible vantage points in the Bay, remains fenced off and inaccessible; much like the exhibits in the third section of the 'Experience', one can see but not touch.[33] The constructed crossing over – 'inhabiting the world' of *Who* as one passes through the viewing screen – is highly circumscribed, following much the same lines as fan–producer relationships where certain websites are granted a degree of access only in order to control what information is released.[34] Fans can buy a controlled proximity to *Doctor Who*, but in so doing they are firmly placed as consumers rather than producers:[35] denied entry to the media world (of TV production) they are instead led by 'commercial logic into looking on as a tourist'.[36]

Despite this, the Porth Teigr location of the 'Experience' also sustains its symbolic closeness to *Doctor Who* in another way. For example, when travelling to the 'Experience', one constantly passes by or through various filming locations. The first of these, for those coming into Cardiff by rail, appears at Cardiff Central. The station itself was a filming location for 'Boom Town' (2005) but also, in the summer of 2012, featured adverts for the 'Experience' on its ticket barriers. Thus, one of the first things one would see upon arrival in Cardiff was a filming location plastered with commercials for a *Who*-based site. Once one arrived in Cardiff Bay, this intertwining of commodified and non-commodified cult geography only increased. Though only the Oval Basin and '*Torchwood* Tower' have appeared in the series as themselves ('Boom Town', 'Utopia', 'Last of the Time Lords', and 'The Stolen Earth'), the two main walking routes from either the Oval Basin or the Red Dragon Centre pass the Millennium Centre ('New Earth', and 'Vincent and the Doctor'), the New Assembly building ('The Lazarus Project') and the Atradius Building ('Rose' and 'The Runaway Bride'). The fan-visitor is likely to be interacting imaginatively with cult geography even before he or she arrives at the 'Experience' itself. Ironically, then, *fans' non-commodified affective play as they travel through Cardiff Bay actually provides part of the value and logic of the commodified 'Experience'*. The fact that Cardiff's filming locations can be freely wandered around does not damage the *'Doctor Who* Experience' as a commercial proposition; rather, its proximity to these spaces and places – 'The Experience Continues', as its brochure says – means that fans effectively cooperate in positioning the walk-through/exhibition as auratic. Fans' agency is not quite reduced by this commodification, but nor is it strictly co-opted; instead playful fan experience adds value to the 'Experience'.

The *'Doctor Who* Experience' thus reinforces fans' anchoring of the diegetic to the physical world, developing 'new relations between reality and fiction' as 'transformative capabilities of pairing fandom and the mundane' (for example Cardiff City Council and BBC Worldwide) are highlighted.[37] Such implicit collaboration, where fans are just as invested in reading and re-circulating the *Who*/Cardiff symbiosis as BBC Worldwide or council authorities – albeit for different reasons and through differing practices – maintains Cardiff's identity as the 'home of *Doctor Who*'. Fans in Cardiff, tourists and residents alike, constantly engage with both city and programme brands, as well as with the combinatorial '*Doctor Who*-ishness' of the city.

Conclusion

This chapter has examined the role played by the '*Doctor Who* Experience' in the commodification of Cardiff Bay. What I have shown is that matters are more complex than a simple binding of city and programme brands, or attempts to make money from fan activity by BBC Worldwide (its commercial enterprises ex-nominated by connotations of 'worldwide' reach and inclusivity). Instead, it is the 'cooperative transformation' played out by authorities (here governmental/broadcasting/corporate) *and* 'fans and citizens'[38] that results in the prioritising of a particular, selective image of the city, infused with and reinforced by associations with *Doctor Who*. That image, however, is presented and reproduced at the expense of elements of the city's heritage that have been deemed unhelpful, like its multicultural, impoverished past, or overly complex, like multiple iterations of Welsh identity. More than simply a matter of whose pockets are lined by tourism, it is finally a question of whose – *Who*'s – cultural–geographical meanings are disseminated, reinforced or silenced.

NOTES

1. Visit Cardiff, 'The home of *Doctor Who*', (2012), available at: http://www.visitcardiff.com/the-home-of-doctor-who, accessed 1 June 2013.
2. Hankinson, Graham, 'Location branding: a study of the branding practices of 12 English cities', *Journal of Brand Management*, iv/2 (2001), pp. 127–42; Hankinson, Graham, 'The brand images of tourism destinations: a study of the saliency of organic images', *Journal of Product Brand Management* xiii/1 (2004), pp. 6–14; Hankinson, Graham, 'The management of destination brands: Five guiding principles based on recent developments in corporate branding theory', *Journal of Brand Management*, xiv/3 (2007), pp. 240–54; Maitland, Robert, 'Tourism and changing representation in Europe's historic capitals', *Rivista di Scienze del Turismo* (2010), pp. 103–20.
3. There has been an even longer history of such exhibitions elsewhere, of course. Over the years, Blackpool, Longleat and Llangollen have all hosted significant *Who* exhibitions, while Longleat was also infamously home to the 1983 event '*Doctor Who* – A Celebration: Twenty Years of a Time Lord'.
4. '*Doctor Who* exhibit opens to fans in Cardiff', *BBC News* (20 July 2012), available online at: http://www.bbc.co.uk/news/uk-wales-18,900040, accessed 1 June 2013; Foster, Chuck, 'Cardiff exhibition closes', *Dr Who News* (27 March 2011), available online at http://www.doctorwhonews.net/2011/03/dwn270311135508-cardiff-exhibition.html, accessed 1 June 2013.

THE '*DOCTOR WHO* EXPERIENCE' (2012–)

5   Experience Design, 'Up Close', *Experience Design* (2009) available online at http://www.experiencedesign.co.uk/#/ATTRACTIONS-04-09/, accessed 1 June 2013.
6   Foster: 'Cardiff exhibition closes.'
7   Ibid.
8   Bukatman, Scott, 'Zooming out: the end of offscreen space' in J. Lewis (ed.), *The New American Cinema* (Duke University Press, Durham, 1998), p. 266.
9   Hills, Matt (2012), Personal communication.
10 Doctor Who Team, 'A town called Cardiff', *BBC.co.uk* (30 August 2012), available online at: http://www.bbc.co.uk/blogs/doctorwho/articles/A-Town-Called-Cardiff, accessed 1 June 2013.
11 Maitland: 'Tourism and changing representation in Europe's historic capitals', pp. 104–5.
12 Hannigan, John, 'Symposium on branding, the entertainment economy and urban place building: Introduction,' *International Journal of Urban and Regional Research* xxvii/2 (2003), pp. 352–60.
13 Cowell, Richard and Thomas, Huw, 'Managing nature and narratives of dispossession: Reclaiming territory in Cardiff Bay', *Urban Studies* xxxix/7 (2002), p. 1245.
14 Hall, Tim, *Urban Geography* (Routledge, London, 1998); Cowell and Thomas: 'Managing nature and narratives of dispossession: Reclaiming territory in Cardiff Bay'; Carless, Tonia, 'Reclaiming public space: A critical architecture', *Proceedings of the Conference held at the University of Brighton* (2–4 July 2009); Dicks, Bella, *Culture on Display: The Production of Contemporary Visitability* (Open University Press, Maidenhead, 2003).
15 Dicks: *Culture on Display: The Production of Contemporary Visitability*, pp. 84–8.
16 Ibid., pp. 84–8.
17 See Knowles, Anne Kelly, 'Migration, nationalism, and the construction of Welsh identity', in G. H. Herb and D. H. Kaplan (eds), *Nested Identities: Nationalism, Territory and Scale* (Rowman and Littlefield, Oxford 1999), pp. 289–316.
18 Dicks, Bella, *Heritage, Place and Community* (University of Wales Press, Cardiff, 2000); Smith, Anthony, *Nationalism and Modernism: A Critical Survey of Recent Theories of Nations and Nationalism* (Routledge, London, 1998); Kumar, Krishan, *The Making of English National Identity* (Cambridge University Press, Cambridge, 2003); Delanty, Gerard and O'Mahoney, Patrick, *Nationalism and Social Theory* (Sage, London, 2002); Knowles: 'Migration, nationalism, and the construction of Welsh identity', p. 289; Blandford, Steve, *Film, Drama and the Break-Up of Britain* (Intellect, Bristol, 2007); Fevre, Ralph and Thompson, Andrew, 'Social theory and Welsh identities' in R. Fevre and A. Thompson (eds), *Nation, Identity & Social Theory: Perspectives from Wales* (University of Wales Press, Cardiff, 1999), pp. 3–24.
19 Anderson, Benedict, *Imagined Communities*, Second Edition, (Verso, London, 2010).
20 Maitland, Robert, 'Introduction: National capitals and city tourism', in R. Maitland and B. W. Richie (eds), *City Tourism: National Capital Perspectives* (CABI, Wallingford, 2009), pp. 7–8.

21 Hannigan: 'Symposium on branding, the entertainment economy and urban place building: Introduction'.
22 Maitland: 'Introduction: National capitals and city tourism'.
23 Hills, Matt, *Fan Cultures* (Routledge, London & New York, 2002), pp. 144–57.
24 See http://www.doctorwholocations.net/ and http://www.visitcardiff.com/, accessed 1 June 2013.
25 Marcus, '*Doctor Who* tour' (28 April 2010) Available at http://www.doctorwhonews.net/2010/04/doctor-who-tour.html, accessed 1 June 2013; see also Porter, Lynnette, *The Doctor Who Franchise: American Influence, Fan Culture and the Spinoffs* (McFarland, Jefferson, 2012), pp. 26–7.
26 See http://www.bbc.co.uk/thingstodo/walks, accessed 1 June 2013.
27 See Fiske, John, *Television Culture* (Routledge, London, 1987); Jenkins, Henry, *Textual Poachers: Television Fans and Participatory Culture* (Routledge, London, 1992); Jenkins, Henry, *Convergence Culture: Where Old and New Media Collide* (NYU Press, London, 2006); Tulloch, John and Jenkins, Henry, *Science Fiction Audiences: Watching Doctor Who and Star Trek* (Routledge, London, 1995); Abercrombie, Nicholas and Longhurst, Brian J., *Audiences* (Sage, London, 1998); Tulloch, John, *Watching Television Audiences: Cultural Theories & Methods* (Arnold, London, 2000); Hills: *Fan Cultures*; Sandvoss, Cornell, *Fans: The Mirror of Consumption* (Polity, Cambridge, 2005); and Zubernis, Lynn and Larsen, Katherine, *Fandom at the Crossroads: Celebration, Shame and Fan/Producer Relationships* (CSP, Newcastle, 2010), among many others.
28 Hills: *Fan Cultures*, pp. 104–6, Beattie, Melissa, 'A most peculiar memorial: Cultural heritage and fiction', in J. Schofield (ed.), *Who Needs Experts? Counter-Mapping Cultural Heritage* (Ashgate, Aldershot, 2013).
29 Beattie: 'A most peculiar memorial'.
30 See Fiske: *Television Culture*; Jenkins: *Textual Poachers*, *Convergence Culture: Where Old and New Media Collide*.
31 In the summer of 2013, the '*Doctor Who* Experience' in fact began offering its own 'Walking Tour' where paying customers were accompanied by a physical Tour Guide working to a script prepared by Gary Russell. This tour was seemingly timed to coincide with the UK's school summer holidays, forming part of a commercial strategy to maximize revenue from holidaying families.
32 Couldry, Nick, 'On the set of *The Sopranos*: "Inside" a fan's construction of nearness' in J. Gray, C. Sandvoss and C. Lee Harrington (eds), *Fandom: Identities and Communities in a Mediated World* (New York University Press, New York, 2007), p. 146.
33 Along with the 'Walking Tour', BBC Worldwide also sold tickets for a 'TARDIS Set Tour' in the summer of 2013. For a limited time only (again coinciding with the UK's school summer holiday period), paying fans were escorted around the permanent TARDIS set in Roath Lock's Studio 4, although the TARDIS console itself was roped off and visitors were, indeed, warned not to touch it.
34 See Johnson, Catherine, *Telefantasy* (BFI, London, 2005); Murray, Simone, '"Celebrating the story the way it is": Cultural studies, corporate media and the contested utility of fandom', *Continuum* xviii/1 (2004), pp. 7–25;

Théberge, Paul, 'Everyday fandom: Fan clubs, blogging, and the quotidian rhythms of the Internet', *Canadian Journal of Communication* xxx/4 (2005), available at http://www.cjc-online.ca/index.php/journal/article/view/1673/1810, accessed 1 June 2013; Perren, Alisa, 'Acafandom and beyond: Week two, part one', (29 August 2011) available at: http://henryjenkins.org/2011/08/aca-fandom_and_beyond_jonathan.html, accessed 1 June 2013; Zubernis and Larsen: *Fandom at the Crossroads: Celebration, Shame and Fan/Producer Relationships*.

35 *Contra* the emphasis in fan studies on fans-as-producers; see, for example, the arguments of McKee, Alan, 'How to tell the difference between production and consumption: A case study in *Doctor Who* fandom' in S. Gwenllian-Jones and R. E. Pearson (eds), *Cult Television* (University of Minnesota Press, Minneapolis, 2004), pp. 167–86.
36 Couldry: 'On the set of *The Sopranos*', p. 145
37 Hoskinson, Katie, 'Escape to ambiguity: The *Twilight* fan's playground' in G. Schott and K. Moffat (eds), *Fanpires: Audience Consumption of the Modern Vampire* (New Academia Publishing, Washington, 2011), p. 199
38 Ibid.

10

REMEMBERING SARAH JANE
Intradiegetic Allusions, Embodied Presence/Absence and Nostalgia

Ross P. Garner

Since its successful return, *Doctor Who* (BBC 2005–) has regularly acknowledged what has become known as its 'classic' incarnation that ran on British television between 1963 and 1989. The re-launched series has, for example, retained its 'structuring *icons* such as the Daleks, the TARDIS and above all the Doctor himself,' while other monsters such as the Autons and the Silurians have been granted reappearances.[1] At the same time, on special occasions, actors associated with iconic roles from the classic series, such as Peter Davison's fifth Doctor and Nicholas Courtney's (now knighted) Brigadier Lethbridge-Stewart, have reappeared across *Doctor Who*'s 'three distinct continents' that included spin-off series *Torchwood* (BBC 2006–) and *The Sarah Jane Adventures* (BBC 2007–11).[2] However, in terms of human characters from 'classic *Who*' returning to its post-2005 incarnation, none have been as prominent as Sarah Jane Smith (played by Elisabeth Sladen). Sarah Jane first appeared in *Doctor Who* in the 1973 story 'The Time Warrior' as companion to Jon Pertwee's third

Doctor and stayed with the programme until 'The Hand of Fear' in 1976, appearing in many of the stories that fans believe make up the 'golden age' of the programme during the mid-1970s.[3] The character then returned to the series 30 years later in the episode 'School Reunion' (2006) before making appearances in series four finale 'The Stolen Earth/Journey's End' (2008) and having a cameo role in 'The End of Time, Part Two' (2009). What's more, Sarah Jane also found renewed popularity with a younger audience via *The Sarah Jane Adventures*, which ran for five series on CBBC (the BBC's outlet for children's television) until Elisabeth Sladen's unexpected passing in 2011.[4]

Sarah Jane clearly holds a position of continuing affection within *Doctor Who* fandom, as she regularly appears in fan-produced lists of favourite ever companions,[5] and when the character's return in 'School Reunion' was announced then extratextual fan discourses approached the episode as the reappearance of 'pretty much [the] Officially Best Companion Ever'.[6] However, beyond the immediate fan community Sarah Jane's return was highlighted by wider press discourses as a key point in promoting the episode,[7] suggesting that the character has become part of generational and/or televisual popular memory by becoming linked to 'the more dominant perceptions of [television – RPG] history that circulate in a society'.[8] Given Sarah Jane's positioning as part of a 'golden age' of *Doctor Who* in both fan and popular discourses, and that 'key tropes to nostalgic rhetoric are the notion of a Golden Age and a subsequent Fall',[9] it could be argued that the character's return would be a prime target for nostalgia. This certainly seemed to be the case when considering audience responses to 'School Reunion', since nostalgia was a term regularly drawn upon by fans to describe their feelings towards the episode.[10] However, such responses are interesting as Sarah Jane's initial characterisation in both 'School Reunion' and 'Invasion of the Bane' (2007) – the pilot episode of *The Sarah Jane Adventures* – hardly constructs her nostalgically: in 'School Reunion' the structuring of characters[11] does not subscribe to the favouring of past over present that is intrinsic to feeling nostalgic.[12] Instead 'the present', as represented by Rose (Billie Piper), is regularly seen as equal to 'the past' (Sarah Jane), therefore undercutting a potential discourse of nostalgia within the episode.[13] Moreover, the characterisation of Sarah Jane in 'Invasion of the Bane' initially positions her unsympathetically, as a loner who visually connotes a 'retro' sensibility, most obviously through the car she drives and the design of her computer Mr Smith (voiced by Alexander Armstrong).

The first aim of this chapter is to account for how, and why, audiences would become nostalgic about the return of Sarah Jane to the diegetic world of *Doctor Who* in 2006. What exactly was it that stimulated feelings of nostalgia among audiences watching 'School Reunion'? To answer this question involves first considering something that TV studies has had little to say about, and that is how the return of a character to a diegetic world might be theorised at the level of the text. Through engaging with theories of intertextuality, and extending Ian Gordon's analysis of *Lois and Clark: The New Adventures of Superman* (ABC 1993–7), I argue that the return of a character to a diegetic world can be considered what I am terming an 'intradiegetic allusion', since it is a reference to a programme's past within its present.[14] As will become evident, however, the concept of intradiegetic allusions requires refining to consider why audiences would become nostalgic about the return of Sarah Jane *specifically* instead of other allusions within the new series of *Doctor Who*. To do this, I argue that the key differential was the *embodied presence* of Elisabeth Sladen reprising the role she had left 30 years earlier. The final part of this chapter then reflects upon reactions to Sladen's death and considers why, again, the loss of her embodied presence resulted in further expressions of nostalgia among *Doctor Who* fans. This section draws upon Anthony Giddens's work on ontological security,[15] and discussions of this concept in relation to television,[16] to support my arguments and explore links between nostalgia, mourning and identity. Here I argue that fans negotiated the anxiety caused by Sladen's passing by nostalgically recalling memories of her from their individual pasts.

Using discussions of intertextuality to theorise the return of a character makes it, as Graham Allen notes,[17] inevitable that the following discussion will intersect with theories of postmodernism, and this is doubly the case when discussing nostalgia since Fredric Jameson has been the key writer on this concept within postmodern theory.[18] However, rather than subscribe to Jameson's position, this chapter instead responds to Janet Staiger's call for increased consideration of the 'functions of cognition and affect for the reading subject who experiences' intertextuality.[19] What this means, then, is that closer attention should be given to how processes of intertextuality operate for audiences. This is because, as Staiger suggests,[20] recognising allusions within a text may also cue affective responses in audience members, such as stimulating nostalgic feelings in the case of Sarah Jane's return. Through considering such affective responses from audiences, and the importance of embodied presence in the stimulus of nostalgic feelings, this chapter argues against some of Jameson's more extreme takes on postmodern society, such as the 'waning of affect' and po-mo 'schizophrenia'.[21] However, before engaging in these wider discussions, it is first necessary to consider how the return of a television character to a diegetic world can be thought about at the level of the text.

'Bringing Something Back'

As many discussions of television drama form agree,[22] '[u]sing key characters and locations week after week is [...] standard in television'[23] since regular characters provide 'familiarity and identification' for audiences during their tenure on that programme.[24] However, little academic attention has been paid to what happens when a character *returns* to the on-going diegesis of a programme after a period of absence. Some academic work mentions this concept but it has not been properly theorised. For example, Dorothy Hobson touches upon the idea of 'bringing something back' at an institutional and promotional level by considering press discourses surrounding the return of a programme for a new series.[25] She states that press coverage usually focuses upon the core elements of a returning programme so as to (re)familiarise audiences with its premise and, in turn, follow the norms of television journalism through highlighting the unique characteristics of that particular show.[26] This journalistic focus was arguably identifiable in the discourses surrounding Sarah Jane's return, since the character was singled out as *Doctor Who*'s 'best ever companion'. Yet discussion of the return of a *character* to a *programme* remains absent from Hobson's study.

On the rare occasions that the return of a character has been mentioned within academic work, such discussions have avoided considering this in relation to the text, since such returns are either glossed over as 'retro, TV-based continuity',[27] or devalued through the use of commercially-focused ratings discourses. Of course, there is nothing to say that Sarah Jane's reintroduction in 'School Reunion' could not be read as an attempt to secure viewers for *Doctor Who*'s second series[28] or for *The Sarah Jane Adventures*.[29] However, subscribing to such readings means that any consideration of how a returning character affects the text, and audiences' responses to that character's return, remains absent.

Yet work on soap operas and contemporary 'quality'/cult television offers starting points for thinking about how the return of a character may impact upon the text. Soap opera criticism has long recognised that when a character leaves the programme it does not necessarily mean they will never return to the diegesis; the potential for a character's return assists the future-orientated focus of the soap's 'continuous serial' narrative.[30] Arrivals and departures of characters in a soap opera, however, result in the programme accruing considerable back-story, which leaves '[t]he serial [...] operating in a situation in which it must be accessible to all viewers while, at the same time, be accurate about its own accumulated past'.[31] The same has also been said about recent 'quality' and cult TV shows since these forms have been discussed in similar terms, generating detailed programme histories which individual viewers will display different levels of familiarity with.[32] In both instances, then, the same tension occurs. While an on-going serial is expected to satisfy its dedicated audience through narrative and character consistency, this consistency should not come at the expense of alienating casual viewers via constant reference to events and characters from past episodes.[33] *Doctor Who* provides a good example of this on-going tension between continuity and wider audience accessibility, since it has often been noted that, from the late 1970s onwards, the programme broadcast 'stories that required detailed fan knowledge' due to the production team responding to fans' desire for greater continuity between stories.[34]

While these discussions are useful for identifying the 'burden' that a serial's past may carry for its production team, textual analysis of how the past is handled (formally and representationally) remains absent.[35] An exception to this tendency, and a way into considering how a programme's past may impact upon its present, can be located in the analysis of *Lois and Clark* provided by Ian Gordon. Gordon notes how *Lois and Clark* 'appealed to audiences for whom Superman['s ...] many guises [...] were familiar figures', observing how the series' producers drew upon preceding versions of the Superman narrative, such as films, comic books and television series, as a way of activating audience memories and drawing a variety of age-based demographics to the programme.[36] By designating these aspects of the text 'nostalgic references', Gordon's study suggests a way in which the return of Sarah Jane to *Doctor Who* can be textually analysed.[37]

'Nostalgic References' as Intradiegetic Allusions

Gordon's use of 'nostalgic' refers to the postmodern Jamesonian understanding of the term.[38] Through noting elements as 'references', Gordon introduces the concept of intertextuality as a way of discussing the appearance of a text's past within its present. It should be recalled, though, that the narrative form of *Lois and Clark* differs to new *Doctor Who*: while *Lois and Clark* used intertextuality to reference *previous incarnations* of Superman, *retelling* the story for a modern audience, new *Doctor Who* constitutes a *continuation* of the on-going narrative that started onscreen in 1963. New *Doctor Who* is therefore more in line with the continuous narrative form associated with soap operas, since the series regularly references its past. These references occur in a variety of ways, ranging from the reintroduction of classic characters such as Davros (Julian Bleach), the Daleks and, indeed, Sarah Jane, to more subtle citations of past stories such as the Doctor mentioning the London Underground to the villainous Great Intelligence in 'The Snowmen' (2012).

Thus, while both *Doctor Who* and *Lois and Clark* draw upon the 'citationism' of intertextuality,[39] there are differences between the types of intertextuality displayed by these programmes. Although the use of intertextuality in both shows highlights 'notions of relationality, interconnectedness and interdependence [between texts – RPG] in modern cultural life,'[40] *inter*textuality focuses upon 'the relationship between a text and *other texts and discourses*' (my emphasis).[41] What this means, then, is that a key assumption behind the theory of intertextuality is that a text refers *outwards* to another text or to the 'world of texts'. This assumption holds for the example of *Lois and Clark*, as it refers outwards to previous versions of the Superman story. However, the continuous narrative structure adopted by *Doctor Who* means that character returns function as an *internal reference to the history of that text*. Matt Hills has noted such intertextuality in relation to the horror movie franchise *Scream* (1996, 1997, 2000), calling it instead '*intra*textuality'[42] (my emphasis) since 'audience knowledge of the [...]

franchise itself [...] comes to supplant audience knowledge of [a world of texts such as] 1970s/80s stalker films'.[43] However, the term intratextuality has been deployed elsewhere to refer to internal character consistency within a narrative.[44] As a result, I would argue that explicit reference to a series' past within a continuous narrative structure – for example the return of Sarah Jane to *Doctor Who* – should be specified as an 'intradiegetic allusion' since it is a direct reference to *that text's past within its present*, instead of an outward reference to another text.[45]

Some TV studies' academics, for instance Charlotte Brunsdon, view intradiegetic allusions as 'displaying a slightly panicky self-cannibalism [...] recycl[ing] fragments of old programmes' which, in this case, would involve 'self-cannibalising' the history of *Doctor Who*.[46] This line of argument leads back to the intersection of intertextuality with postmodernism, and the work of Fredric Jameson. Jameson noted the rise, in 1970s Hollywood cinema, of 'the moment of pastiche in which energetic artists who now lack both forms and content cannibalise the museum and wear the masks of extinct mannerisms'.[47] It is here that Ian Gordon's use of the term 'nostalgic' becomes relevant.[48] This is because Jameson argues that the 'cannibalisation' of old forms to produce new texts is representative of a 'contemporary "nostalgia" culture [... of] pastiche which, in a category mistake that confuses content with form, sets out to reinvent the style, not of an art language, but of a whole period'.[49] This 'nostalgia culture' has arisen due to the (post)modern world that contemporary subjects inhabit, since Jameson believes that instead of being able to 'cognitively map' – or comprehend and articulate their social and historical milieu in textual form – subjects represent it through characters and genres lifted from the past.[50] Hence why Gordon deemed *Lois and Clark* 'nostalgic' since it combines elements of past versions of its source material to create a postmodern Superman narrative.[51]

The negative weighting academics ascribe to Jamesonian nostalgia can be seen in the above attitude of Charlotte Brunsdon, and in Hills's designation of returning TV characters as 'retro' continuity.[52] This negativity stems from the fact that Jameson's argument started as a 'complaint' against forms of cinema[53] where he perceived certain cultural objects to represent a waning of affect.[54] In essence, Jameson's argument relates to his belief that '[a]s capitalism's modernising project evolved, [...] its corresponding intensification of the process of reification' increased.[55] This intensified reification (or emptying out of the traces of human autonomy from cultural artefacts produced under capitalism) leads Jameson to view postmodern cultural objects as affectively 'depthless' when compared to past equivalents.[56] Fred Davis demonstrates Jameson's argument well when discussing 'contemporary nostalgia'.[57] Davis discusses this form of nostalgia through mass media products, and argues that the nostalgia constructed in, say, film and television does not have 'quite the same diversity of reference and individuality of association as do more private forms of memory generated in more private settings'.[58] Akin to Jameson, then, Davis suggests that the nostalgia constructed through popular cultural forms is a reified, waning version of the feeling since it is linked to industrial production rather than to subjective recollection (although exactly how critics might quantitatively or qualitatively differentiate between these affective states remains absent from both arguments).

Such arguments can be applied to the reappearance of Sarah Jane in *Doctor Who*, with the character's return being taken to represent the postmodern inability to conceive new narratives articulated with contemporary experience, or as the failure of producers to create characters responding to the postmodern world. However, grand-theoretical dismissals are less than helpful, leading to key questions regarding intertextuality, cognition, and affect being overlooked.

An unstated assumption guiding theories of intertextuality is that the viewing subject cognitively recognises and interprets intertextual references, thus casting them in the role of 'amateur semiotician'.[59] Intertextual reading practices therefore require audiences to exercise their accumulated cultural knowledge(s); through doing so, their 'symbolic capital' and sense of identity as part of an educated imagined community are subjectively reaffirmed.[60] In the case of intradiegetic allusions, then, such pleasures stem from recognising that one belongs to an imagined community of knowledgeable fans. This is because, as Barbara Klinger argues, '[w]atching a film or other media text inevitably brings into play innumerable variables drawn from [...] intertextual zones'[61] and, as previous work on *Doctor Who* has shown, one of the key 'intertextual zones' for fandom concerns intradiegetic allusion.[62]

The propensity for fans to read intradiegetically appeared in their responses to 'School Reunion'. While the reappearance of Sarah Jane and K-9 constituted the most obvious intradiegetic allusions in the episode, fans nonetheless recognised other potential references to *Doctor Who*'s past. For instance, the school location was seen as a potential allusion to the location of both 'An Unearthly Child' (1963),[63] the very first *Doctor Who* episode, and the 1988 story 'Remembrance of the Daleks'.[64] Similarly, Matt Michael saw Sarah Jane and K-9's departure at the end of the episode as reminiscent of the closing scene of 'Survival' (1989), the last *Doctor Who* story before its cancellation.[65]

Fans' tendency to read for intradiegetic allusions seems to support Barbara Klinger's assertion that when reading texts 'autobiography [...] outweighs the power of language to control and shape the reader's thoughts'.[66] Klinger calls attention here to the role that personal memory and affect may play in relation to intertextuality and audience interpretation of texts. Lynn Spigel has noted that 'the comparative nature of memory [...] calls for a dialogue between past and present,' and recognising intertextual references similarly involves negotiation between the text being read in the present and those previously encountered in the past.[67] Since negotiation between 'past' and 'present' lies at the centre of feeling nostalgic, linking this idea to fans' propensity to read for intradiegetic allusions suggests that such allusions open up a space for the fan audience to become nostalgic about affective attachments to *Doctor Who*. Sara Gwenllian Jones has argued that serialised narrative plays a central role in establishing and maintaining the links that fans have with their object of fandom,[68] and likewise intradiegetic allusions open up spaces where dedicated viewers can affectively negotiate their on-going relationship with a serial.

So far, this essay has demonstrated that consideration of 'bringing a character back' to a television series has been relatively overlooked within TV studies. Explicit references to a continuing serial's past can be theorised textually as intradiegetic allusions. Such allusions rely on, and satisfy, the fan inclination to read intradiegetically and facilitate the affective negotiation of fans' commitment to 'their' programme. However, such questions as 'why would audiences become nostalgic about the return of Sarah Jane specifically?' and 'why might the same ideas not also apply to the return of the Autons or the Daleks?' remain unexplored. The next section addresses these questions.

Embodied Presence, or Why Sarah Jane?

The serial nature of (cult) television programmes has been seen as an important factor contributing to the affective attachment of audiences.

Within on-going narratives, TV studies has further recognised that '[t]he constant repetition of a character means that characters "live" in similar time scales to their audience',[69] helping to create the impression that fictional narrative time runs parallel to that experienced by the viewer and so 'intensif[ying] the audience's imaginative engagement with the cult text'.[70] While such an assumption is slightly complicated by the use of cliff-hanger endings that freeze narrative time between episodes, seriality has nevertheless been seen as important to the appeal of cult shows and mainstream soaps.

However, an additional aspect of television characters' appeal stems from the actors who embody them.[71] It has regularly been argued that, in television drama, the character takes primacy over the actor (unlike film stardom where the reverse is supposedly true). Yet it still seems that part of the audience appeal of TV characters strongly relates to the actors who play them.[72] This is especially so for cult television series since, as Ina Rae Hark notes of the *Star Trek* films that featured the original cast, actors from the original *Trek* had 'become practically welded to their characters by the show's cult status and numerous [...] conventions'.[73] Thus, if cult TV intensifies the bond between character and actor for fans, I would argue that the return of an actor provides just as much stimulus to nostalgic sentiment as does their returning character. An actor reprising his or her role also emphasises the passing of (extra-)diegetic time, as the ageing body of the performer – in this instance Elisabeth Sladen as Sarah Jane – affects nostalgic responses by recognisably, but differentially, embodying the character.[74]

This addresses why fan audiences would become nostalgic about the return of Sarah Jane over and above many other intradiegetic allusions in the world of *Doctor Who*. To start with, consider the references that fans noted between 'School Reunion' and 'An Unearthly Child', 'Remembrance of the Daleks' and 'Survival'.[75] The fact that fans discern these references in 'School Reunion' further supports Klinger's argument that reading positions are established through the autobiography of individual readers. However, from the perspective of nostalgia, the key difference between these allusions and the return of Sarah Jane Smith is that the embodied presence of Elisabeth Sladen reprising her role provides an additional, powerful stimulus to nostalgic feeling. While 'School Reunion' may offer intertextual links to myriad past *Doctor Who* stories, such links do not carry this extra level of embodiment that intensifies nostalgic sentiment. Moreover, the embodied presence of Elisabeth Sladen also provides the differentiating factor between Sarah Jane's return and other intradiegetic allusions within *Doctor Who*, such as returning classic monsters. Although these monsters have retained familiar elements of their iconography, they have all been redesigned to make them appear more 'substantial' and modern than their previous onscreen incarnations.[76] Extratextual discourses surrounding the programme have regularly emphasised aspects of the series' iconography that have been redesigned.[77] This is presumably a method of discouraging audiences from the 'mass camp' reading position that discursively positioned classic *Who* as having wobbly sets and men in rubber suits.[78] However, where monsters are made to carry contemporaneous meanings, Elisabeth Sladen illustrates the nature of human physiology. This means that physical signs of ageing connote a sense of passing time that the programme's redesigned monsters cannot. Indeed, nor can returning but re-cast characters such as the Master and the Doctor, as different (notably younger) actors have been used to play these roles meaning that, again, they lack the embodied presence of original actors. Thus, just as Hills argues that for fans listening to Big Finish audios it is the conserved *textual* form of 'classic' *Who* that stimulates nostalgic sentiments, similarly it is the returning 'form' of Elisabeth Sladen – combined with the sense of past/present time she connotes – that generates nostalgic feelings among (fan) audiences.[79]

The story goes on, however... On the evening of Tuesday 19 April 2011, reports emerged that, at the age of 65, Elisabeth Sladen had passed away after succumbing to cancer. As a point of scholarly enquiry, Sladen's passing raises multiple research issues. These include how memories of the actress were constructed across different media[80] targeting alternative audiences (for example mainstream press obituaries, officially-licensed and unofficial fan publications), how communal mourning practices were performed among *Doctor Who* fans and, given Sarah Jane's popularity with younger generations, how the BBC mobilised its public service responsibilities for protecting children.[81] However, as this essay has focused upon embodied presence and nostalgia, I will consider how fans nostalgically remembered Elisabeth Sladen when embodied presence gave way to tragic absence.[82]

Tears for Sarah Jane: Grief, Ontological Security and Nostalgia

Robert Turnock, examining responses to Diana, Princess of Wales's death, considers the authenticity of audiences' mourning the passing of media figures by asking whether 'people's responses to [... Diana's] death were not specifically grief, but another kind of emotional or psychological response'.[83] The crux of Turnock's argument here is whether 'it [is] possible to grieve over someone that you have never met?'[84] Fan reactions to Elisabeth Sladen's death are more complex, however, as posters to the 'Elisabeth Sladen R.I.P [1946–2011]' thread on Gallifrey Base[85] and comments published in *Doctor Who Magazine* frequently recalled instances where fans had either directly met and formed friendships with Sladen, or had attended one of her public appearances.[86] Reactions to Sladen's death may, on the one hand, be viewed as symbolic of the 'non-reciprocal intimacy [...] which underlines [...] the relationship between fan and star,' but on the other hand reactions to her passing also demonstrate varying levels of proximity to, and perceived intimacy with, the actress due to her long association with *Doctor Who*.[87] Moreover, multiple posters drew upon discourses of grief (whether explicitly or otherwise) when articulating their response to Sladen's death:

> Before the forum collapses under the weight of grief, I have to say what sad news this is, and that my thoughts are with her friends and family.[88]

> A total shock! Devastating news. This has been the hardest Who related news I have ever heard. RIP Elisabeth Sladen.[89]

One way of accounting for these expressions of mourning can be provided by linking Sladen's embodied presence, and then absence, to Anthony Giddens's concept of ontological security. Ontological security arises from the social and historical conditions of contemporary society (what Giddens characterises as 'late' modernity[90]) where:

> ... technological change and industrialisation have changed most humans' significant relations from being primarily face-to-face to being increasingly mediated and dependent on abstract systems of effective management of risks.[91]

In other words, 'modern danger is often impersonal and faceless' as it is linked to geographically- and/or temporally-distant events and locations that people have little or no control over.[92] This results in social subjects being aware of 'perceived threats to the integrity of [...] the individual' on a day-to-day basis but,[93] arising from an 'awareness of risks associated with globalisation',[94] contemporary subjectivity is characterised by a 'changed [...] nature of trust'.[95] Responding to anxieties emerging from a fragmented, dispersed social world, people subsequently mobilise and articulate a coherent self-narrative that enables them to gain reassurance about the world they operate in.[96] Ontological security helps to uphold an individual's sense of basic trust (in the world) and self-coherence since, as Giddens argues:

> [a]ll individuals develop a framework of ontological security of some sort, based on routines of various forms. People handle dangers, and the fears associated with them, in terms of the emotional and behavioural 'formulae' which have come to be part of their everyday behaviour and thought.[97]

Elsewhere, television been theorised as a medium that supports ontological security in that it 'contributes to ordering everyday life, especially in its embeddedness in routines and rituals'.[98] Due to its location within domestic spaces of the home, the familiarity generated through its schedules, and the fact that 'watching confirms, affirms, reaffirms and reinforces that life still goes on as normal',[99] television supports an individual's understanding of – and trust in – the external world.[100] David Tennant's foreword to *Elisabeth Sladen: The Autobiography* demonstrates ontological security's relevance to television and embodied presence. Reflecting upon anxieties felt during his first day as the tenth Doctor, Tennant derives basic reassurance – or Giddens would say, ontological security – from Sladen's embodied presence:

> And there, just across from me and down to my left, a face from my childhood leapt out from among the throng [...] Sarah Jane Smith was quietly leafing through a script and composing herself for the afternoon ahead [...] all I remember is the sense that in that moment someone familiar, someone comforting and someone slightly magical had come to make sure everything was going to be all right.[101]

Tennant's self-narrative emblematises how television 'contributes towards ontological security by representing and reflecting aspects of daily life that are familiar to viewers' as recognising a figure from his childhood allows him to uphold a coherent self-narrative.[102] Sladen's embodied presence eased anxieties 'then' just as it does 'now'.

If the embodied presence of TV actors 'help[s] constitute ontological security [by...] negotiating a continual sense of self',[103] it is unsurprising that the shocking loss of a favoured actor/character would generate feelings of grief among fans. Embodied presence generates ontological security by providing television audiences with 'a sense of co-temporality' since '[c]haracters [...] on television [... operate] like age cohorts [...providing] an awareness of a shared chronology'.[104] Feelings of nostalgia generated by Sladen's return to *Doctor Who* demonstrate this – holding 'a powerful resonance' for fans, and affirming a sense of shared temporal progression.[105] The loss of embodied presence temporarily ruptures ontological security and fans' self-continuity. It is for these reasons, then, that *Doctor Who* fans responded to Sladen's death with expressions of grief; the performer's sudden 'absence [would be] hard to comprehend' for these viewers.[106] As Joanne Garde-Hansen argues about ageing celebrities and personal memory, as the favoured star 'ages, we age, and thus we are reminded of our own mortality'.[107]

However, as well as offering condolences to Elisabeth Sladen's family, fans also articulated nostalgia via childhood memories of watching Sladen:

> Sarah Jane was by far my favourite companion, probably because of her indomitable spirit, which obviously came from Lis herself. Being my mum's age, she was like a second mother to me. My mum always took us on great adventures at home; Lis did this in the realms of time and space.[108]

> One of my earliest memories includes Sarah Jane, a spider, and Jon Pertwee's regeneration – and it's safe to say that since then I have never liked those eight-legged creatures. I wasn't watching these episodes in the 1970s however, but via a video player with my dad in the 90s, yet Sarah Jane was as much a part of my childhood as she was of the generation she originally entertained.[109]

> Awful news, terrible.

> She was my first companion, back in the heady days of the 1970's, and like your first love, or first kiss, you never forget your first companion.

> RIP Liz.[110]

Rebecca Williams has recognised that 'fan reactions to the cessation of fan objects have received little academic attention'.[111] At the same time, Laura Impert and Margaret Rubin have also observed, from the perspective of psychoanalytical practice, that there has been 'scant attention [...] to nostalgia and its relationship to mourning'.[112] Instead, where direct links between nostalgia and loss have occurred, these studies have taken place in disciplines including economics[113] and experimental social psychology.[114] Interpretive issues concerning how nostalgia and mourning interact in terms of constructing self-identity, and the media's role in these processes, have therefore been largely overlooked. Nevertheless, mentions of nostalgia in relation to processes of mourning and identity formation are observable. Elizabeth Hallam and Jenny Hockey recognise that '[d]eath is a phase of transition involving loss and adjustment'[115] and that '[i]f death is regarded as loss, departure or journey – displacements that create distance, either spatial or temporal – memories stand as mediators'.[116] Given that one of nostalgia's contemporary understandings is as a form of remembering that arises in reaction to 'an anxious present', is it not possible that nostalgia overlaps with the grieving process?[117]

The above fan responses allow for associations between nostalgia and death to be explored by returning to the concept of ontological security and arguing that, when faced with anxiety arising from Sladen's embodied absence, fans reacted by reconfiguring their self-narratives via re-appropriating memories of Sladen. For example, the above statements all indicate how the fan object is 'indelibly interwoven with the[ir...] lives and histories' and so contributes to their self-actualisation via narrative construction.[118] Thus, given that '[a] person with a reasonably stable sense of self-identity has a feeling of biographical continuity which she is able to grasp reflexively and [...] communicate to other people',[119] the shock of Sladen's death resulted in fans constructing what Williams names a 'reiteration discourse'.[120] Reiteration discourses occur when the fan object (and the ontological security that it generates) comes under threat and so fans 'reassert their identities, offering stories of how the [object...] impacted upon their lives and [...] revealing large amounts of detail' such as, in this case, memories of childhood and family members.[121] However, this aspect of maintaining self-continuity and ontological security via reiterating the importance of the fan object involves articulating feelings of nostalgia. This is because, as Fred Davis posits in relation to nostalgia's role in maintaining self-identity, 'nostalgia clearly attends [...to ...] pleas for continuity'.[122] Moreover, although not directly mentioning nostalgia, Giddens alludes to attributes associated with the concept when discussing how social subjects re-narrate their self-identity in times of upheaval such as divorce.[123] Reviewing Judith Wallerstein and Sandra Blakeslee's study, which posits that following the breakdown of a marriage a phase of mourning sets in,[124] Giddens argues that a re-narration of the self takes place as subjects reach into past experiences and locate images there that help to construct a 'new self'.[125] The implication is that since nostalgia can be seen as 'a form of idealised remembrance', a new sense of self is forged – and continuity is restored to the subject – by incorporating idealised images of one's past into a reconfigured self-narrative.[126] Garde-Hansen makes a related point when discussing fan memories of Madonna, arguing that '[t]he ability to remember Madonna's early days as a breakthrough act legitimises [...] the fan's [...] identity as a follower over a long period of time'.[127] Fan comments offered in reaction to Sladen's death demonstrate this; reacting to her embodied absence, fans maintained ontological security – and asserted long-term fandom – via nostalgically remembering Elisabeth Sladen's presence in their subjective past(s). Continuity was therefore established between the remembered 'past' and losses of the 'present'. Thus, whereas Sladen's reappearance in *Doctor Who* provoked feelings of nostalgia via her embodied presence, her untimely passing also provoked feelings of nostalgia – only this time in aid of easing anxiety and preserving fans' coherent self-narratives.

Conclusion: Countering Postmodern 'Schizophrenia'

I have considered why audiences of *Doctor Who* became nostalgic about the return of Sarah Jane Smith/Elisabeth Sladen, as well as after the actress's death. I've suggested that the return of a character to the world of a television programme can be considered as an intradiegetic allusion that opens up space for nostalgia to enter into reading positions. However, I have also argued that key to stimulating this nostalgic response was the embodied presence of Elisabeth Sladen playing the same role she left 30 years before. Her returning body displayed physical signs of time passing, yet remained highly recognisable and so supported fans' ontological security. However, while Sladen's return generated feelings of nostalgia among fans, her sudden death in 2011 also generated expressions of nostalgia – albeit for different reasons. Sladen's passing was felt as a rupture to ontological security and, to counter the anxiety caused by this news, fans reiterated their identities by constructing nostalgic childhood memories of watching the actress on TV, thereby managing her loss and maintaining a coherent sense of self.

These arguments concerning nostalgia, embodied presence/absence and temporality indicate a need to return to debates surrounding postmodernism that have lingered across this chapter and so, in closing, I would like to consider how embodied presence/absence may counter one of the defining characteristics of the postmodern: schizophrenia.

According to Fredric Jameson, the postmodern experience involves a decline in any clear historical perspective which, he argues, means 'we seem condemned to seek the historical past through our own pop images and stereotypes about that past'.[128] Jameson's position here ties in with his argument about contemporary 'nostalgia culture', since he posits that as a result of our failure to comprehend or represent the present, cultural objects feed intertextually off images of the past. This then creates a form of 'disorientation'[129] – which Jameson names 'schizophrenia'[130] – as a result of contemporary subjects inhabiting a 'perpetual present' where differences between 'past' and 'present' become indistinguishable.[131] This timey-wimey postmodernist argument could easily be applied to the redesigned Daleks and Cybermen. These monsters seemingly represent the past–present–future temporal collapse that Jameson identifies, since they are 'old' monsters that retain aspects of their past design, but they have also been futuristically updated for present audiences. This blurring of times is especially evident with the 2006 Cybermen, since they were consciously styled with a 1930s art-deco feel to connote the fascistic nature of their diegetic world of origin in 'Rise of the Cybermen'/'The Age of Steel'.[132] Meanwhile, the 2010 Daleks harked back to the brighter colour schemes and bulkier shapes of 1960's movie Daleks, while the theoretical, sociological concept of a 'perpetual present' is directly coded (in science-fictional, diegetic terms) in 'The Wedding of River Song' (2011), perhaps the most Jamesonian *Doctor Who* story ever.

In marked contrast to temporal collapse, however, the embodied presence – and then absence – of Elisabeth Sladen in her role as Sarah Jane Smith helps restore 'the experience of temporality [. . .] the] existential or experiential feeling of time itself' to the postmodern experience, providing an alternative to the 'reified' form of nostalgia that has been perceived as characteristic of po-mo media texts.[133] It appears that through the body, the signs it connotes, and its eventual, sad demise, a way of resisting the perceived impact of the postmodern may be located.

NOTES

1. Britton, Piers D., *TARDISbound: Navigating the Universes of Doctor Who* (I.B.Tauris, London, 2011), p. 26.
2. Perryman, Neil, '*Doctor Who* and the convergence of media: A case study in "transmedia storytelling"', *Convergence: The International Journal of Research into New Media Technologies* xiv/1 (2008), p. 36.
3. See Hills, Matt, '"Gothic" body parts in a "postmodern" body of work? The Hinchcliffe/Holmes era of *Doctor Who* (1975–77)', *Intensities: The Journal of Cult Media* iv/December (2007) available at: http://intensities.org/Essays/Hills.pdf, accessed 2 June 2013. See also McKee, Alan, 'Which is the best *Doctor Who* story? A case study in value judgements outside the academy', *Intensities: The Journal of Cult Media* i/December (2007), available at: http://intensities.org/Essays/McKee.pdf, accessed 2 June 2013.
4. See Garner, Ross P., '"Don't you forget about me": Intertextuality and generic anchoring in *The Sarah Jane Adventures*', in R. P. Garner, M. Beattie and U. McCormack (eds), *Impossible Worlds, Impossible Things: Cultural Perspectives on Doctor Who, Torchwood and The Sarah Jane Adventures* (Cambridge Soholars Publishing, Newcastle upon Tyne, 2010), pp. 161–81.
5. See Digital Spy. Favourite companion? – Doctor Who and Torchwood. *Digital Spy Forums* (15 October 2006), available at: http://www.digitalspy.co.uk/forums/showthread.php?t=724532&highlight=doctor+who%26quot%3B+%26quot%3Bschool+reunion, accessed 2 June 2013.
6. Cook, Benjamin, 'Holding back the years', *Doctor Who Magazine* 369 (2006), p. 12.
7. See, for example, Chater, David, 'TV guide', *The Times: Features: The Knowledge*, 29 April 2006, p. 45 or Griffiths, Nick, 'Friends reunited', *Radio Times* 29 April 2006–5 May 2006, p. 15.
8. Spigel, Lynn 'From the Dark Ages to the Golden Age: Women's memories and television reruns' *Screen* xxxvi/1 (1995), p. 22.
9. Tannock, Stuart, 'Nostalgia critique', *Cultural Studies* ix/3 (1995), p. 454.
10. See Digital Spy. Doctor Who – School Reunion – Doctor Who and Torchwood. *Digital Spy Forums* (15 October 2006), available at: http://www.digitalspy.co.uk/forums/showthread.php?t=37,0106&highlight=doctor+who%26quot%3B+%26quot%3Bschool+reunion&page=16, accessed 1 June 2013.
11. Fiske, John, *Television Culture* (Methuen, London, 1989), p. 153.

12. This understanding of nostalgia can be identified in both Fred Davis, *Yearning for Yesterday: A Sociology of Nostalgia* (Free Press, New York, 1979) and Tannock: 'Nostalgia critique'.
13. For an example of the inversion of this structuring of characters, see the discussion of the *Star Trek* movies by Hark, Ina Rae, 'The wrath of the original cast: Translating embodied television characters to other media' in D. Cartmell and I. Whelehan (eds), *Adaptations: From Text to Screen, Screen to Text* (Routledge, London, 1999), p. 178.
14. Gordon, Ian, 'Superman on the set: The market, nostalgia and television audiences', in M. Jancovich and J. Lyons (eds), *Quality Popular Televisoon: Cult TV, The Industry and Fans* (Routledge, London, 2003).
15. Giddens, Anthony, *Modernity and Self-Identity: Self and Society in the Late Modern Age* (Polity, Cambridge, 1991).
16. Silverstone, Roger, *Television and Everyday Life* (Routledge, London, 1991); Turnock, Robert, *Interpreting Diana: Television Audiences and the Death of a Princess* (BFI, London, 2000); and Williams, Rebecca, '"This is the night TV died": Television post-object fandom and the demise of *The West Wing*', *Popular Communication* ix/4 (2011), pp. 266–79 are all relevant studies in this area.
17. Allen, Graham, *Intertextuality: The New Critical Idiom* (Routledge, London, 2000), p. 181.
18. See Jameson, Fredric '*The Shining*', *Social Text* iv (1981), pp. 114–25; Jameson, Fredric, *Postmodernism, or The Cultural Logic of Late Capitalism* (Verso, London, 1991); and Jameson, Fredric 'Postmodernism and consumer society' in H. Foster (ed.), *The Anti-Aesthetic: Essays on Postmodern Culture* (Pluto Press, London, 1991).
19. Staiger, Janet, 'Hitchcock in Texas: Intertextuality in the face of blood and gore' in E. Mathijs and X. Mendik (eds), *The Cult Film Reader* (Open University Press, Maidenhead, 2008), p. 248.
20. Staiger: 'Hitchcock in Texas', p. 248.
21. Jameson: *Postmodernism*, p. 12.
22. See, for example, Creeber, Glen, 'The mini-series' in G. Creeber (ed.), *The Television Genre Book* (BFI, London, 2001), p. 35 and Smith, Greg, 'Serial narrative and guest stars: *Ally McBeal*'s eccentrics' in M. Hammond and L. Mazdon (eds), *The Contemporary Television Series* (University of Edinburgh Press, Edinburgh, 2001), p. 102.
23. Thornham, Sue and Purvis, Tony, *Television Drama: Theories and Identities* (Palgrave, Basingstoke, 2005), p. 166.
24. Fiske: *Television Culture*, p. 155.
25. Hobson, Dorothy, *Crossroads: The Drama of a Soap Opera* (Methuen, London, 1982), p. 25.
26. Fiske: *Television Culture*, p. 164.
27. Hills, Matt, 'Televisuality without television? The Big Finish audios and discourses of tele-centric *Doctor Who*' in D. Butler (ed.), *Time and Relative Dissertations in Space: Critical Perspectives on Doctor Who* (Manchester University Press, Manchester, 2007), p. 290.
28. See Ros Jennings, '*Coronation Street*' in G. Creeber (ed.), *Fifty Key Television Programmes* (Arnold, London, 2004), p. 56.

29. See Ndalianis, Angela, 'Television and the neo-baroque' in M. Hammond and L. Mazdon (eds), *The Contemporary Television Series* (Edinburgh University Press, Edinburgh, 2005), p. 90.
30. Geraghty, Christine, 'The continuous serial – a definition' in R. Dyer, C. Geraghty, M. Jordan, T. Lovell, R. Paterson and J. Stewart (eds), *Coronation Street: Television Monograph* (BFI, London, 1981), p. 11.
31. Geraghty: 'The continuous serial – a definition', p. 16.
32. See, for example, Jancovich, Mark and Lyons, James, 'Introduction' in M. Jancovich and J. Lyons (eds), *Quality Popular Television: Cult TV, The Industry and Fans* (BFI, London, 2003), p. 1.
33. Geraghty: 'The continuous serial – a definition', p. 17.
34. Hills, Matt, *'Doctor Who'* in G. Creeber (ed.), *Fifty Key Television Programmes* (Arnold, London, 2004), p. 56.
35. See also Geraghty: 'The continuous serial – a definition', p. 18.
36. Gordon: 'Superman on set', p. 151.
37. Gordon: 'Superman on set', p. 156.
38. Gordon: 'Superman on set', p. 156.
39. Peter Phillips, 'Biblical studies and intertextuality: Should the work of Genette and Eco Broaden our horizons' available at: http://postmodernbible.blogs.com/Intertxtuality.doc, accessed 3 June 2013.
40. Allen: *Intertextuality*, p. 5.
41. Metz, Walter, 'Toward a post-structural influence in film genre study: Intertextuality and "The Shining"', *Film Criticism* xxii/1 (1997), available at: http://find.galegroup.com/itx/retrieve.do?contentSet=IAC-Documents&resultListType=RESULT_LIST&qrySerId=Locale%28en%2CUS%2C%29%3AFQE%3D%28JN%2CNone%2C16%29%22Film+Criticism%22%3AAnd%3ALQE%3D%28DA%2CNone%2C8%2919970922%24&sgHitCountType=None&inPS=true&sort=DateDescend&searchType=PublicationSearchForm&tabID=T002&prodId=EAIM&searchId=R1&currentPosition=3&userGroupName=ucw_itc&docId=A19927508&docType=IAC, accessed 4 April 2008.
42. Hills, Matt, *The Pleasures of Horror* (Continuum, London, 2005), p. 188.
43. Hills: *The Pleasures of Horror*, p. 188.
44. See Dawson, David, 'Allegorical Intratextuality in Bunyan and Winstanley', *The Journal of Religion* lxx/2 (1990), p. 190–1 or Shen, Dan and Xu, Dejin, 'Intratextuality, extratextuality, intertextuality: Unreliability of autobiography versus fiction', *Poetics Today* xxviii/1 (2007), pp. 43–87.
45. The term 'allusion' is deployed here because of Noel Carroll's use of it. See Carroll, Noel, 'The Future of Allusion: Hollywood in the Seventies (and Beyond)' in E. Mathijs and X. Mendik (eds), *The Cult Film Reader* (Open University Press, Maidenhead, 2008), p. 241.
46. Brunsdon, Charlotte, 'Taste and Time on Television', *Screen* vl/2 (2004), p. 115.
47. Jameson: *'The Shining'*, p. 114.
48. Gordon: 'Superman on set', p. 156.
49. Jameson: *'The Shining'*, p. 115.
50. For further discussion of 'cognitive mapping', see Jameson, Fredric, 'Cognitive mapping' in M. Hardt and K. Weeks (eds), *The Jameson Reader*

(Blackwell, Oxford, 2000) and Jameson, Fredric, 'Class and allegory in contemporary mass culture: *Dog Day Afternoon* as a political film' in M. Hardt and K. Weeks (eds), *The Jameson Reader* (Blackwell, Oxford, 2000).
51. Gordon: 'Superman on set', p. 153–4.
52. See Brunsdon: 'Taste and time on television', p. 115 and Hills: '"Gothic" body parts in a "postmodern" body of work', online.
53. Brooker, Peter and Brooker, Will, 'Introduction' in P. Brooker and W. Brooker (eds), *Postmodern After-Images: A Reader in Film, Television and Video* (Arnold, London, 1997), p. 7.
54. See Jameson: *Postmodernism*, pp. 11–16.
55. Homer, Sean, *Frederic Jameson: Marxism, Hermeneutics, Postmodernism* (Polity, Cambridge, 1998), p. 122.
56. See Homer: *Frederic Jameson*, pp. 22–3 for a more detailed discussion of Jameson's ideas on reification.
57. Davis: *Yearning for Yesterday*, p. 122.
58. Davis: *Yearning for Yesterday*, p. 130.
59. Tolson, Andrew, *Mediations: Text and Discourse in Media Studies* (Arnold, London, 1996), p. 12.
60. Hills: *The Pleasures of Horror*, p. 170.
61. Klinger, Barbara, 'The art film, affect and the female viewer: *The Piano* Revisited', *Screen* iiil/1, p. 25.
62. See Tulloch, John and Jenkins, Henry, *Science Fiction Audiences: Watching Doctor Who and Star Trek* (Routledge, London, 1995), pp. 121–43.
63. Cook, Benjamin, 'TV preview: School Reunion', *Doctor Who Magazine* 369 (2006), p. 19.
64. See Digital Spy. Doctor Who – School Reunion – Doctor Who and Torchwood. *Digital Spy Forums* (15 October 2006) available at: http://www.digitalspy.co.uk/forums/showthread.php?t = 370106& highlight=doctor+who%26quot%3B+%26quot%3Bschool+reunion, accessed 3 June 2013.
65. Michael, Matt, 'Never can say goodbye: Episode 3: School Reunion', *Doctor Who Magazine* 371 (2006), p. 54.
66. Klinger: 'The art film, affect and the female viewer', p. 25.
67. Spigel, Lynn, 'Communicating with the dead: Elvis as medium', *Camera Obscura* xxiii (1991), p. 187.
68. Gwenllian Jones, Sara, 'Starring Lucy Lawless?', *Continuum: Journal of Media and Cultural Studies* xiv/1 (2000), p. 11.
69. Fiske: *Television Culture*, p. 150.
70. Gwenllian Jones: 'Starring Lucy Lawless?', p. 11.
71. Hark: 'The wrath of the original cast', p. 172.
72. See, for example, Ellis, John, *Visible Fictions: Cinema, Television, Video* (Routledge, London, 1984) and Gwenllian Jones: 'Starring Lucy Lawless?'.
73. Hark: 'The wrath of the original cast', p. 177.
74. Again, this is something that has been alluded to in extratextual discourses. See Arnopp, Jason, 'Adventure playground!', *Doctor Who Magazine* 388 (2007), p. 13.
75. See Cook: 'TV preview: School Reunion', and Michael: 'Never can say goodbye'.

76　See Chapter 2 in this volume. The Autons are, for example, still walking mannequins with flip-down handguns while the Daleks remain the same basic shape. See also Arnopp, Jason 'Smash Hits!', *Doctor Who Magazine* 370 (2006), p. 16 on executive producer Russell T Davies's statements concerning the need to retain iconic 'handlebars' on the helmets of the Cybermen.

77　See, for example, Cook, Benjamin, 'Dummy run', *Doctor Who Magazine* 355 (2005), pp. 14–20 or Griffiths, Nick, 'Tinpot dictator', *Radio Times* 29 April– 5 May 2006, pp. 18–21.

78　Brunsdon: 'Taste and time on television', p. 118. Piers D. Britton addresses the 'responsible modernisation' of monsters in Chapter 2.

79　Hills: 'Televisuality without television?', p. 282. See also Holdsworth, Amy, *Television, Memory and Nostalgia* (Palgrave, Basingstoke, 2011), pp. 111–2 on how reusing the form of 'past' channel idents can help stimulate nostalgia among audiences.

80　And for a discussion of how United States fans mourned Sladen, where 'memorials were personal and private instead of national and television-worthy', see Porter, Lynnette, *The Doctor Who Franchise: American Influence, Fan Culture and the Spinoffs* (McFarland, Jefferson, 2012), pp. 128–30.

81　See Messenger Davies, Maire, *Dear BBC: Children, Television Storytelling and the Public Sphere* (Cambridge University Press, Cambridge, 2001) for further discussion of the BBC's responsibilities towards children. Responses to Sladen's death through the CBBC website are available at 'CBBC – Newsround – Your memories of *Sarah Jane* star Elisabeth Sladen', http://news.bbc.co.uk/cbbcnews/hi/newsid_9460000/newsid_ 9463000/9463099.stm, accessed 3 June 2013.

82　Hallam, Elizabeth and Hockey, Jenny, *Death, Memory and Material Culture* (Berg, Oxford, 2001), p. 18.

83　Turnock: *Interpreting Diana*, p. 35.

84　Ibid.

85　Gallifrey Base. Elisabeth Sladen – R.I.P. [1946–2011]. *Gallifrey Base*, available at: http://gallifreybase.com/forum/showthread.php?t=102749 &highlight=elisabeth+sladen+death&page=5, accessed 3 June 2013.

86　Uncredited, 'Our Sarah Jane...', *Doctor Who Magazine* 435 (2011), pp. 13–14.

87　Thompson, John B., *The Media and Modernity: A Social Theory of the Media* (Polity, Cambridge, 1995), p. 208.

88　'Radioactive hamster' in *Gallifrey Base: Elisabeth Sladen – R.I.P. [1946–2011]*, available at: http://gallifreybase.com/forum/showthread.php?t=102749& highlight=elisabeth+sladen+death&page=5, accessed 12 December 2012.

89　'Yeti attack' in *Gallifrey Base. Elisabeth Sladen – R.I.P. [1946–2011]*, available at http://gallifreybase.com/forum/showthread.php?t=102749& highlight=elisabeth+sladen+death&page=5, accessed 12 December 2012.

90　Giddens: *Modernity and Self-Identity*, pp. 14–21.

91　Georgiou, Myria, 'Seeking ontological security beyond the nation: The role of transnational television', *Television and New Media* x/10 (2012), p. 3.

92 Zaretsky, Eli, 'Trauma and dereification: September 11 and the problem of ontological security', *Constellations* ix/1 (2002), p. 100.
93 Giddens: *Modernity and Self-Identity*, pp. 44–5.
94 Georgiou: 'Seeking ontological security beyond the nation', p. 3.
95 Zaretsky: 'Trauma and dereification', p. 100.
96 See also Williams: '"This is the night TV died"', p. 269.
97 Giddens: *Modernity and Self-Identity*, p. 44.
98 Georgiou: 'Seeking ontological security beyond the nation', p. 4.
99 Turnock: *Interpreting Diana*, p. 38.
100 See also Silverstone: *Television and Everyday Life* and Georgiou: 'Seeking ontological security beyond the nation', pp. 4–5.
101 Tennant, David, 'Foreword: *It was Always the Doctor and Sarah Jane*' in E. Sladen with J. Hudson, *Elisabeth Sladen: The Autobiography* (Aurum Press, London, 2011), p. ix.
102 Turnock: *Interpreting Diana*, p. 38.
103 Ibid.
104 Turnock: *Interpreting Diana*, p. 48.
105 Ibid.
106 Turnock: *Interpreting Diana*, p. 47.
107 Garde-Hansen, Joanne, *Media and Memory* (Edinburgh University Press, Edinburgh, 2011), p. 131.
108 JP Goodwin in Uncredited: 'Our Sarah Jane...', p. 13.
109 Laura in Uncredited: 'Our Sarah Jane...', p. 13.
110 'Sword of Orion' in *Gallifrey Base: Elisabeth Sladen R.I.P. [1946–2011]*, available at: http://gallifreybase.com/forum/showthread.php?t=102749&highlight=elisabeth+sladen+death&page=5, accessed 12 December 2012.
111 Williams: '"This is the night TV died"', p. 266. Sladen's passing differs from Williams' example (fan negotiations of the final episode of *The West Wing*) in that it is the loss of a key cast member rather than the loss of '*Doctor Who* itself'.
112 Impert, Laura and Rubin, Margaret, 'The mother at the glen: The relationship between mourning and nostalgia', *Psychoanalytic Dialogues: The International Journal of Relational Perspectives* xxi/6 (2011), p. 692.
113 Matheson, Victor A. and Baade, Robert A., '"Death effect" on collectible prices', *Applied Economics* xxxvi/11 (2004), pp. 1151–5.
114 Routledge, Clay, Arndt, Jamie, Sedikides, Constantine and Wildschut, Tim, 'A blast from the past: The terror management function of nostalgia', *Journal of Experimental Social Psychology* ivl (2008), pp. 132–40.
115 Hallam and Hockey: *Death, Memory and Material Culture*, p. 1.
116 Hallam and Hockey: *Death, Memory and Material Culture*, p. 25.
117 Davis: *Yearning for Yesterday*, p. 58. See Boym, Svetlana, *The Future of Nostalgia* (Basic Books, New York, 2001), pp. 3–18 or Sprengler, Christine, *Screening Nostalgia: Populuxe Props and Technicolor Aesthetics in Contemporary American Film* (Berghahn, New York, 2011), pp. 11–37 on historical developments concerning nostalgia's meanings.
118 Williams: '"This is the night TV died"', p. 272.
119 Giddens: *Modernity and Self-Identity*, p. 54.

120 Williams: '"This is the night TV died"', p. 273.
121 Williams: '"This is the night TV died"', p. 273.
122 Davis: *Yearning for Yesterday*, p. 33.
123 Giddens: *Modernity and Self-Identity*, pp. 10–11.
124 See Wallerstein, Judith and Blakeslee, Sandra, *Second Chances* (Ticknor & Fields, London, 1989).
125 Giddens: *Modernity and Self-Identity*, pp. 11.
126 Grainge, Paul, 'Nostalgia and style in retro America: Moods, modes and media recycling', *Journal of American & Comparative Cultures* xxiii/1 (2000), p. 28.
127 Garde-Hansen: *Media and Memory*, p. 126.
128 Jameson: 'Postmodernism and consumer society', p. 135.
129 King, Geoff and Krzywinska, Tanya, *Science Fiction Cinema: From Outerspace to Cyberspace* (Wallflower, London, 2000), p. 56.
130 Jameson: 'Postmodernism and consumer society', p. 136.
131 King and Krzywinska: *Science Fiction Cinema*, p. 56.
132 Arnopp: 'Smash Hits!', p. 17.
133 Jameson: 'Postmodernism and consumer society', p. 137.

11

ANNIVERSARY ADVENTURES IN SPACE AND TIME
The Changing Faces of *Doctor Who*'s Commemoration

Matt Hills

Doctor Who's 50th anniversary falls on 23 November 2013, the programme having previously celebrated its 10th birthday with 'The Three Doctors' (1972–3) and its 20th via 'The Five Doctors' (1983). Bringing different eras and various lead actors together, *Who*'s history of anniversaries has rarely been theorised within TV studies, where the very topic of television anniversaries has also languished somewhat, perhaps assumed to be self-explanatory and in need of no further thought. Despite accurately noting in *Television, Memory and Nostalgia* that TV 'itself is marked by and generates our obsession with commemoration and anniversaries, through its repetition and continual re-narrativisation',[1] Amy Holdsworth doesn't go on to address TV anniversaries in any depth. And even a book-length study of cultural anniversaries, William Johnston's *Celebrations*, rules out studying media-oriented festivities:

ANNIVERSARY ADVENTURES IN SPACE AND TIME

> Many anniversaries, particularly ones concerning television [...] and celebrities, serve no other purpose than to justify media coverage. This book largely ignores campaigns by the media to commemorate its own earlier creations.[2]

In this chapter I want to put the TV anniversary back under consideration. As Holdsworth has usefully pointed out:

> ... it is the longevity of *Doctor Who* which has led scholars to respond to the series as a 'receptacle' for multiple forms of history, memory and identity. For example [...] its ability to 'map the shifting cultural landscape' (Chapman 2006, p.201) [...] might also be utilised to map a shifting television landscape.[3]

Rather than tracing how *Who*'s assorted anniversaries might 'map' changing cultural contexts across its 50-year life — and, after all, substantive work has already been carried out on the programme's overall cultural history[4] — my interest lies instead in how industry practices of 'the TV show anniversary' have themselves altered along with the television landscape between 1973 and 2013. Far from stressing 'the appeal of repetition in precise multiples, whether of days, months or years [... where the] cult of anniversaries meets the need to experience repeatability on a large scale,'[5] I will argue that anniversaries do not merely record empty, calendrical 'multiples' of time, but instead take on different meanings within reconfigured industry/audience contexts. I will therefore analyse *Doctor Who*'s multiple incarnations of 'the anniversary' by drawing on John Ellis's tripartite model of television eras, dubbed those of scarcity, availability and plenty,[6] as well as relating *Who*'s different celebrations to 'the evolution of fan discourse from [...] the 1970s through to today'.[7] My argument is that *Doctor Who* has entertained four ideal-types of anniversary across its 50 years:

(i) the mainstream media event with little or no sense of targeting 'fandom' as an audience category, and far less time-sensitivity than we would expect today;
(ii) variations on the hybrid anniversary planned both as 'something for the fans'[8] and as consensus TV;
(iii) variations on the purely fan-oriented, consumer anniversary (usually happening off-air and in audio/novel media tie-ins); and
(iv) the rise of the anniversary conceptualised as an extended branding and marketing campaign.

These modes of TV anniversary – naive, hybrid, niche, and hyped – have played out across *Who*'s many commemorations, for example the 10th, 20th, 25th, 30th, 35th, 40th, 45th and 50th, hence according with William Johnston's recognition that the 'media of mass culture have [...] contrived] anniversaries of events at a distance of as little as five and ten years'.[9] Yet the unfolding texts of *Doctor Who*'s multiple anniversaries call for a theorization of industry and fan practices, and it is to these that I will now turn.

Naive and Hybrid Celebrations

The notion of celebrating a *Who* milestone first occurs in 1972—3 four-parter 'The Three Doctors', uniting William Hartnell, Patrick Troughton and the then-current Doctor, Jon Pertwee. But although this team-up was '[n]ominally the story marking *Doctor Who*'s tenth birthday [...] it was actually broadcast shortly after its ninth',[10] running from 30 December 1972 to 20 January 1973.[11] This is remarkable by the standards of today's TV anniversaries, which tend to be carefully timed and promoted so as to maximise audience awareness of specific dates and moments. The TV industry of 1973, however, seems to have operated with a far less developed sense of time-stamped event television, with *Doctor Who*'s 10th anniversary special actually being a season opener, and hence garnering publicity as much for *Who*'s return as for its birthday. Seasonal scheduling in both senses – times of year, and new seasons of TV shows – formed a major part of the United Kingdom TV industry's common-sense, ritualistic practices through the 1970s.[12] But within television's ephemeral, here-today and gone-tomorrow broadcasting system, the focus tended to be on rhythms and cycles of ritual return, such as the seasonal premiere, rather than assuming detailed or archival TV memories on the part of audiences. This is attributable to the fact that 1970's United Kingdom TV was still in the first era of John Ellis's historical schema: 'characterized by a few channels broadcasting for part of the day only. It was the era of scarcity, which lasted for most countries until the late 1970s or early 1980s.'[13] *Doctor Who* fan expert J. Jeremy Bentham recalls this TV age:

> The past isn't always rose tinted [...] there were no domestic VCRs, no satellite stations showing reruns, and no public access whatsoever to

visually recorded media: just a stark choice between watching ITV or BBC in real time.[14]

Media scholar Mark Bould relates Ellis's work directly to *Who*, noting how the 'back-story and detail of *Doctor Who*'s story world [...] were created in an ad hoc manner, appropriate to the unrecoverable, ephemeral flow of television in the era of scarcity'[15] characterising the 1960s and 70s. In such a cultural and technological context, the concept of a TV show anniversary would have carried significantly different meanings to those circulating around TV celebrations in the twenty-first century. 'The Three Doctors' wasn't only less time-sensitive (23 November is not marked out as a key transmission date); it also made unrecoverable TV drama partially recoverable for its audiences. As fan-turned-*Radio-Times*-journalist Nick Griffiths recounts in his memoirs: 'To me, at the age of eight, *The Three Doctors* felt like a once-in-a-lifetime chance to be able to glimpse the past and treasures I had missed'.[16] In an age without video, DVD, streaming and downloading, special multi-Doctor episodes could almost offer a form of imaginative time-travel, allowing new audiences who could only read or hear about earlier periods of the programme to experience prior portrayals of the title character for the very first time. And fans that missed the story's 1972–3 broadcast would have to rely on a Target novelization until its 1981 transmission as part of the *Five Faces of Doctor Who* run of repeats. Gary Gillatt's cleverly mimetic fan review from 2002 alludes to this scarcity, representing his two former selves as follows:

> November 1981[: ...] *The Three Doctors* is very good, and certainly the best of the old stories I've seen so far. Everyone at school agrees. The good thing about this *Five Faces of Doctor Who* season of repeats is that it lets you see things you thought you'd never get a chance to see [...]. August 1979[:] *Doctor Who and the Three Doctors* is just amazing, and my favourite story of the six I've read so far. [...] I wish I could see this adventure on the TV. I bet it's really good.[17]

Unlike all later *Who* anniversaries, 'The Three Doctors' is also unique insofar as it was made without any real concept of catering to fandom as a specific interpretive community. *Doctor Who*'s producers were evidently aware of an emergent fandom, since Keith Miller who was in charge of the Official Doctor Who Fan Club had been invited to watch the story being recorded:

> November 27, 1972 [...] Lennie Mayne [...] leant forward and spoke into his microphone. "Run telecine" and the recording of the first episode of The Three Doctors commenced [.... Later it] was coming to the time when Pat Troughton was to join the action. Terrance appeared beside me, as did Dudley, who introduced me to Katy's manager. They all crowded round as Pat cheekily reappeared in the Tardis, to a giant cheer from the production team in the gallery. I hope Jon [Pertwee] didn't hear it.[18]

But 'The Three Doctors' wasn't designed to particularly appeal to a fan audience; rather, its founding assumption was that the mass, general audience would appreciate seeing Hartnell, Troughton and Pertwee brought together for a one-off special. In *Inside the TARDIS*, James Chapman examines production memos relating to the story, pointing out that script editor Terrance Dicks had to significantly re-direct writers Bob Baker and Dave Martin after their initial ideas paid homage to Ingmar Bergman's *The Seventh Seal* and the horror genre:

> 'I'm afraid the general feel of the piece is more suited to Hammer than to us [...]. The whole atmosphere of mass suicides, corpse filled morgues, lumbering ghastly zombies and man-eating fungus will give our viewers nightmares and our Head of Department apoplexy' [wrote Dicks]. The story was reworked to turn the [chess-playing] 'Death' figure into a renegade Time Lord, Omega.[19]

Omega and Time Lord history emerge as story points not out of a sense of catering to fan interests, but rather as a solution to Dicks' specific production problem: how to avoid content deemed inappropriate for the general/family audience. For – as Miles Booy has recently argued – at around the time of 'The Three Doctors' 'the show, its fans, and its spin-off products were discrete entities with few sustained points of connection. Fandom – such as it was – was invisible to the general public' as well as being acknowledged but not especially courted by the show's producers.[20] In the TV age of scarcity, then, *Who* fandom was basically a private phenomenon, with fan discourse not having any wider cultural currency or public circulation.

'The Three Doctors' can be described as a 'naive' anniversary as a result of these three factors, and not because its production somehow lacks sophistication. It isn't precisely tied into an anniversary date, instead working more tellingly as part of TV's ritualised, seasonal patterns;[21] it is first broadcast as part of an unrecoverable, ephemeral and thus 'scarce' TV show, rather than as a purchasable commodity-text;

and it lacks any address to fandom as an imagined, distinct audience rather than targeting fan-consumers with an encyclopaedic knowledge of continuity and series' memory.

In the ten years between 1973 and 1983, however, this situation changed radically. By the 1980s, the era of televisual scarcity had given way to one of availability in the United Kingdom,[22] with a far greater number of channels broadcasting around the clock, terrestrial TV supplemented by satellite services, and video recording technology finally entering the mass market. The meanings of *Doctor Who*'s 20th anniversary were thus a world apart from those of 'The Three Doctors'. Now, actors invited to appear in the anniversary special were urged by producer John Nathan-Turner to 'Think of the fans [...]. That was so typical of John [...] "Think of the fans" might have been his catchphrase.'[23]

By this point fandom constituted an identifiable sector of the audience, meaning that unlike its anniversary predecessor, 'The Five Doctors' was called upon to make sense to devoted fans, less committed followers, and the casual or general audience. This hybridized audience address led to the programme's anniversary – 23 November – being given greater prominence since fans would be highly conscious of it, although the special was actually shown on this date only on American PBS television, being broadcast in the United Kingdom two days later as part of Friday 25 November's 1983 *Children in Need* line-up. Furthermore, 'The Five Doctors' was unexpectedly available as a Target novelization before its United Kingdom transmission date, suggesting that effective brand management had yet to become a routinized part of *Doctor Who*'s industrial existence. Writing before the BBC Wales' series, Lawrence Miles and Tat Wood argue this 'was the last time that a *Doctor Who* episode was widely perceived as a big event'.[24] Its hybrid fan/mainstream position would very soon fragment, something also attested to by Kim Newman's latter-day verdict:

> *Who* essentially sank to doing its own fan fiction. The most extreme example is the 'anniversary special', 'The Five Doctors' [...]. 'The Three Doctors' (1973) managed to be significant in the evolution of the series at the time, but 'The Five Doctors' is just a celebratory runabout.[25]

Here, 'The Five Doctors' allegedly fails to unite its hybrid audiences, and errs on the side of fandom. But Miles Booy's historicized analysis of shifting fan discourse is rather more nuanced than Newman's outright castigation, noting that paratextual merchandise accompanying the programme's 20th anniversary, such as Peter Haining's coffee table reference book *Doctor Who: A Celebration*:

> ... was a 'big tent' within which everyone could find a space, either revelling in new information or in seeing it repackaged in a glossy format [...]. The [20th] anniversary celebrations, however, were papering over sizeable cracks, and the moment when such an approach worked – when the diverse interests of different groups could be so easily reconciled – was a brief one.[26]

For Booy, and for Wood and Miles before him, 'The Five Doctors' succeeds in temporarily arresting the industrial and audience slide towards niche, targeted consumer markets. However, as James Chapman adds, it is also possible to interpret this special episode as the beginning of the end for a coalition audience made up of fandom and mainstream viewers:

> ... invested with a sense of the series' history [... and] preoccupied with the theme of memory [...] the long-term significance of 'The Five Doctors' is that it anticipated, and perhaps even started, the increasing tendency to self-referentiality that characterised the series in the later 1980s.[27]

As such, this hybrid anniversary could rely on shared memory and knowledge among fans. 'The Three Doctors', though featuring a Time Lord enemy, put forward Omega as a new invention whereas 'The Five Doctors' includes returning Time Lord characters such as President Borusa and the Master. Its reliance on returning elements makes it rather run-of-the-mill for fan critic Dave Owen: 'Following a season that had already featured Gallifrey, the Brigadier and the Master, *The Five Doctors* is not so much a special, as a typical.'[28] For Owen, 'The Five Doctors' displays a 'paucity of invention [...] repeating the premise of the previous decade's reunion [... and] unsubtly inviting comparison with the earlier story'.[29]

The 20th anniversary also paratextually imitated its predecessor by once again featuring a *Radio Times Special* to commemorate the event. Where the *Tenth Anniversary Special* included an early episode guide, helping to consolidate and shape emergent fan knowledge rather than targeting it,[30] the *Twentieth Anniversary Special* anticipated fannish

ANNIVERSARY ADVENTURES IN SPACE AND TIME

interest in continuity and series history, for example by including a short story 'Birth of a Renegade' by then-script editor Eric Saward (itself presenting an origin story for the first Doctor and Susan's departure from Gallifrey). Each of these *Radio Times Specials* is greatly valued, if not fetishized, by fans:

> My best moment of *Doctor Who* isn't even watching it. It's about being in that motorway café [Foxton Services in late October, 1983] and finding the *Radio Times 20th Anniversary Special* for sale. [...] The whole of that 20 years' of history seemed crammed into that glossy mag.[31]

If 'The Five Doctors' and its (limited) merchandising seem, on the face of it, to copy 'The Three Doctors', this impression is somewhat misleading. The industry/audience context in which each story operates is crucially different. By coming up with another multi-Doctor story, 1983 *Doctor Who* generates an illusion of self-continuity and self-identity, but the 1983 anniversary special works in a fundamentally changed way to the 1972—3 one. By 1983, *Doctor Who*'s scarcity is about to cease: it will shortly become a consumer object in the form of home video, 'the BBC Enterprises market research team [having] canvassed opinion on which stories to release' at the '*Doctor Who* Celebration' event held at Longleat on 3 and 4 April 1983.[32] And socially-organised fandom had been cataloguing and debating the show since at least the mid-70s, learning and fixing 23 November as the show's anniversary date, rather than, say, 27 September 1963 when the first version of the opening episode was recorded, 18 October 1963 when this pilot was remounted for 23 November broadcast, or even 20 August 1963 when the very first (title sequence) filming was done for *Doctor Who*.[33] 'The Five Doctors' is therefore compelled to reflexively engage with fandom and its knowledge of the series, appropriating 23 November as a vital date in the TV calendar for the first time, while catering for more casual audiences through the story's fantasy/quest structure.

Along with the uneasy hybrid anniversary of 'The Five Doctors', which threatened to potentially alienate the mass audience, classic *Who* also celebrated its 25th and 30th birthdays via new TV drama material, namely 'Silver Nemesis' (1988) and 'Dimensions in Time' (1993). An industrial sense that hybrid anniversaries had had their day hung over both, with Tat Wood arguing that '[n]obody in the wider world outside fandom cared about 23rd of November' by the late 80s,[34] despite the date being worked into the diegesis of 'Silver Nemesis'. Meanwhile, 'Dimensions in Time' was made for BBC1 only after discussions had already occurred around the idea of pursuing a direct-to-video special, *The Dark Dimension*, positioned as sell-through merchandise in order to maximise profit from the fan target-market. This notion was eventually rejected as inappropriate for BBC Enterprises, but it was evidently given serious thought.[35]

James Chapman echoes communal fan sentiment when he writes that '[i]n the event the [30th] anniversary was marked by a woeful pantomime piece for *Children in Need* [...] *Dimensions in Time*'.[36] Scholar-fans and fan writers have variously rejected 'Dimensions in Time' as a 'charity skit'[37] or a 'charity sketch',[38] with its canonical status as *Doctor Who* marking one of fandom's recurrent controversies, particularly given that it involves a crossover with *EastEnders*'s characters and settings. Although 'Dimensions in Time' is effectively the final hybrid anniversary prior to *Who*'s return at BBC Wales, it is notable for prefiguring the brand awareness of later anniversary campaigns. In this case, rather than constituting a programme brand spearheading its own paratexts and hype,[39] *Doctor Who* was instead subordinated, as a legacy brand, to other then-current BBC shows. It was narratively fused to *EastEnders* (presumably in the hope of carrying it to a mass audience), broadcast in 3D as part of *Children in Need*, and had its audience-selected second episode shown as part of *Noel's House Party*. A few years before the BBC's Charter renewal of 1996, one might be forgiven for wondering whether this outing for *Doctor Who* was aimed less at commemorating the series than at collating an intertextual array of BBC brands, and promoting the Beeb simultaneously as engaged in charitable works, as forward-looking (thanks to 3D and audience phone-vote interaction), and as possessing historical/nostalgic value for audiences. To dismiss 'Dimensions in Time' simply as a poor substitute for 'a "proper" 30th anniversary special'[40] misses the fact that it was working against industrial contexts that had begun to increasingly stress branding and niche marketing rather than 'big tent' anniversaries in the mode of 'The Five Doctors'. Attempting to work as a hybrid anniversary when the consensus audience had fractured into a fan market plus an uninterested – or at best nostalgic – general public meant that 'Dimensions in Time' felt somehow out of time, and out of step with the TV industry as well as fan expectations. All subsequent anniversaries, at least until the 50th, would go on to be niche affairs aimed purely at *Who*'s loyal, enduring fan base, as well as happening outside the realms of BBC television, often in a curiously 'meta' fashion.

Niche and Hyped Celebrations

Between *Doctor Who*'s 30th anniversary in 1993 and its 45th in 2008, the show's birthdays were not celebrated by TV specials, but the notion of commemorative adventures lived on in BBC Books (*The Infinity Doctors*, 1993), Big Finish Audios (*Zagreus*, 2003; *Forty-Five*, 2008), DVD releases (*The Three Doctors*, 2003; *The Five Doctors 25th Anniversary Edition*, 2008), and web-hosted stories (*The Scream of the Shalka*, 2003). Despite BBC Wales' *Doctor Who* being on air in 2008, it is only the 50th anniversary that has drawn the current show into explicitly celebratory mode. Prior to this, the multi-Doctor 'event' episode was gestured at, and symbolically contained, by virtue of appearing only as a *Children in Need* mini-episode, 'Time Crash', rather than as part of a *Doctor Who* series or as a fully-fledged special. As Robert Smith? has noted: 'This mini-episode can afford to have all the in-jokes about the past that the new show can't do.'[41] The multi-Doctor tale has therefore been preserved post-2005, but sometimes disarticulated from anniversary commemorations, as in *The Forgotten*, a six-part IDW comic book series (August 2008–January 2009) where the tenth Doctor has to remember his former selves and their adventures. Like 'The Five Doctors' before it, this too was preoccupied with the theme of memory, but its narrative hinged on fan-readers possessing detailed knowledge of continuity. Unlike 'The Five Doctors', *The Forgotten* – featuring the Doctor arriving in a museum seemingly dedicated to himself – is essentially and purely written for fans; it is targeted at, and draws on, detailed fan knowledge. Indeed, its narrative makes little sense unless the reader brings such knowledge to the table.

If multi-Doctor stories have become an 'event' in fan-targeted transmedia paratexts and media tie-ins, rather than in the TV show itself (even 'Time Crash' is securely positioned outside the main text of new *Who*), then these narratives can be viewed as a form of fan service reinforcing the fact that fandom's interpretive community reads differently to the mainstream, mass audience.

Niche anniversary celebrations, marketed and sold to fans outside *Doctor Who*'s TV text, amount to products of the 'commemoration industry'.[42] Across the 1980s, and especially in the wake of *Who*'s 1989 cancellation:

> The very meaning of collecting merchandised *Who* shifted considerably. It had previously entailed searching second-hand shops [...]. From this point onwards, it would mean visits to specialist stores [...] and keeping up with the latest releases of products aimed at the interests of fan-consumers. The downside of this [...] was that the proliferation of books, models and toys was no longer any index of genuine public interest.[43]

As part of this reconfiguration of industry and fan discourses, *Doctor Who*'s anniversaries similarly became 'products aimed at [...] fan-consumers'. *The Infinity Doctors*, a BBC Worldwide novel that celebrated 'the thirty-fifth anniversary of *Doctor Who*',[44] played with the convention of titles constructed along the lines of 'The N Doctors' by taking this to its logical, yet absurdist, conclusion. In the event, writer Lance Parkin didn't actually build his tale around infinite incarnations of the Doctor, but instead displayed such 'super-adherence to established continuity' – including all its contradictions and versions – that the novel was 'impossible to place at a particular point in continuity without contradicting something established elsewhere' in cross-media *Doctor Who*.[45] Parkin's 'Infinity Doctor' therefore dialogically intersects with fan knowledge of the Whoniverse, gaming fan cultural capital as 'key elements in the vast narrative of *Doctor Who* are somehow rendered strange, [and] altered through [...] refraction'.[46]

Fan-targeted, niche anniversary products became increasingly concerned with avoiding celebratory clichés, and thus with offering something new to fan-consumers likely to be highly familiar with all previous celebrations. Even paratexts such as the 40th anniversary *Doctor Who Magazine Special Edition* went out of their way to advertise their difference from prior special issues:

> And besides, a special issue detailing every story was published for the thirtieth anniversary. And the twentieth. And the tenth... So then, some exclusive interviews perhaps? But so many of *Doctor Who*'s talented writers, performers and other major contributors have spoken about their work in the pages of DWM and elsewhere that, again, it would seem too much like repetition.[47]

At the same time, Big Finish audio were also making a 40th anniversary story featuring many actors who had played the Doctor, again to be sold directly into the fan market. This production, *Zagreus*, refrained from functioning as an archetypal multi-Doctor story, instead casting the Doctor and companion actors as new characters or as garbled, mis-remembered projections of familiar figures:

> Why not a more traditional multi-Doctor tale in the vein of *The Three Doctors*, *The Five Doctors*, or, ahem, *Dimensions in Time*? 'Because it's all been done before,' insists [*Zagreus* director and co-writer Gary] Russell, 'and to varying degrees of success'.[48]

Targeted, niche anniversaries have thus come up against the issue of intertextual 'position-takings':[49] in order to act as new, exciting products for discerning fan-consumers, they attempt to work out novel ways of doing an anniversary tale that simultaneously display awareness both of previous takes and *Doctor Who*'s established continuity. Such intertextual position-taking has also been extended to re-releasing and repurposing previous anniversary stories, making the 'meta-anniversary' – or the anniversary of an anniversary – one subgenre of niche commemoration. 'Nostalgia squared', as Gary Gillatt puts it, reviewing the DVD release of a 30th anniversary documentary in *Who*'s 50th year.[50] To give another example, the *Radio Times Tenth Anniversary Special* was reprinted and reissued as part of 40th anniversary merchandising:

> For those who missed it the first time around, or whose copy was lost in the mists of time, we're pleased to be republishing the 68-page [tenth anniversary] special in its original format [...] This special edition is being produced in a limited print run, so don't delay placing your order.[51]

And BBC Worldwide's 40th anniversary campaign also involved re-commodifying 'The Three Doctors' in a 'highly collectable DVD package, released on 24 November [... with] a Corgi replica model of the Doctor's car, Bessie'.[52] Interpellating fan-consumers for whom 24 November was just a day after the 40th, this meta-anniversary release branded the tenth birthday story with a '*Doctor W40*' logo designed for the 2003 commemorations. In the absence of any televised special that year, 'The Three Doctors' could be appropriated and recontextualised via fan nostalgia for past anniversaries, and sold as a 'collectable' DVD release. The same fate befell 'The Five Doctors' in 2008. Set against the absence of any 45th birthday TV special, the 20th anniversary story was itself reissued as a '25th Anniversary Edition' complete with a hidden Easter Egg DVD commentary involving the actor then playing the Doctor, David Tennant. While BBC Worldwide has exploited *Doctor Who*'s back catalogue by repurposing prior anniversaries, other niche celebrations, such as Big Finish's *Forty-Five*, avoided the multi-Doctor story altogether, instead creating an innovative tale based around repetition of the signifiers 'forty-five' and riffing intertextually on Time Lord mythology via a character dubbed 'the Word Lord'.

Amy Holdsworth has argued that '"milestone moments" often function as [...] self-reflexive spaces within serial drama that "reference back" on their own long perspectives,'[53] and it could certainly be argued that 'milestone moments' occur in naive and hybrid anniversary TV episodes. But niche anniversaries cut adrift from *Doctor Who*'s televisual existence, or even the re-selling of older TV specials and documentaries, lack this sense of significance. Hybrid anniversaries are nostalgically remembered and looked back upon when they become niche re-issues, whereas new niche products are primarily concerned with intertextually and dialogically varying established patterns of 'the anniversary story'/multi-Doctor tale. In each case, the 'milestone moment' is subordinated either to *Doctor Who*'s TV history, or to intricate fan knowledge of that very history. By buying (into) niche anniversaries, fandom buys (back) its own concerns, knowledge, and reading protocols.

By the time of the 40th anniversary, *Who* was already industrially positioned as 'one of BBC Worldwide's most enduring and well-loved brands,' with its press pack keen to make the case for *Doctor Who*'s currency even while it wasn't on the air as a going concern: 'As well as making headlines it continues to win awards'.[54] But if *Who* was firmly conceptualized as a brand, complete with a reworked anniversary logo for its 2003 merchandise and DVDs aimed at consumer-fans,[55] by the time of the 50th anniversary the series was in a fundamentally different position again. Now it was a flagship BBC television programme – a scenario that could only be dreamt of by fans back in 1993 and 2003. As a result, the show's 50th birthday seems to return it to days gone by, generating the possibility of a twenty-first century 'hybrid' anniversary for the first time, and a TV special addressing both fans and the mass TV audience. The closest comparison would be with 'The Five Doctors', and its capacity to unite fandom and general viewers in 1983. However, in 1983 *Doctor Who* had not yet become a 'first-order commodity'[56] in its own right – in other words directly purchasable by viewers – since it would take consumer home video to cement such a development. Nor had the show been permeated by industrial discourses of branding.

These cultural, technological shifts make the 50th unique: this is the first celebrated anniversary, in fact, when *Doctor Who* has been *both* an active, popular, mass-audience TV show *and* subject to rigorous practices of brand management. John Ellis recognises that in the third era of television – the era of plenty, with its 'crowded media environment' and 'almost infinite choice'[57] – the value of television brands becomes paramount. Brands can 'cut [...] through problems of consumer recognition',[58] as well as creating 'an extended relationship with viewers over time'.[59] By commemorating its 50th, *Doctor Who* hence accrues further brand value via emphasising its longevity, at the same time as using this birthday to anchor a transmedia array of planned, coordinated merchandise and events. Celebrating a hyped, brand anniversary also gives *Who* a temporarily-enhanced capacity to 'cut through' media culture by rendering it especially newsworthy and timely. What Robert van Krieken refers to as the 'attention-capital'[60] characterising celebrity in the cultural context of 'scarcity of attention, and [...] oversupply of information'[61] similarly characterises anniversary brands. Becoming a celebrated text across 2013 lends *Doctor Who* additional 'attention-capital' thanks to the transmedia hype of a major birthday campaign. Such 'hype and surrounding texts [...] establish frames and filters'[62] through which the TV show can be positioned and interpreted.

In stark contrast to the naive anniversary of 'The Three Doctors', broadcast in December 1972 and January 1973, and even 'The Five Doctors' with its hybrid anniversary preceded by 1983's Longleat '*Doctor Who* Celebration' in April, cross-media 50th festivities have been designed to extend from January to at least November 2013, with each month thematically coordinated around its numerically-corresponding Doctor. 'The First Doctor' was commemorated at a BFI Southbank event in the first month of the year, just as a new first Doctor audio adventure was released as part of the 11-part 'Destiny of the Doctor' sequence.[63] At the same time, a first Doctor comic book was published as part of IDW's 'Prisoners of Time',[64] and a first Doctor short story made electronically available by Puffin/Penguin.[65] In turn, February saw the second Doctor celebrated via a BFI screening, a second Doctor ebook, and the release of parts two of 'Destiny of the Doctor' and 'Prisoners of Time' starring the Patrick Troughton Doctor.

There is thus a commercial, brand logic given to the 2013 calendar, and to month-by-month product releases that stretch systematically across the year, as *Doctor Who*'s framing hype and paratextual density sequentially build up to the 11th Doctor in the 11th month, followed by the 12th in the 12th. Rather than merely being recognised as an anniversary date, 23 November thus becomes one culminating point within an integrated cross-media campaign incorporating ebooks, comics, audio, screenings and the like. Extending the anniversary across the year partly displaces the multi-Doctor cliché by treating all incarnations as part of a sequential, collectable set – a gesture captured particularly acutely by the Royal Mail's commemorative stamps.[66] However, it also allows multi-Doctor stories both on TV and in other media – timed to coincide with November's big date – to effectively crown or cap these extended celebrations. Indeed, Big Finish's audio 'The Light at the End' (2013), uniting all surviving classic series Doctors, was introduced in *Doctor Who Magazine* in exactly these terms: 'We've saved the best till last. The jewel in the crown of the non-TV anniversary celebrations.'[67]

In short, unlike all previous anniversaries this is a coordinated, hyped commemoration, wholly integrated into the 'commemoration industry', and hinging on the branding equation of *Doctor Who*'s consumer value with its public service value to British (TV) culture. Although fans and academics have speculated over the diegetic content of *Who*'s 50th anniversary special,[68] in a sense the show's cultural omnipresence across 2013, and thereby its framing as a unification of consumerism and public value, are more significant developments. Rather than mirroring social media and media use, as Paul Booth argues is the case for temporalities represented in *Doctor Who*,[69] temporality represented *by* the show is just as crucial. As a hyped anniversary, *Who*'s 50th marks a further 'evolution of fan discourse' along with industry discourse,[70] filtering *Doctor Who* explicitly into territories of cultural value and vigorously marrying it to calendrical time. The programme has a chance to reinforce its 'historical' worth as a public good, recontextualising lifelong fans as amateur historians and popular curators rather than obsessives,[71] as well as reinforcing its commercial worth as a consumer good. The ideological value of a brand anniversary lies, at least in part, in this pre-planned, scheduled unification; something far more culturally potent than the hybrid anniversary's bringing together of fans and mainstream audiences.

Conclusion

Across this chapter I have argued that *Doctor Who*'s anniversaries can be productively analysed in relation to their changing industry/fan contexts. Rather than viewing anniversary texts and paratexts simply as self-explanatory celebrations undeserving of academic study – and somehow remaining the remit of passionate fans only – I have sought to restore the subject matter to theoretical consideration. Furthermore, I have suggested that *Doctor Who*'s many anniversaries can be variously categorised as naive, hybrid, niche and hyped TV events, intersecting with television's ages of scarcity, availability and plenty,[72] as well as being inflected by shifting fan discourses. Textually-celebrated anniversaries may well offer up milestone moments, but meanings and practices of 'the anniversary' have themselves reached particular milestones across *Doctor Who*'s history, attaining new dimensions of commemoration such as purely fan-targeted and primarily brand-led specials.

NOTES

1. Holdsworth, Amy, *Television, Memory and Nostalgia* (Palgrave-Macmillan, Basingstoke and New York, 2011), p. 1.
2. Johnston, William M., *Celebrations: The Cult of Anniversaries in Europe and the United States Today* (Transaction Publishers, New Brunswick and London, 1991), p. 5.
3. Holdsworth: *Television, Memory and Nostalgia*, p. 127.
4. Chapman, James, *Inside the TARDIS: The Worlds of Doctor Who* (I.B.Tauris, London and New York, 2006); Cull, Nicholas J., '"Bigger on the inside...": *Doctor Who* as British cultural history' in G. Roberts and P. M. Taylor (eds), *The Historian, Television and Television History* (University of Luton Press, Luton, 2001), pp. 95–111.
5. Johnston: *Celebrations*, p. 31.
6. Ellis, John, *Seeing Things: Television in the Age of Uncertainty* (I.B.Tauris, London and New York, 2000), p. 39.
7. Booy, Miles, *Love and Monsters: The Doctor Who Experience, 1979 to the Present* (I.B.Tauris, London and New York, 2012), p. 2.
8. Sladen, Elisabeth with Hudson, Jeff, *Elisabeth Sladen: The Autobiography* (Aurum Press, London, 2011), p. 294.
9. Johnston: *Celebrations*, p. 31.

10   Wood, Tat, *About Time: The Unauthorized Guide to Doctor Who, Expanded 2nd Edition 1970-1974, Seasons 7-10* (Mad Norwegian Press, Illinois, 2009), p. 291.
11   Howe, David J. and Walker, Stephen James, *Doctor Who: The Television Companion* (BBC Worldwide, London, 1998), p. 235.
12   See, for example, on the 1971-8 *Ghost Story for Christmas*: Wheatley, Helen, *Gothic Television* (Manchester University Press, Manchester and New York, 2006), pp. 47-8.
13   Ellis: *Seeing Things*, p. 39.
14   Bentham, J. Jeremy, 'S.O.S.', *Doctor Who Magazine Special Edition: The Complete Fourth Doctor – Volume One* (2004), p. 32
15   Bould, Mark, '*Doctor Who*: Adaptations and flows' in J.P. Telotte and G. Duchovny (eds), *Science Fiction Film, Television and Adaptation* (Routledge, New York and London, 2012), p. 152.
16   Griffiths, Nick, *Dalek I Loved You: A Memoir* (Gollancz, London, 2007), p. 173.
17   Gillatt, Gary, 'The Three Doctors: Yesterday once more', *Doctor Who Magazine Special Edition: The Complete Third Doctor* (2002), p. 50
18   Miller, Keith, *The Official Doctor Who Fan Club Volume 1 The Jon Pertwee Years* (Lulu Publishing, Raleigh, 2012), pp. 115, 117, and 118.
19   Chapman: *Inside the TARDIS*, p. 96.
20   Booy: *Love and Monsters*, p. 2.
21   Scannell, Paddy, *Radio, Television and Modern Life* (Basil Blackwell, Oxford, 1996), p. 153.
22   Ellis: *Seeing Things*, p. 61.
23   Sladen with Hudson: *Elisabeth Sladen*, p. 268.
24   Miles, Lawrence and Wood, Tat, *About Time: The Unauthorized Guide to Doctor Who 1980-1984, Seasons 18-21* (Mad Norwegian Press, Illinois, 2005), p. 233.
25   Newman, Kim, *BFI TV Classics: Doctor Who* (BFI Publishing, London, 2005), p. 100.
26   Booy: *Love and Monsters*, p. 87.
27   Chapman: *Inside the TARDIS*, p. 152; see also Burt, Simon in May, David (ed.), *Views From behind the Sofa* (Lulu Publishing, Raleigh, 2007), p. 569.
28   Owen, Dave, 'The Five Doctors: Sweet dreams (are made of this)', *Doctor Who Magazine Special Edition: The Complete Fifth Doctor* (2002), p. 41.
29   Ibid.
30   Booy: *Love and Monsters*, pp. 24-5.
31   Magrs, Paul in Berry, Steve, *Behind the Sofa: Celebrity Memories of Doctor Who* (Matador, Kibworth Beauchamp, 2012), p. 166.
32   Miles and Wood: *About Time*, p. 231; BBC Enterprises, *The Doctor Who Celebration: Twenty Years of a Time Lord, Commemorative Programme* (Warminster Press, Warminster, 1983).
33   See Chapman: *Inside the TARDIS*, p. 24, and Howe, David J., Stammers, Mark and Walker, Stephen James, *Doctor Who: The Sixties* (Virgin Publishing, London, 1993), p. 11.
34   Wood, Tat, *About Time: The Unauthorized Guide to Doctor Who 1985-1989, Seasons 22-26, The TV Movie* (Mad Norwegian Press, Illinois, 2007), p. 270.

35 See Lofficier, Jean-Marc, *The Nth Doctor* (Virgin Publishing, London, 1997), p. 165–88.
36 Chapman: *Inside the TARDIS*, p. 175.
37 Newman: *BFI TV Classics: Doctor Who*, p. 100.
38 Levesque, Lissa in Southall, J.R. (ed.), *You and Who: A Doctor Who Fan Anthology* (Miwk Publishing, Tadworth, 2012), p. 193.
39 Gray, Jonathan, *Show Sold Separately: Promos, Spoilers, and Other Media Paratexts* (New York University Press, New York and London, 2010).
40 May: *Views from Behind the Sofa*, p. 573.
41 Smith R., in Burk, G. and Smith, R., *Who Is the Doctor: The Unofficial Guide to Doctor Who, The New Series* (ECW Press, Toronto, 2012), p. 189; see also Basu, Balaka, 'When worlds continue: The Doctor's adventures in fandom and metatextuality' in C. Hansen (ed.), *Ruminations, Peregrinations and Regenerations: A Critical Approach to Doctor Who* (Cambridge Scholars Publishing, Newcastle upon Tyne, 2010), p. 167 and Holdsworth: *Television, Memory and Nostalgia*, p. 148.
42 Johnston: *Celebrations*, p. 63.
43 Booy: *Love and Monsters*, p. 81.
44 Parkin, Lance, *The Infinity Doctors* (BBC Worldwide, London, 1998): back cover.
45 Parkin, Lance and Pearson, Lars, *AHistory: An Unauthorised History of the Doctor Who Universe* (3rd edition) (Mad Norwegian Press, Des Moines, 2012), p. 713; see also Parkin, Lance, 'Canonicity matters: defining the *Doctor Who* canon' in D. Butler (ed.), *Time and Relative Dissertations in Space: Critical Perspectives on Doctor Who* (Manchester University Press, Manchester and New York, 2012), p. 246–62.
46 Britton, Piers, *TARDISbound: Navigating the Universes of Doctor Who* (I.B.Tauris, London and New York, 2011), p. 210.
47 Hickman, Clayton, 'Welcome!', *Doctor Who Magazine 40th Anniversary Special Edition: We ♥ Doctor Who* (2003), pp. 6–7.
48 Cook, Benjamin, *Doctor Who the New Audio Adventures: The Inside Story* (Big Finish Productions, Maidenhead, 2003), p. 226.
49 Hills, Matt, *The Pleasures of Horror* (Continuum, London and New York, 2005), p. 167.
50 Gillatt, Gary, 'The Legacy Collection', *Doctor Who Magazine* 456 (2013), p. 69.
51 Anonymous, 'RT shop: Doctor Who offers', *The Radio Times* 22–28 November, *Radio Times Doctor Who 40th Anniversary Special* (2003), p. 16.
52 Ibid.
53 Holdsworth: *Television, Memory and Nostalgia*, p. 36.
54 BBC Worldwide Press Pack, *Doctor Who 40th Anniversary 1963–2003* (BBC Worldwide Press Office, London, 2003), p. 15.
55 This was prefigured by *Doctor Who*'s 1993 VHS releases, a number of which also carrying a reworked '30th anniversary' logo.
56 Dunleavy, Trisha, *Television Drama: Form, Agency, Innovation* (Palgrave Macmillan, Basingstoke and New York, 2009), p. 241.
57 Ellis: *Seeing Things*, pp. 167 and 169.
58 Ibid., p. 167.

59 Johnson, Catherine, *Branding Television* (Routledge, London and New York, 2012), p. 178.
60 van Krieken, Robert, *Celebrity Society* (Routledge, London and New York, 2012), p. 61.
61 Ibid., p. 55.
62 Gray: *Show Sold Separately*, p. 3.
63 Tostevin, Dan, 'Anniversary fever!', *Doctor Who Magazine* 456, pp. 26–31.
64 Kelly, Karl, '11 Doctors inhabit Scott & David Tipton's *Doctor Who: Prisoners of Time*' (28 December 2012), *Comic Book Resources*, available at: http://www.comicbookresources.com/?page=article&id=42842 accessed 3 June 2013.
65 Lazarus, Susanna, 'Series of Doctor Who short stories announced to celebrate 50th anniversary' (3 January 2013), *Radio Times*, available at: http://www.radiotimes.com/news/2013-01-03/series-of-doctor-who-short-stories-announced-to-celebrate-50th-anniversary, accessed 3 June 2013.
66 See http://www.royalmail.com/DoctorWho, accessed 3 June 2013.
67 Tostevin: 'Anniversary fever!', p. 30.
68 See, for example, Sleight, Graham, *The Doctor's Monsters: Meanings of the Monstrous in Doctor Who* (I.B.Tauris, London and New York, 2012), p. 197.
69 Booth, Paul, *Time on TV: Temporal Displacement and Mashup Television* (Peter Lang, New York, 2012), p. 136.
70 Booy: *Love and Monsters*, p. 2.
71 Indeed, the National Media Museum in Bradford hosts an exhibition 'Fifty Years of *Doctor Who* Fans' from 12 November 2013 to 2 March 2014, having invited fans to contribute memorabilia to the display.
72 Ellis: *Seeing Things*.

FURTHER READING
A Selective Bibliography

Aldridge, Mark and Murray, Andy, *T is for Television: The Small Screen Adventures of Russell T. Davies* (Reynolds and Hearn Ltd, Kew Gardens, 2008).
Baym, Nancy, *Personal Connections in the Digital Age* (Polity, Cambridge, 2010).
Beattie, Melissa, 'A most peculiar memorial: Cultural heritage and fiction', in J. Schofield (ed.), *Who Needs Experts? Counter-Mapping Cultural Heritage* (Ashgate, Aldershot, 2013).
Bignell, Jonathan, 'The child as addressee, viewer and consumer in mid-1960s Doctor Who' in D. Butler (ed.), *Time and Relative Dissertations in Space: Critical Perspectives on Doctor Who* (Manchester University Press, Manchester and New York, 2007).
Bignell, Jonathan, and Andrew O'Day, *Terry Nation* (Manchester University Press, Manchester, 2004).
Booth, Paul, *Digital Fandom* (Peter Lang, New York, 2010).
────── *Time on TV: Temporal Displacement and Mashup Television* (Peter Lang, New York, 2012).
────── *Fan Phenomena: Doctor Who* (Intellect, Bristol, 2013).
Booy, Miles, *Love and Monsters: The Doctor Who Experience, 1979 to the Present* (I.B.Tauris, London and New York, 2012).
Born, Georgina, *Uncertain Vision: Birt, Dyke and the Reinvention of the BBC* (Secker & Warburg, London, 2006).
Bould, Mark, 'Doctor Who: Adaptations and Flows' in J.P. Telotte and G. Duchovny (eds), *Science Fiction Film, Television and Adaptation* (Routledge, New York and London, 2012) pp. 143–63.
Bradshaw, Simon, Keen, Antony, and Sleight, Graham (eds) *The Unsilent Library: Essays on the Russell T. Davies Era of the New Doctor Who* (Science Fiction Foundation, London, 2011).

Britton, Piers D., *TARDISbound: Navigating the Universes of Doctor Who* (I.B.Tauris, London, 2011).

Britton, Piers and Simon Barker, *Reading Between Designs: Visual Imagery and the Generation of Meaning in The Avengers, The Prisoner and Doctor Who* (University of Texas Press, Austin, 2003).

Burdge, Anthony S., Burke, Jessica and Larsen, Kristine (eds), *The Mythological Dimensions of Doctor Who* (Kitsune Books, Crawfordville, 2010).

Burk, Graeme and Smith, Robert, *Who is the Doctor: The Unofficial Guide to Doctor Who, the New Series* (ECW Press, Toronto, 2012).

Chapman, James, *Inside the TARDIS: The Worlds of Doctor Who* (I.B.Tauris, London, 2006).

Charles, Alec, 'The crack of doom: the uncanny echoes of Steven Moffat's *Doctor Who*' in *Science Fiction Film and Television* iv/1 (2011), pp. 1–23.

Cherry, Brigid, 'Squee, Retcon, Fanwank and the Not-We: computer-mediated discourse and the online audience for Nu*Who*' in C. Hansen (ed.), *Ruminations, Peregrinations, and Regenerations: A Critical Approach to Doctor Who* (Cambridge Scholars Publishing, Newcastle upon Tyne, 2010), pp. 209–32.

Chin, Bertha and Hills, Matt, 'Restricted confessions? Blogging, subcultural celebrity and the management of producer-fan proximity', *Social Semiotics* xviii/2 (2008), pp. 253–72.

Collins, Frank, *The Pandorica Opens: Exploring the worlds of the Eleventh Doctor* (Classic TV Press, Cambridge, 2010).

Cornea, Christine, 'Showrunning the *Doctor Who* franchise: A reply to Denise Mann' in V. Mayer, M. J. Banks and J. Thornton Caldwell (eds), *Production Studies: Cultural Studies of Media Industries* (Routledge, New York and London, 2009), pp. 115–22.

Cranny-Francis, Anne and Tulloch, John, 'Vaster than empire(s), and more slow: the politics and economics of embodiment in *Doctor Who*' in P. Harrigan and N. Wardrip-Fruin (eds) *Third Person: Authoring and Exploring Vast Narratives* (MIT Press, Massachusetts, 2009), pp. 343–55.

Cull, Nicholas J., '"Bigger on the Inside …" *Doctor Who* as British cultural history,' in *The Historian, Television and Television History* (University of Luton Press, London, 2001).

——— 'Tardis at the OK Corral: *Doctor Who* and the USA' in J. R. Cook and P. Wright (eds), *British Science Fiction Television: A Hitchhiker's Guide* (I.B.Tauris, London and New York, 2006), pp. 52–70.

Deller, Ruth, 'Twittering on: Audience research and participation using Twitter', *Participations* 8/1 (May 2011), available at: http://www.participations.org/Volume%208/Issue%201/deller.htm, accessed 3 June 2013.

Donnelly, Kevin J., 'Between prosaic functionalism and sublime experimentation: *Doctor Who* and musical sound design', in D. Butler (ed.), *Time And Relative Dissertations In Space: Critical perspectives on Doctor Who* (Manchester University Press, Manchester, 2007), p. 190.

Dunleavy, Trisha, *Television Drama: Form, Agency, Innovation* (Palgrave Macmillan, Basingstoke and New York, 2009).

Ellis, John, *Seeing Things: Television in the Age of Uncertainty* (I.B.Tauris, London and New York, 2000).

FURTHER READING

Evans, Elizabeth, *Transmedia Television: Audiences, New Media and Daily Life* (Routledge, London, 2011).
—— 'The evolving ecosystem: Interview with Victoria Jaye' in P. Grainge (ed.), *Ephemeral Media: Transitory Screen Culture from Television to YouTube* (BFI Publishing, London, 2011).
Garner, Ross P., Beattie, Melissa, and McCormack, Una (eds), *Impossible Worlds, Impossible Things: Cultural Perspectives on Doctor Who, Torchwood and The Sarah Jane Adventures* (Cambridge Scholars Publishing, Newcastle upon Tyne, 2010).
Geraghty, Lincoln, 'From balaclavas to jumpsuits: The multiple histories and identities of *Doctor Who*'s Cybermen', *Atlantis: Journal of the Spanish Association of Anglo-American Studies*, xxx/1 (2008), pp. 85–100.
Hadas, Leora, 'The Web planet: How the changing Internet divided *Doctor Who* fan fiction writers', *The Journal of Transformative Works and Cultures* xxx (2009) available at: http://journal.transformativeworks.org/index.php/twc/article/view/129, accessed 3 June 2013.
Hansen, Chris (ed.), *Ruminations, Peregrinations, and Regenerations: A Critical Approach to Doctor Who* (Cambridge Scholars Publishing, Newcastle upon Tyne, 2010).
Hayles, N. Katherine, *How We Became Posthuman: Virtual Bodies in Cybernetics, Literature, and Informatics* (Chicago University Press, Chicago, 1999).
Hills, Matt *Fan Cultures* (Routledge, London & New York, 2002).
—— '"Gothic" body parts in a "postmodern" body of work? The Hinchcliffe/Holmes era of *Doctor Who* (1975–77)', *Intensities: The Journal of Cult Media* iv (2007), available at http://intensities.org/Essays/Hills.pdf, accessed 3 June 2013.
—— 'Televisuality without television? The Big Finish Audios and discourses of tele-centric *Doctor Who*', in D. Butler (ed.), *Time and Relative Dissertations in Space: Critical Perspectives on Doctor Who'* (Manchester University Press, Manchester, 2007).
—— 'The dispersible television text: theorising moments of the new *Doctor Who*', *Science Fiction Film and Television* i/1 (2008), pp. 25–44.
—— 'Absent epic, implied story arcs, and variation on a narrative theme: *Doctor Who* (2005) as cult/mainstream television' in P. Harrigan and N. Wardrip-Fruin (eds), *Third Person: Authoring and Exploring Vast Narratives* (MIT Press, Massachusetts, 2009), pp. 333–42.
—— *Triumph of a Time Lord: Regenerating Doctor Who in the Twenty-First Century* (I.B.Tauris, London and New York, 2010).
—— '*Doctor Who*' in D. Lavery (ed.), *The Essential Cult TV Reader* (University Press of Kentucky, Lexington, 2010), pp. 97–103.
—— 'A showrunner goes to war: *Doctor Who* and the almost fans' in *Antenna*, 6 June 2011, available at: http://blog.commarts.wisc.edu/2011/06/06/a-showrunner-goes-to-war-doctor-who-and-the-almost-fans/, accessed 3 June 2013.
—— '*Torchwood*'s trans-transmedia: Media tie-ins and brand "fanagement"', *Participations: Journal of Audience and Reception Studies* ix/2 (2012), available at: http://www.participations.org/Volume%209/Issue%202/23%20Hills.pdf, accessed 3 June 2013.

Holdsworth, Amy, *Television, Memory and Nostalgia* (Palgrave-Macmillan, Basingstoke and New York, 2011).
Hoge, Charles William, 'Whodology: Encountering *Doctor Who* fan fiction through the portals of play studies and ludology', *Journal of Transformative Works and Cultures* viii (2011), available online at http://journal.transformativeworks.org/index.php/twc/article/view/262/223, accessed 3 June 2013.
Howe, David J. and Walker, Stephen James, *Doctor Who: The Television Companion* (BBC Worldwide, London, 1998).
Jenkins, Henry, *Textual Poachers: Television Fans and Participatory Culture* (Routledge, London, 1992).
Johnson, Catherine, *Telefantasy* (BFI Publishing, London, 2005).
────── *Branding Television* (Routledge, London and New York, 2011).
Layton, David, *The Humanism of Doctor Who: A Critical Study in Science Fiction and Philosophy* (McFarland, Jefferson, 2012).
Leach, Jim, *Doctor Who: TV Milestones* (Wayne State University Press, Detroit, 2009).
Leitch, Gillian I. (ed.), *Doctor Who in Time and Space: Essays on Themes, Characters, History and Fandom, 1963–2012* (McFarland, Jefferson, 2013).
Lewis, Courtland and Smithka, Paula (eds), *Doctor Who and Philosophy* (Open Court Publishing, Chicago, 2011).
Lury, Celia, *Brands: The Logos of the Global Economy* (Routledge, London, 2004).
Lyon, J. Shaun, *Back to the Vortex: The Unofficial and Unauthorised Guide to Doctor Who 2005* (Telos, Tolworth, 2005).
────── *Second Flight: The Unofficial and Unauthorised Guide to Doctor Who 2006* (Telos, Tolworth, 2006).
Magrs, Paul, 'Afterword: My adventures' in D. Butler (ed.), *Time and Relative Dissertations in Space: Critical Perspectives on Doctor Who* (Manchester University Press, Manchester and New York, 2007), p. 308.
Marlow, Christopher, 'The folding text: *Doctor Who*, adaptation and fan fiction' in R. Carroll (ed.), *Adaptation in Contemporary Culture: Textual Infidelities* (Continuum, London, 2009), pp. 46–57.
May, David (ed.), *Views From Behind the Sofa* (Lulu Publishing, Raleigh, 2007).
McKee, Alan, 'Which is the best *Doctor Who* story? A case study in value judgements outside the Academy', *Intensities: The Journal of Cult Media* i/December 2001, available at: http://intensities.org/Essays/McKee.pdf, accessed 3 June 2013.
────── 'How to tell the difference between production and consumption: A case study in *Doctor Who* fandom' in S. Gwenllian-Jones and R.E. Pearson (eds), *Cult Television* (University of Minnesota Press, Minneapolis, 2004), pp. 167–86.
Miles, Lawrence and Wood, Tat, *About Time: The Unauthorised Guide to Doctor Who 1970–1974 Seasons 7 to 11* (Mad Norwegian Press, Illinois, 2004).
────── *About Time: The Unauthorized Guide to Doctor Who 1980–1984, Seasons 18–21* (Mad Norwegian Press, Illinois, 2005).
Miller, Keith, *The Official Doctor Who Fan Club Volume 1 The Jon Pertwee Years* (Lulu Publishing, Raleigh, 2012).
Newman, Kim, *BFI TV Classics: Doctor Who* (BFI Publishing, London, 2005).
O'Day, Andrew, *Doctor Who, The Eleventh Hour* (I.B.Tauris, London and New York, 2013).

FURTHER READING

O'Mahony, Daniel, '"Now how is that wolf able to impersonate a grandmother?" History, pseudo-history and genre in *Doctor Who*' in D. Butler (ed.), *Time and Relative Dissertations in Space: Critical Perspectives on Doctor Who* (Manchester University Press, Manchester, 2007).

Parkin, Lance, 'Canonicity matters: defining the *Doctor Who* canon' in D. Butler (ed.), *Time and Relative Dissertations in Space: Critical Perspectives on Doctor Who* (Manchester University Press, Manchester and New York, 2007) p. 246–62.

────── 'Truths universally acknowledged: how the "rules" of *Doctor Who* affect the writing' in P. Harrigan and N. Wardrip-Fruin (eds), *Third Person: Authoring and Exploring Vast Narratives* (MIT Press, Massachusetts, 2009), pp. 13–24.

Parsons, Paul, *The Science of Doctor Who* (Icon Books, Cambridge, 2006).

Peacock, Steven, 'Against *Dr. Who*' in *CST Online*, 8 June 2011, available at: http://cstonline.tv/against-dr-who, accessed 3 June 2013.

Perryman, Neil, '*Doctor Who* and the convergence of media: A case study in "transmedia storytelling"', *Convergence: The International Journal of Research into New Media Technologies* xiv/1 (2008), pp. 21–39.

Porter, Lynnette, *Tarnished Heroes, Charming Villains and Modern Monsters: Science Fiction in Shades of Gray on 21st Century Television* (McFarland, Jefferson, 2010).

────── *The Doctor Who Franchise: American Influence, Fan Culture and the Spinoffs* (McFarland, Jefferson, 2012).

Robb, Brian J., *Timeless Adventures: How Doctor Who Conquered TV* (Kamera Books, Harpenden, 2009).

Rose, James, 'The suffering of the skin: The uncanny nature of the Cybermen in the Russell T. Davies Era of *Doctor Who*' in C. Hansen (ed.), *Ruminations, Peregrinations, and Regenerations: A Critical Approach to Doctor Who* (Cambridge Scholars Publishing, Newcastle upon Tyne, 2010), pp. 283–98.

Ross, Sharon Marie, *Beyond the Box: Television and the Internet* (Blackwell, Malden and Oxford, 2008).

Sarachan, Jeremy, '*Doctor Who* fan videos, YouTube, and the public sphere' in C. Hansen (ed.), *Ruminations, Peregrinations, and Regenerations: A Critical Approach to Doctor Who* (Cambridge Scholars Publishing, Newcastle upon Tyne, 2010), pp. 249–61.

Selznick, Barbara, 'Rebooting and re-branding: The changing brands of *Doctor Who*'s Britishness' in C. Hansen (ed.), *Ruminations, Peregrinations, and Regenerations: A Critical Approach to Doctor Who* (Cambridge Scholars Publishing, Newcastle upon Tyne, 2010), pp. 68–84.

Shimpach, Shawn, *Television in Transition* (Wiley-Blackwell, Malden, 2010).

Short, Sue, *Cult Telefantasy Series* (McFarland, Jefferson, 2011).

Sleight, Graham, 'The big picture show: Russell T. Davies' writing for *Doctor Who*', in S. Bradshaw, A. Keen and G. Sleight (eds), *The Unsilent Library: Essays on the Russell T. Davies Era of the New Doctor Who* (Science Fiction Foundation, Chippenham, 2011), pp. 15–27.

────── *The Doctor's Monsters: Meanings of the Monstrous in Doctor Who* (I.B.Tauris, London and New York, 2012).

Stanish, Deborah and Myles, L.M. (eds), *Chicks Unravel Time: Women Journey Through Every Season of Doctor Who* (Mad Norwegian Press, Illinois, 2012).

Thomas, Lynne M. and O'Shea, Tara (eds), *Chicks Dig Time Lords: A Celebration of Doctor Who by the Women Who Love It* (Mad Norwegian Press, Illinois, 2010).

Suvin, Darko, *Metamorphoses of Science Fiction* (Yale University Press, New Haven and London, 1979).

Théberge, P., 'Everyday fandom: Fan clubs, blogging, and the quotidian rhythms of the internet,' *Canadian Journal of Communication*, xxx/4 (2005).

Thornham, Sue and Purvis, Tony, *Television Drama: Theories and Identities* (Palgrave Macmillan, Basingstoke, 2005).

Tulloch, John, *Watching Television Audiences: Cultural Theories & Methods* (Arnold, London, 2000).

Tulloch, John, and Manuel Alvarado, *Doctor Who: The Unfolding Text* (Macmillan, Basingstoke, 1983).

Tulloch, John and Jenkins, Henry, *Science Fiction Audiences: Watching Doctor Who and Star Trek* (Routledge, London, 1995).

Vint, Sherryl, *Bodies of Tomorrow: Technology, Subjectivity, Science Fiction* (University of Toronto Press, Toronto, 2007).

Wheatley, Helen, *Gothic Television* (Manchester University Press, Manchester, 2006).

Williams, Rebecca, 'Desiring the Doctor: Identity, gender and genre in online fandom' in T. Hochscherf and J. Leggott (eds), *British Science Fiction Film and Television: Critical Essays* (McFarland, Jefferson, 2011), pp. 167–77.

Wood, Tat, *About Time: The Unauthorized Guide to Doctor Who 1985–1989, Seasons 22–26, The TV Movie* (Mad Norwegian Press, Illinois, 2007).

——— *About Time: The Unauthorized Guide to Doctor Who, Expanded 2nd Edition 1970–1974, Seasons 7–10* (Mad Norwegian Press, Illinois, 2009).

Wright, Peter, 'Expatriate! Expatriate! *Doctor Who: The Movie* and commercial negotiation of a multiple text' in T. Hochscherf and J. Leggott (eds), *British Science Fiction Film and Television: Critical Essays* (McFarland, Jefferson, 2011), pp. 128–42.

Zubernis, Lynn and Larsen, Katherine, *Fandom at the Crossroads: Celebration, Shame and Fan/Producer Relationships* (Cambridge Scholars Publishing, Newcastle upon Tyne, 2012).